Guatemala Journey
Among the Ixil Maya

Overlooking Nebaj on road from Sacapulas

Guatemala Journey Among the Ixil Maya

SUSANNA BADGLEY PLACE

Copyright © 2013 Susanna Badgley Place

All Rights Reserved. International copyright reserved in all countries. No part of this book may be reproduced in any form without written permission from the publisher.

Library of Congress Control Number: 2012920741

ISBN 978-0-9884876-0-4

Design by Blue Design (www.bluedes.com)
Printed in China

*This book is dedicated to the weavers
of Nebaj, Chajul, and Cotzal.
They hold in their hearts and minds,
sturdy looms and nimble fingers,
the ancient threads of the Ixil Maya culture.*

CONTENTS

ACKNOWLEDGMENTS 10
AUTHOR'S NOTE 10
INTRODUCTION: THE INVITATION 13
GEOGRAPHY OF THE IXIL REGION 19
WINDOWS INTO IXIL HISTORY 23
Pre-Hispanic Ixil History and Culture (500 BC–AD 1524) . . . 24
Decoding the Legacy of the Ancient Maya. 27
Three Centuries of Spanish Colonial Rule (1524–1821). 36
Independence to Civil War (1821–1960). 40
Civil War (1960-1996) 45
Postwar Challenges for the Ixil Region 52

PLANNING THE JOURNEY 59
Maps and Guides 60
Transportation 61
When to Travel 62
Travel Tips. 62
Route to Nebaj 64

NEBAJ 75
Visitor Services in Nebaj. 78
Explorations in Nebaj. 84
  History of the Catholic Church and the Central Plaza 84
  Market Day in Nebaj and Basic Ixil Foods 86
  Weaving Traditions in Nebaj 88
  Nebaj's Cultural Center and Artisanal Market 92
  Postwar Poverty and Recovery 93
  Indigenous Community Radio. 98
  Doctoring in the Ixil region. 100
  Trekking and Touring in Nebaj's Aldeas 103
  Ixil Religion: A Blend of Ancient and Modern Faiths 109
  Sacred Spaces in Nebaj 115

CHAJUL 121
  Directions to Chajul 122
Visitor Services in Chajul. 125
Explorations in Chajul. 131
  Walking through History in Chajul 131

  Market Extravaganza in Chajul .136
  Asociación Chajulense: An Engine for Economic Development 138
  Chajul Traditional Dress:
    Fusion of Myth, Art, and Manual Dexterity 139
  Weaving Lessons with a Master .141
  Cooking Lessons. 143
  Hiking to Cerro San Andrés 146
  Hiking Cerro Paxil, "Mountain of the Sacred Maize" 147
  Soaking in the Maya Sauna 150
  Traditional Music in Chajul. 150
  Exploring Northern Chajul 153
  Limitless Horizons for the Ixil:
    Expanding Educational Opportunities 165

COTZAL 169
  Directions to Cotzal 170
Visitor Services in Cotzal. 173
Explorations in Cotzal. 176
  Transforming Cotzal's Colonial Plaza 176
  Preserving Ixil Language
    and Identity 177
  Ixil Marriage Customs. 182
  Birth traditions in an ixil family 184
  Continuity and Change in Cotzal Weaving 187
  Cooling off in Cotzal's Waterfalls and Swimming Holes 191
  Ixil Gold: Certified Fair Trade Organic Coffee in Santa Avelina . . .193
  Maguey: The Fiber of Commerce 194
  Development in the Cotzal River Valley:
    The Case of Finca San Francisco 195
  Navigating the Skyline Frontier in Southeastern Cotzal 199
  Breaking the Cycle of Poverty:
    Agros International's Development Model. 202
  Celebrating Cotzal's Annual Fiesta 207

NEXT STEPS IN THE IXIL JOURNEY 211
APPENDIX 1: CALENDAR OF FIESTAS IN THE IXIL REGION. 214
APPENDIX 2: GLOSSARY OF COMMONLY USED WORDS 219
BIBLIOGRAPHY 223
ENDNOTES 231

ACKNOWLEDGMENTS

When I decided to write this guidebook, I set out to find a research assistant in Nebaj to help me document aspects of Ixil Maya culture, geography, and history. I tentatively floated the idea among a few Ixil contacts. Such was the enthusiasm for this project that I promptly harvested a talented team with abundant expertise. Juan Clemente Raymundo Velasco of Nebaj, a graduate of the University of San Carlos and former director of the European Union–funded Project Ixil, took the lead in organizing the investigations, interviewing community leaders, and providing analysis of economic and social trends. Ana Laynez, president of the Association of Maya Ixil Women, contributed information on the history, organizations, and traditions of Chajul. Beth Lentz, a former U.S. Peace Corps volunteer in Cotzal, with a master's in international relations, documented cultural traditions, education, health, and social issues in Cotzal. Miguel Ceto Raymundo of Nebaj, with a master's in social development from the University of Rafael Landívar, educated me about Ixil religious customs, traditional community authorities, and land-ownership issues. The contributions of this team were invaluable, and their voices resonate throughout these pages. I cannot thank them enough for their insights and friendship. Out of respect for my hosts' privacy and for reasons of political and cultural sensitivity, I purposely wrote this guidebook in first-person. The opinions expressed here are my own, as are any shortcomings.

I also want to thank my family and friends for their encouragement in this first book-writing endeavor. Many have accompanied me on these Ixil explorations, adding eyes and ears and valuable perspectives. Several contributed fabulous photos, including Chris Percival, Michel de la Sabliere, and Scott Stoll. Stephen and Elaine Elliot added valuable historical and linguistic insight. My daughter, Louise Place, commented on numerous rough drafts, and Melissa Hayes masterfully put the manuscript in its final form. Julianna Stoll provided expert graphic and website design, and Tom Morgan skillfully combined text and photos into the final book design. I am deeply indebted to my late husband, David, whose boundless interest in the natural and cultural world led us to explore beyond the comfort zone of most travelers, and to Scott Stoll, whose local knowledge of Quiché from his former U.S. Peace Corps experience made him a skillful navigator, patient translator, and ready adventurer for this Ixil journey.

My long-time friend and Spanish teacher, Verónica Judith Ortega Zarazúa de Xicay, of Antigua, Guatemala, provided a graceful translation for the Spanish edition, entitled *Viajando entre los Mayas Ixiles de Guatemala*, to be available in both print and e-book versions in 2013.

AUTHOR'S NOTE

The Ixil Maya people constitute one of twenty-four distinct linguistic communities in Guatemala today, including twenty-one Maya communities, plus the Garifuna, Xinca, and the exclusively Spanish-speaking population.

Ixil is pronounced "ee-SHEEL," [iʃil] in the International Phonetic Alphabet.

The term *Maya* is used as both a noun and adjective.

The average US$–GTQ (Quetzal) exchange rate in 2011: US$ 1 = Q7.8

All altitudes are stated as from sea level.

Photo Credits: Photos that illustrate this guide were taken by the author, unless otherwise noted in the photo captions.

Website: www.GuatemalaIxilJourney.org

Ana Laynez, President of Association of Ixil Maya Women (ADMI) in Chajul, with author Susanna Place.

Introduction: The Invitation

OPPOSITE: While foreign visitors usually stand out in a crowded Ixil market, my experience suggests that the curiosity is mutual and that Ixil Maya families welcome the chance to show off their culture, produce (even piglets!), and exchange greetings with visitors.

Twenty years ago, in the early 1990s, Maya weavers from the Ixil-speaking region of northwestern Guatemala invited me to visit their homeland. Due to my life's circuitous path, it took me fifteen years to accept this invitation. When I did, I was captivated by the beauty and soul of the Ixil countryside and culture. Now, I would like to pass this invitation on to other travelers.

I initally traveled to Guatemala to learn more about the Maya textile traditions I had admired in books and museums. I was an utter novice, largely ignorant about the causes and course of the civil war that had gripped this country for thirty years, and naively exploring Guatemala's western highlands via crowded "chicken buses." With only meager Spanish, I counted on my former U.S. Peace Corps experience and skill at charades to get by. Looking back, I now admit that these early expeditions were perhaps foolhardy, if not reckless. What I saw and experienced, however, was unforgettable.

In the bustling indigenous market of Chichicastenango, I encountered weavers from Nebaj, Chajul, and Cotzal, the three Ixil-speaking municipalities in northern Department of Quiché that make up this linguistically distinct Maya subculture. I was mesmerized by the Ixil weavers' bold use of forest greens, mountain blues, chili reds, and maize yellows; symbols of sacred mountains and cultural myths crowded the canvases of their masterful handwoven blouses, called huipiles (also written as *güipiles*).

These Ixil weavers urged me to journey home with them, a rugged day's drive north into the heart of the Cuchumatanes Mountains. At that time, the government and the opposition forces under the Guatemalan National Revolutionary Unity (URNG) were negotiating the conditions for peace, and the western highlands remained tense and traumatized. It was not a good time for me to venture further north, I decided. Nonetheless, the memory of this tantalizing invitation returned with me to Boston, like a stowaway, deeply enmeshed in the silky tassels of a weathered Ixil shawl.

In January of 2005, almost a decade after the 1996 signing of the Guatemalan Peace Accords, I was determined to follow up on the invitation to visit the

BELOW: Chajul, young girl waits for friends outside the traditional adobe brick and clay roof-tiled house.

RIGHT: Prepare for the daily deluge and cool nights during the rainy season in the high Cuchumatanes. **FAR RIGHT:** Visitors will enjoy savory Ixil foods and can engage local women for a culinary lesson in preparing a traditional meal. **BELOW RIGHT:** Gathering and transporting firewood for cooking is a daily chore. **BELOW:** Speckled duck eggs for sale or barter.

Ixil region. I spent an amazing—and far too short—week in Nebaj, Chajul, and Cotzal. The journey was eye-opening and ear-popping, as I poked along rutted roads in mist-enshrouded valleys and hiked high mountain paths into remote Ixil villages. The region's diverse ecology proved endlessly fascinating: tropical cloud forests, cascading waterfalls, delicate orchids, howler monkeys, and iridescent quetzals. In Spanish and through Ixil translators, conversations with Ixil weavers, farmers, professionals, and schoolchildren were heartwarming and thought-provoking. As afternoon shadows deepened in the courtyards of their adobe houses, Ixil mothers bent intently over their backstrap looms and weary men delivered the days' harvest of chopped wood or field-dried maize.

Children stacked firewood, invented games, and finished homework in the fading light. Within every household, I learned, civil war survivors struggled to rebuild shattered lives. By the end of my first trip to the Ixil region, I was already planning to return.

One visit led to another, and eventually spawned the idea of writing this guidebook. Although increasingly accessible by an improved road system, Nebaj, Chajul, and Cotzal lie far off the beaten track for most foreign tourists and remain unfamiliar to many Guatemalans. As I have discovered, a journey into this ancient Ixil homeland offers wonderful opportunities to explore Ixil culture and countryside on an unusually personal level.

This is not your typical guidebook. While I

suggest specific places of geographic, historical, and cultural interest for visitors, I believe that the real richness of the Ixil region is best appreciated by learning about its history, and through direct experience with the vibrant Ixil culture and local economy. When I embarked on this project, there was almost nothing written for the tourist about the Ixil region. I had to start from scratch. That turned out to be fortuitious. With the help of my Ixil friends and colleagues, I am able to introduce the Ixil region in ways that emphasize what is most important to the Ixil people—to write about their traditions and sacred mountains, their place in ancient and modern history, and their quest to build sustainable livelihoods and preserve the unique Ixil identity.

The first three chapters of this guidebook introduce the visitor to the Ixil region's geography and history, and present the logistics of traveling to the region from La Antigua. The heart of the guidebook is found in the three chapters dedicated to each of the three Ixil-speaking municipalities—Nebaj, Chajul, and Cotzal. These chapters include an overview of each municipality's dominant characteristics and information about local lodging, food, and logistics, followed by a menu of in-depth exploration into the area's history, culture, geography, economy, and rhythms of daily life.

I encourage travelers to visit local schools that are educating the next generation of Ixil leaders; hire a guide to learn about traditional sacred sites; buy a meal in the market; learn to weave; and visit with nonprofit organizations leading the region's economic and social development. The explorations I have profiled in this guidebook afford keen insight into the historical forces that have shaped indigenous communities across Guatemala. The millenia-old civilization of the Maya is evident in the physical and cultural landscape of this region: the crumbling ancient temples, smoking ceremonial altars, oral histories passed down through generations, and the Maya vision of the universe portrayed in Ixil weaving. The story of the Spanish conquest of Guatemala and of postcolonial incursions into Ixil country are also etched, often discordantly, into the architecture of colonial towns and the patterns of land owership and development.

Observations and conversations with Ixil men and women, entrepreneurs and schoolchildren reveal much about the prospects for the cultural and economic future of the Ixil community. On the one hand are strong testimonies to resurgent Ixil pride and community development, such as indigenous coffee cooperatives, boisterous bilingual schools, and vibrant community radio. On the other hand are the daunting challenges to Ixil traditional values and livelihoods posed by rapid population growth, deforestation, national unrest, and economic globalization. This is an exciting and defining time for an ancient and resilient culture entering another historic transition.

I believe that cultural, ecological, and volunteer tourism can both honor the Ixil identity and contribute to the sustainable development of this majestic region. The goal of this guidebook is to make the Ixil region and culture more accessible, and to serve as a springboard for travelers to venture beyond the routes and suggestions in these pages. My hope is that visitors will discover opportunities to cultivate their own ties to the Ixil Maya and pass this invitation onward.

¡Tiichal a xaane'!
Have a wonderful journey!
¡Buen Viaje!
—**SUSANNA BADGLEY PLACE**

CHAPTER 1

Geography of the Ixil Region

OPPOSITE: Cotzal River Valley, much of this magnificent tropical cloud forest was coverted to coffee cultivation by outsiders in the early 1900s. **ABOVE LEFT:** Abudant Ixil biodiversity. **ABOVE RIGHT:** Traditional thatched maize granary.

The ancestral homeland of the Ixil Maya occupies 2,314 square kilometers (893 square miles) in the Cuchumatanes Mountains of northwestern Guatemala, and three of the twenty-one municipalities (*municipios*)[*] in the Department of Quiché: Nebaj, Chajul, and Cotzal. Although this area is sometimes referred to as the "Ixil Triangle," this term has negative connotations within the region, as it is associated with the army's assault on Ixil communities during the recent civil war. Roughly the size of Luxembourg, or half the area of the smallest U.S. state of Rhode Island, the Ixil region's mountainous terrain and minimal roads make distances deceiving and lend an impression of vastness.

Nebaj, Chajul, and Cotzal are cut off from the southern half of Quiché

---

[*] *The Guatemalan municipio is a geographic and political unit consisting of an administrative center, or cabecera, and the surrounding land area formally titled to the municipality. Municipalities vary greatly in size, and in many areas of the country roughly approximate the historical boundaries of indigenous communities at the time of formal land registration in the late 1800s and early 1900s.*

ABOVE: Moist clouds settle into Ixil valleys as night approaches.

by a sheer escarpment of 2,800 meters, towering above the town of Sacapulas. To the west of Nebaj, mountain ridges climb to 3,500 meters (11,500 feet) near the village of Chortis, situated at the crossroads of trails to Todos Santos Cuchumatán in the Department of Huehuetenango. Along Cotzal's eastern border, a series of mountain ridges run north-south at 2,400 meters (7,874 feet) above the Cotzal and Chipal river valleys to form the boundary with Uspantán municipality. In northern Chajul, the mighty Cuchumatanes descend into the tropical lowlands of the Ixcán municipality, extending north to the Usumacinta River and the Mexican border.

Within the sequestered Ixil region, high cloud forest, dramatic slopes, and lush river valleys translate into myriad microclimates, supporting rich biodiversity and a wide range of agricultural potential.[1] At the higher altitudes, temperatures range between 15 to 17 degrees Celsius (59 to 62 degrees Fahrenheit)—cool at night, and only a bit warmer at midday. This *tierra fria* describes much of the highland Nebaj and all but the far northern villages (*aldeas*) of Chajul, supporting one annual crop of maize, some wheat and oats, potatoes, sheep, and cattle. Conifers, oaks, liquidambar, alders, sweet gum, and other deciduous hardwoods cloak the upper slopes of the mountains in this zone. Where altitudes dip to between 800 and 1,500 meters in sunny valleys, the moderate climate is described as *tierra templada*. With temperatures

LAND AREA	NEBAJ	CHAJUL	COTZAL
Km²	608	1,524	182
Hectares	60,801	152,411	18,200
Caballerías	1,341	3,361	401

Note: Land measurement equivalents actually vary within different communities in Guatemala. This guidebook applies the following measurements, used by anthropologist David Stoll and corroborated by engineer Juan Clemente Raymundo Velasco of Nebaj.

1 caballería = 64.5 manzanas = 45.35 hectares = 112.07 acres

1 manzana = 16 cuerdas

1 cuerda = 25 varas² = 437.5 m²

averaging 18 to 23 degrees C (65 to 75 degrees F), this zone supports an expansion of traditional crops to include coffee on the warmer slopes, plums, apples, peas, and temperate greens and vegetables. Large areas of eastern Cotzal and several northern villages (*aldeas*) of Chajul are classified as tropical lands, *tierra caliente*. Where the altitude is less than 800 meters, the average temperature hovers around 25 degrees C (77 degrees F), but can be sweltering in the noonday sun. The *tierra caliente* climate supports two maize crops per year, coffee, sugarcane, cardamom, maguey (agave or "century plant"), avocados, and other tropical fruits.

Historically, the dense forest cover of Ixil territory and predictable rainfall has nourished an extensive watershed area of northern Guatemala. The region is renowned for its spectacular waterfalls and year-round abundance of water. Since ancient times, the many tributaries sourced in these high mountain cloud forests have fed the region's major rivers: the Xak'b'al River that runs northward through Nebaj and Chajul municipalities, and the Chipal, Chama, and Cotzal rivers flowing northeast through Cotzal. Today, this all-important watershed is threatened by development, including logging, slash-and-burn agriculture, and the damming of the Xak'b'al and Cotzal rivers by foreign-owned companies for hydroelectric power generation. It remains to be seen whether Ixil communities and the government can come to an agreement and develop a sustainable plan to steward these critical natural resources for the benefit of the region and communities downstream.

There are two main seasons in Guatemala. The rainy season, referred to as *invierno*, stretches from late May to mid-October, with a daily deluge most often in the afternoon. The dry season, *verano*, settles in by November and gradually parches the earth by mid-May. In the higher altitudes of the Ixil region, however, rain and fog are common well into February. Annual rainfall averages between 2,000 and 3,000 millimeters (80 to 112 inches). Travelers should be prepared for wide swings in temperatures and pack rain gear even in the dry season.

BELOW: Ixil packhorses ready for trek to distant maize fields and woodlots.

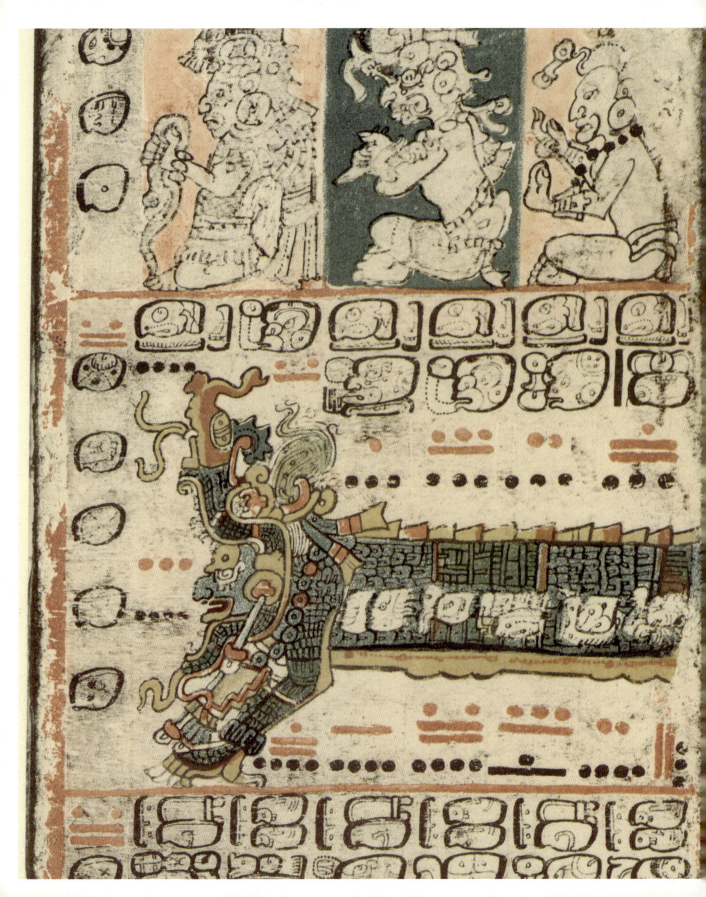

CHAPTER 2

Windows into Ixil History

OPPOSITE: Drawing/(Photograph) by Linda Schele, ©David Schele, courtesy Foundation for the Advancement of Mesoamerican Studies, Inc., www.famsi.org. Detail from the Förstemann version of the ancient Yucatecan Maya hieroglyphic divinatory almanac, known as the Dresden Codex. **ABOVE LEFT:** Contemporary Ixil weaving recreates and reinterprets ancient mythical figures and symbols. **ABOVE RIGHT:** Fragment of pre-Hispanic funerary urn from Nebaj, from the collection of the National Museum of Ethnology and Archaeology of Guatemala.

I set off for my first visit to Nebaj in 2005 with little knowledge of Ixil history and culture. Several articles in the Sunday section of Guatemala's leading newspaper, *Prensa Libre*, had piqued my interest. One recounted the Ixil Maya's rich legends and storytelling culture, while another advanced

the etymological interpretation of *Ixil* as "place of the jaguar."[2] In a stroke of serendipity, I met anthropologist Benjamin Colby and learned of his 1960s research on Ixil ethnicity and the perseverance of pre-Hispanic beliefs and rituals. Both sources gave the impression of a deeply traditional Maya society, still removed physically and culturally from the main currents of modern Guatemala. I was aware, however, that the relative isolation of Ixil communities had already been shattered, first by land- and labor-hungry outsiders in the early twentieth century, and second, by devastating civil war violence perpetrated by both government and opposition forces during the thirty-six-year civil war (1960–96). These initial windows into the Ixil past, in turn,

[23]

opened doors to further inquiry and exploration.

Since 2005, I have gathered oral histories and stories from Ixil elders, engaged in conversations with youth and young professionals about postwar changes and challenges, and delved into academic literature and museums. The following thumbnail history of the Ixil Maya is presented through the wide-angle lens of Guatemala's political, social, and economic evolution, with a close-up focus on the distinctive Ixil culture and homeland where sources makes this possible. I believe these windows into history may help travelers to direct their exploration with more understanding, and to conduct local conversations with greater appreciation and sensitivity. (For more in-depth study, please consult the bibliography.)

Foreigners—linguists, ethnographers, archaeologists, anthropologists, human rights groups, and itinerant adventurers—have authored the majority of written source material on the Ixil region. I know of only a few Guatemalan investigators, notably Ixil teachers and members of the Academy of Mayan Languages, who have documented aspects of Ixil history, culture, and the sacred and war-scarred landscapes. Just as the ancient Ixil temple mounds erode with each passing season, when the current elders pass on, much of the rich detail of Ixil heritage that is not preserved in written, photographic, or audio form will disintegrate into dust. At present, few among the Ixil are looking back. Attention is on the future—education, land, jobs, mobility, and survival. For those interested in historic documentation or preservation, there is a wonderful—and very brief—opportunity to contribute time, energy, or resources to help document the extraordinary Ixil legacy.

Pre-Hispanic Ixil History and Culture (500 BC–AD 1524)

LATE PRECLASSIC PERIOD (400 BC–AD 200): IXIL ANCESTORS SETTLE IN NORTHERN QUICHÉ

Ancient ruins and artifacts unearthed in the present-day *aldea* (district) of Ilom, in northern Chajul municipality, place the earliest Ixil settlements in the present region by about 500 BC. This period saw the rise of the first large Maya centers in the Petén lowlands to the north, including Tikal (previously known as Mutal), Nak'be, Izapa, Waxaktun, and El Mirador. Teotihuacan's power was simultaneously rising in central Mexico, and its distant ally, Kaminaljuyú, whose ruins lie within Guatemala City limits today, dominated the central Guatemalan highlands to the southeast. By the turn of the millennium, powerful Maya rulers were enthroned as "holy lords" (as in *K'ul Mutul Ajaw*, "Holy Tikal Lord"); their political and military alliances were reinforced by elaborate trade and tribute collection networks extending over hundreds of miles.[3]

The origin of the early Ilom settlers remains an unresolved puzzle. Some cultural historians believe that the first Ixil migrated into northern Chajul from El Mirador or Tikal, navigating the Usumacinta River east and branching south into the northern foothills of the Cuchumatanes. Standing on the mountain heights above Ilom (from *Illomb'al*, meaning "lookout" or "place of rest"), one can well imagine why Ixil ancestors selected this locale. The foothills of these dense mountains offered temperate relief from the steaming jungles of the lowlands, a gateway into the territory of the prized quetzal and regal jaguar, and a pathway through the mountains along the Xak'b'al River into the central highlands. Ilom offers a sweeping vista north and east to the rising sun. Stone remnants of early temples and plazas dot the banks of the Xamala' River in Ilom, as it spills from higher ground into the Xak'b'al

ABOVE: Late Classic Period jade pendant from Nebaj, courtesy of the National Museum of Ethnology and Archaeology of Guatemala.

River Valley and winds northward into the humid expanse of the lowlands. Others, including Mayan linguists, point to distant shared roots of Ixil and Mam languages,[4] and argue that the early Ixil must have come from territories settled by the Mam, whose ancient ruling center Zaculeu lies near the present-day city of Huehuetenango. This question cannot be answered without further discoveries or reconstruction of scattered archaeological evidence. Consistent with known patterns of conquest and acculturation, it is quite conceivable that the provenance of early Ixil settlers in the region may have been different from the origins of those who dominated their ruling classes.

CLASSIC PERIOD (AD 200–910): IXIL DEVELOP CULTURALLY COHESIVE SETTLEMENTS

Archaeological evidence and oral history indicate that the Ixil migrated deeper into the Cuchumatán mountain valleys and established a series of small kingdoms and ceremonial centers throughout the present Ixil-speaking region by AD 500, the midpoint

Ancient ceramic funerary urn and fragments from the private Museo Maya Ixil in Chajul, courtesy of collector and curator, Felipe Rivera Caba.

of the Classic Period. One group moved south into the area of present-day Nebaj municipality, which takes its Ixil name from *Naab'a,* meaning "birthplace of water." The principal population and religious center of this group was located near the present town of Nebaj, in an area called Xe'vak. A second group settled further to the east, in the lower altitudes of Cotzal, as evidenced by the archaeology of several early settlements near present-day Chichel and along the Cotzal River Valley. Ixil linguists say that the name *Cotzal* describes a Maya kingdom "between the mountains"; others suggest that its name may derive from the Ixil expression, *Ko'tutz'a'lavitz,* which translates as, "Let's go to the warmer lands." A third group migrated deeper into the high mountain valleys just south and west of Ilom, creating centers at Xak'b'al, Juil, and Onkab' within present-day Chajul, whose Ixil name, *Xo'l laq jul,* is interpreted as *hoya sagrada,* or "sacred valley."

Although Ixil kingdoms developed in areas distant from the major centers of Maya power and culture during the Classic Period, their rulers appear to have shared in the Maya belief systems and patterns of hierarchical rule that predominated in Mesoamerica at this time. Ixil archaeological sites confirm that Ixil rulers designed their civic and ceremonial centers to reflect elements of the Maya Creation myth, and suggest that Ixil kingdoms benefited from the remarkable cultural florescence that accompanied the rise of the Petén lowland Maya city-states.

The Ixil region is dotted with vestiges of ancient settlements and ceremonial sites, but a few have been rigorously investigated or preserved for posterity. I know of only ancient Xak'b'al in northern Chajul that is being actively preserved and partially restored, as a goodwill gesture of foreign investors constructing a nearby hydroelectric dam on the Xak'b'al River. Most of the other ancient sites lie completely neglected and difficult to locate among the overgrowth or maize fields that long ago encroached on these ancient sites.

The best-known Classic Period site in the Ixil region is Xe'vak, encompassing seventeen temple mounds connected by plazas, raised platforms, and at least one ritual ballcourt. The American archaeological team of A. Ledyard Smith and Alfred A. Kidder conducted fieldwork here in the 1950s, excavating two prominent temple mounds that yielded burial chambers of several generations of rulers at Xe'vak. The sequencing of unearthed artifacts enabled Smith and Kidder to document continuous occupation of Xe'vak over a span of about 800 years, from the Early Classic Period to the Early Postclassic Period (AD 200 to about AD 1000). In burial vaults associated with the Classic Period, they uncovered elaborate ceramics, skillfully carved jade, alabaster vessels, and other exquisite artifacts that Smith and Kidder argued were proof of the cultural, if not political, influence of Petén lowland city-states on Ixil ruling elites. They further speculated that the Ixil might have served as an important trading link for Maya city-states north and south of the Cuchumatanes:

> *From the jungle country there probably came copal, rubber, beautiful hard woods, feathers and skins of tropical birds and animals, cotton, and shells from the Gulf of Mexico. In the reverse direction would have passed implements of igneous rocks, such as celts, manos, metates, obsidian, pyrite, Sacapulas black salt, the highly prized quetzal feathers, and Pacific shells. Jade, too, may have been an active commodity . . .*[5]

In the mid-1960s, Pierre Becquelin and colleagues picked up where Smith and Kidder left off, with a reconnaissance of several dozen pre-Hispanic Ixil sites noted by earlier ethnographers, linguists, and anthropologists who explored the region.[6] Their research contains the best (and perhaps only) drawings of about twenty of the major Ixil ceremonial centers from the Classic and Postclassic Periods. Becquelin concluded that the Ixil region constituted a culturally unified area from the Preclassic through the Postclassic Period, with strong cultural influence from the Petén. However, his team found little evidence to support Smith and Kidder's hypothesis of a strong trade relationship between these backwater Ixil kingdoms and the great centers of Maya power north and south of the Cuchumatanes.[7]

Ixil archaeology provides only suggestive clues as to how political upheaval and devastation of the Maya city-states to the north affected Ixil kingdoms. Smith and Kidder determined that the rich funerary traditions practiced by rulers at Xe'vak had ceased by the latter part of the Classic Period. Similarly, Becquelin's team found almost no trace of Postclassic ceramics at Xe'vak or Xak'b'al, suggesting that these two important Ixil centers may have been abandoned by AD 1000. What caused the downfall of Ixil rulers? Were their fates tied by trade, military alliance, or by blood to defeated lowland Maya rulers?

Decoding the Legacy of the Ancient Maya

Following the mid-eighteenth-century rediscovery of ancient Maya cities by the American diplomat and travel writer, John Lloyd Stephens, and his English illustrator companion, Frederick Catherwood, archaeologists and epigraphers, academics and amateurs around the world struggled to unravel the mysteries of this great civilization locked in the elegant hieroglyphics adorning Maya architecture and artifacts. Major progress came in the 1970s, as scholars and passionate laymen put their heads and existing research together to forge a critical breakthrough. The story of this historic and riveting endeavor is brilliantly recounted by one of the foremost scholars of Maya civilization, Michael Coe, in *Breaking the Maya Code* (1992) later made into a spellbinding documentary film by David Lebrun and Night Fire Films of Los Angeles (2008). Two of Coe's colleagues in this quest, Linda Schele and Peter Mathews, described these discoveries as nothing less than a "revolution" in Maya studies:

> *The past four decades have seen the decipherment of the Maya hieroglyphic writing system and the reading of the history of one of the great civilizations of the world. This decipherment has recovered the names of kings, their families, members of their courts, and artists, artisans, and builders who served them. Growing understanding of Maya imagery has combined with increasingly subtle decipherments of the glyphs to give us new insights into courtly life, religious ideas, and the politics of the time, as well as the economies and social mechanisms that allowed Maya civilization to flourish... As epigraphers who have participated in this revolution, we find that our personal relationship to Maya cities has changed forever... How different it is to walk through a ruined city when it has become a historical place—to "read" a building and to know who looks out from a sculptured portrait. The ruins cease to be anonymous places admired only for their beauty and mystery. Instead, they become the works of people who had names and motivations that we can understand, even from our distant points of view.*[8]

Ixil archaeological sites unfortunately remain mute; remnants of ancient architecture and artifacts have yet to yield "readable" portraits of local rulers or their dynastic histories. To understand the broad cultural and political context in which Ixil kingdoms flourished and perished during the first millennium AD, we can, nevertheless, learn from the rich harvest and decoding of extensive archaeological sites in the Petén lowlands and Yucatan.

During the Classic Period, Maya rulers further developed and refined the cultural legacy of their Mesoamerican forbearers to marshal the sciences of architecture, writing, numbers, time, agriculture, and artisanal production to enrich their ruling dynasties and extend their spheres of political power. They derived "divine" authority from the primordial gods and spirits that populated a Creation myth inherited from earlier Mesoamerican cultures. The Classic Maya lords were invested with godlike attributes and ruled from ceremonial and civic centers planned and executed to enhance sacred symbolism. First among the high castes of the royal retinue were the priest-astronomers, who consulted sacred almanacs of celestial orbits to determine propitious days for ceremonial events, military campaigns, and the planting and harvesting of the sacred maize crop. Through the sacred smoke of copal incense, ritual bloodletting, and live sacrifice, rulers and priests communed with Maya deities, intoned their will, and mediated sacred issues of life and death in the mortal world.

Knowledge of the early Mesoamerican Creation myths, together with the epic narratives of the first Maya peoples and their acquisition of patron gods, comes to us through the miraculous preservation of key source material and intense scholarly study. Two important "alphabetic" sources, originally written by Maya nobles after the Spanish conquest in their newly acquired Roman script, include the eighteenth-century *Chilam Balam* ("Jaguar Translator") of the Yucatec Maya and the sixteenth-century *Popol Vuh* (or "Council Book") of the K'iche' of highland Guatemala. It is believed that these post-Conquest versions were transliterations of both oral histories and earlier sacred pictoral and hieroglyphic renditions created on screen-fold bark-paper codices by royal Maya scribes. Other ancient

Late Classic Period ceramic figurine of K'iche' warrior, courtesy of the National Museum of Ethnology and Archaeology of Guatemala.

sources that complement these late-sixteenth- or early-seventeenth-century textual versions of the Creation myth include many examples of the carved and painted inscriptions that embellished ancient Maya architecture and artifacts from the royal courts of ancient Maya capitals, as well as four hieroglyphic codices that survived the ravages of time and the bonfires of zealous missionaries.[9] The Paris, Madrid, Dresden, and Grolier codices recorded planetary, solar and lunar eclipses, and the precession of constellations associated with important gods and events in the Maya sacred, solar, and Long Count calendars.

The *Popol Vuh* narrative that can be consulted today in the Newberry Library in Chicago is the 1703 manuscript copy of an earlier "alphabetic" K'iche' text. This manuscript was prepared in two columns, in both K'iche' and Spanish, by the Dominican priest, Francisco Ximénez, with K'iche' translation assistance, during his parish posting to Santo Tomas Chichicastenango. The manuscript survived Ximénez and the expulsion of the Dominican Order from Guatemala in 1830, and found its way to the University of San Carlos in Guatemala City. Subsequently, it was "permanently borrowed" in 1855 from the University library by a French monk, Charles Étienne Brasseur, who tucked it in his luggage when he returned to France. After Brasseur's death, the manuscript changed hands several times before being purchased by an American antiquarian, who donated his collection of early American and colonial originals to the Newberry Library in 1911. Rescued from potential oblivion in the 1940s by the Guatemalan historian, Adrián Recinos, the *Popul Vuh* has since been resurrected, retranslated, and interpreted by numerous scholars of the ancient Maya and the K'iche'.[10]

The following is a thumbnail sketch of the Maya Creation according to the *Popul Vuh*. For a better understanding of this extraordinary myth, I highly recommend that visitors and students of Maya history and sprituality read Adrián Recino's Spanish translation or Dennis Tedlock's English translation of Ximénez's manuscript. Victor Montejo, a Jakaltek Maya anthropologist and chronicler of Maya legends and history, also offers a simplified and highly accessible interpretation of the *Popul Vuh*, written in Spanish and beautifully illustrated by Luis Garay (see bibliography).

After creating land from a vast sea and the animals and plants of this new paradise, the primordial gods, embodied as "Heart of the Sky," labor to create humans who will populate the earth, obey, and praise their makers. The gods fail in their first two attempts, initally molding humans from clay and then trying to fashion men from wood. The stage is then set for an epic drama preceding the fourth cycle of Creation, as two generations of twin dieties confront belligerent demigods of hubris, destruction, and evil.

With the blessing of Heart of the Sky, the original Maize Twins, One Hunahpu and Seven Hunahpu, depose the haughty diety, Seven Macaw, and his destructive progeny. While the twins have created conditions for greater peace and harmony, they anger the lords of Xib'alb'a, the Underworld, with their noisy playing of the sacred ball game. The Xib'alb'ans challenge the twins to play ball in their court, foreshadowing a prolonged battle between the forces of life and death, retribution, and regeneration. One Hunahpu and Seven Hunahphu fail to perceive the trickery of their adversaries and are quickly defeated and killed. The severed head of One Hunahpu is hung in a tree among squash vines and ripening calabash, where the seeds of the twins' revenge are sown. Upon visiting the forbidden tree, the curious daughter of a Xib'alb'an lord, Ixkik', becomes impregnated by the spit of One Hunahpu. She narrowly

Illustration from *Popol Vuj: A Sacred Book of the Maya*, ©1999 by Luis Garay. Reprinted with permission from Groundwood Books, Toronto.

escapes her father's wrath, abandoning the Underworld and seeking out the mother of deceased twins, Ixmukane, and eventually gives birth to Hunahpu and Xbalanke', known as the Hero Twins. To protect the twins from repeating their predecessors' fate, Ixmukane and Ixkik' conspire to hide the implements of the ball game in the rafters of their house.

It is the Hero Twins's destiny to confront the Lords of the Underworld, to avenge the death of their father and uncle, to vanquish evil, and to make the world safe for the gods' fourth attempt to create humans. Thus, the twins recover the hidden ball and return to the ballcourt, armed with insight from their animal allies about how to beat the Xib'alb'ans at their own games. The Hero Twins cleverly survive a series of ever-deadly challenges, including immolating themselves and then bringing themselves back to life. Ultimately, the envious Lords of Xib'alb'a are tricked into their own death and defeated.

The Hero Twins are unable to revive their father, One Hunahpu, or their uncle, Seven Hunahpu, but declare that they will forever honor their names at the first light of day and the "Place of Ball Game Sacrifice." The Hero Twins are conveyed by canoe and the "Paddler Gods" to an opening in the ballcourt, the place of Creation, and rise into sky as the sun and the full moon.

With the victory of the Hero Twins, the primordial gods can turn to setting the world and universe in motion and proceeding with their Fourth Creation. They "throw" three pivotal hearthstones into the sky (the triad of stars known today as Alnitak, Saiph, and Rigal) and lay the four cornerstones of the universe, with a tree of life at its center. The primordial grandmother, Ixmukane, grinds sacred yellow and white maize with water to mold the four men and four women humans, who will become the founding ancestors of the Maya.

ABOVE: Early Post-Classic Period incense burner from Nebaj, from the collection of the National Museum of Ethnology and Archaeology of Guatemala.

Maya rulers prepared for death and rebirth in the tradition of the Hero Twins, Hunahpu and Xbalanke', and their father, One Hunahpu, whose sacrifice and seed ensures the resurrection of life. From this Creation myth the figure of the all-powerful Maize God emerges, embodying the Sun, regeneration, and life-giving food of the primordial gods and body and blood of the Maya ancestors. The civic and ceremonial centers of the ancient Maya kings mirrored symbolic elements of the Creation myth and their legendary origins in an ancient city of mountains, canyons, and caves.[11] Pyramidal temples with altars at their apex may have represented the volcanoes at the mythical cradle of civilization, thought to be the Tuxtlas volcanoes on the Gulf Coast, the ancient homeland of the Olmec civilization near present-day

Veracruz. Plazas symbolized openings into the primordial sea and the life-giving role of water that the Classic Maya channeled into aqueducts and reservoirs to supply urban centers and adjacent fields. Slope-sided ballcourts represented the place of death and rebirth, the sacred portal through which the Hero Twins descended into the Underworld and were reborn to set the universe in motion. The planning and proportions of Maya architecture and ceremonial space echoed the ancient symmetry of a rectangle defined by a "golden mean," attributed to the divine hand of the primordial gods in laying out the sacred dimensions of the cosmos.[12]

The ancient Maya mastered celestial observation, numbers, and time. Like other early Mesoamerican cultures, the Maya clocked sacred and secular rituals according to highly accurate observation and recording of celestial movements, in particular the rising and setting sun, orbits of the moon and Venus, as well as the arcing of other key constellations in the Milky Way. Incorporating the concept of zero, probably inherited from their Olmec forbearers, the Maya deployed a numerical system of dots, bars, shell-like symbols, and pictorial glyphs to record sacred and linear time.

The Maya observed a sacred 260-day count, called the *tzolk'in*, with 13 periods of 20 days each. Each day in this cycle consisted of a number from 1 to 13 paired with one of 20 ordered daygods. The daygods were portrayed by glyphs that were at once linguistic and astrological, and used in divination. A 365-day solar year was composed of a 360-day period, called a *haab* (*uallab* in Ixil), consisting of 18 named "months" or *winals*, of 20 number/daygod days, plus a brief end-of-year period of 5 "watchful" days, called the *wayeb* (*o'q'ii* in Ixil). After 52 *haabs*, the sequence of 18,980 unique day-month-year combinations came full circle, synchronizing the *tzolk'in* and *haab* cycles in a complete Calendar Round, written by the Maya as a day-sign (number and daygod combination), plus the numbered month in the *tzolk'in* cycle and number and name of the month in the *haab* cycle. One can envision this cyclical calendrical system like a set of three interlocking gears, as in figure 1. At the end of 104 *haabs* (two calendar rounds), the sacred and solar calendars also aligned with another portentous cycle, the alignment of the Earth with Venus and the sun.

In addition to these eternally repeating cycles, the Maya employed a linear calendar, known as the "Long Count," to record important events in ruling dynasties with reference to the beginning of a "Great Cycle," equal to 13 *b'ak'tuns*, associated mythologically with the dawn of Creation. Long Count time was configured in a five-decimal system, in base 20, as follows:[13]

LONG COUNT UNITS	EQUIVALENT	DAYS
1 k'in	1 day	1
1 winal	20 days	20
1 tun	18 uinal	360
1 k'atun	20 tun	7,200
1 b'ak'tun	20 k'atun	144,000
1 "Great Cycle"	13 b'ak'tun	1,872,000

According to surviving hieroglyphic codices and dated inscriptions from Preclassic and Classic Period architecture and artifacts, the Maya believed that three pivotal Hearthstones of Creation were "thrown" into orbit by the primorial gods on 13.0.0.0.0, *4 Ajaw (tzolk'in cycle) 8 Kumk'u (haab cycle)*. The last day of the previous "Great Cycle," calculated as August 13, 3114 BC, marked the dawn of a new era, the Fourth Creation.

On December 23, 2012, the current 13-*b'ak'tun* "Great Cycle" in the Maya Long Count, came to a close on 13.0.0.0.0. 4 Ajaw 3 K'ank'in . . . and a new cycle began. The anticipation of this date has engendered much discussion, as well as apochryphal doomsday predications, about the significance of the 13-*b'ak'tun* cycle to the ancient Maya and early

Mesoamerican cultures. For those interested, I recommend the work of researchers and scholars affiliated with the Maya Conservancy (www.mayaconservancy.org), who have contributed years of intense study to the astronomical advancement of the ancient Maya and their physical and ritual embellishment of place and time within their sacred landscapes, art and architecture, civic and religious life, and rich mythologies.

IMPLOSION OF THE LOWLAND MAYA CITY-STATES

The early Classic Maya city-states were intricately networked by trade, "drum-telegraph," and shifting political alliances. A key military victory of Tikal (or Mutal) over its rival, Uaxactún, in AD 378 consolidated two powerful kingdoms under a new dynastic ruler in Tikal with ties to Teotihuacan (originally known as Puh, or "Place of Reeds") in central Mexico, and Kaminaljuyú in the central Guatemalan highlands.

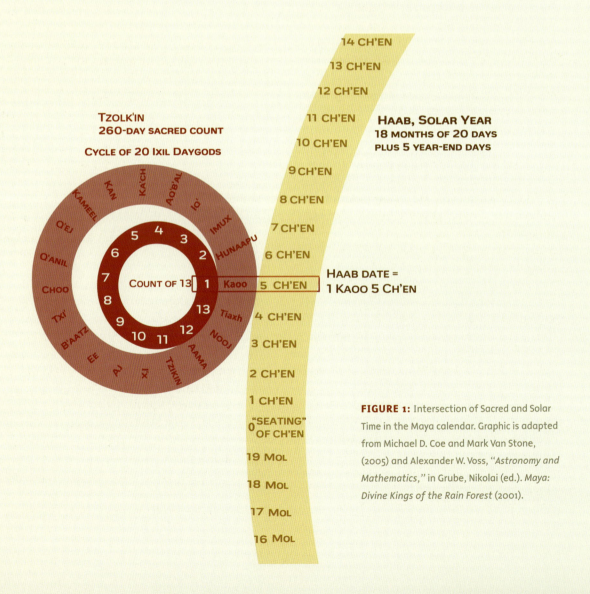

FIGURE 1: Intersection of Sacred and Solar Time in the Maya calendar. Graphic is adapted from Michael D. Coe and Mark Van Stone, (2005) and Alexander W. Voss, "Astronomy and Mathematics," in Grube, Nikolai (ed.). *Maya: Divine Kings of the Rain Forest* (2001).

This power shift led to the polarization of some sixty lowland city-states into two rival alliances—those loyal to Tikal, and others aligned with the powerful kingdom of K'an (Kalak'mul) further north, in the present-day Mexican state of Campeche.

Over time, the kingdoms of the Petén, together with more-distant allied states, were drawn into a protracted feud. In turn, treachery and war led to the demise of these kingdoms, their royal lineages decapitated and their centers pillaged, burned, and depopulated. Archaeologists and climatologists speculate that widespread human destruction, combined with the effects of prolonged drought on an overtaxed and fragile ecology, led to the abandonment of these once-mighty Maya kingdoms of the Petén. Lowland rivalries, battles, and the defeat of major powers reverberated across the Maya world in the latter centuries of the Classic Period. Political alliances were shattered, and trade and tribute networks withered. Survivors straggled out of the Petén between AD 700 and AD 900, leaving a power vacuum in Mesoamerica and heightened insecurity in formerly allied regions.

The latest date in the Maya Long Count that has yet been recovered is AD 909, carved into a royal stela in Toniné, Chiapas; Maya archaeologists associate this date with the end of the Classic Period.

POSTCLASSIC PERIOD (AD 910–1524): RISE AND DECLINE OF K'ICHE' MAYA DOMINANCE

During the Postclassic Period, "Toltec" tribes swept into the western and central highlands of Guatemala from their ancestral homeland of Tollan (or Tula), in the present-day Mexican state of Hidalgo.[14] The K'iche', and related Kaqchikel, Tz'utujil, and Rabinal tribes, subdued other Maya settlements in their path, branding, enslaving, and sacrificing captives to their patron gods. The K'iche' established a fortified capital at Gumarcaah (called Utatlán after the Spanish conquest) just outside of present-day Santa Cruz del Quiché. During the reigns of the divine lord, Gucumatz (AD 1400–1425), and his heir, Kikab' (AD 1425–1475), the K'iche' dominated their brethren nations, Tz'utujil, Kaqchikel, and Rabinal, and implanted key family members to preside over conquered communities. These great K'iche' lords carried the title and insignia of their patron god, Toh'il, represented as the famed "Plumed Serpent" deity common to the Aztecs, Teotihuacan, Yucatec, Toltec, and Maya of Classic Petén kingdoms.

There is strong evidence of K'iche' influence of Ixil kingdoms during this period. Postclassic Ixil settlements were more likely to be located in defensive positions, a pattern consistent with increased tension and militarization under K'iche' rule.[15] Cultural artifacts from this period bore the mark of K'iche' style and influence. In a fortuitous instance of ancient oral tradition preserved to modern day, a fifteenth-century Maya ceremonial drama, *Rabinal Achi*, refers to a captured K'iche' prince as emissary-ruler of Chajul. As this drama opens, the defiant Kawek of the Forest, in a jaguar mask, intones his royal lineage: *I am the brave, I am the man of the lord of foreign Cunén foreign Chajul: the Lord Jaguar Man Jaguar K'iche', the quick one.*[16] The foreshadowing of the dissolution and downfall of the K'iche' empire, the hubris of this fifth son of Kikab', takes center stage, and ultimately he pays with his head for his affront to Lord Five Thunder of the Rabinal Nation.

In the hundred years preceding the arrival of the Spanish in the Americas, the supremacy of the K'iche' was decisively broken by internecine warfare and the reassertion of independent and sparring Maya confederations in the central and western highlands. The confluence of European-borne plague in 1520 and famine literally decimated indigenous communities on the very eve of the Spanish invasion. The *Annals of the Kaqchikels*, a sixteenth-century history of the Kaqchikels compiled by several indigenous nobles in Roman script, describes a devastating epidemic as the "black night [that] enveloped our fathers and grandfathers and us also … the mortality was terrible."[17] These factors weakened the capacity of the Maya confederations to defeat Pedro de Alvarado in 1524, when he marched into the territory of *quauhtimalatlan*, a Nahuatl term interpreted as "land of trees."[18]

Three Centuries of Spanish Colonial Rule (1524–1821)

SPANISH INVADERS DIVIDE AND CONQUER THE MAYA

In February 1524, the Spanish conquistadors arrived in Xepit and Xetulul, near present-day Retalhuleu on Guatemalan's Pacific coast, with 120 mounted cavalry, 300 Spanish infantry, and an army of mercenaries from Cholula and Tlaxcala.[19] On a plain near present-day Quetzaltenango, the Spanish engaged an army of 10,000 K'iche' and other Maya warriors led by the K'iche' commander, Tecún Umán. According to one indigenous account of the battle, the K'iche' leader was adorned "like an eagle, covered with feathers . . . and three crowns of gold, pearls, diamonds and emeralds."[20] After Tecún Umán decapitated Pedro de Alvarado's horse, the Spanish general killed his challenger with a lance through his chest. Indigenous forces greatly outnumbered foreigners, but their bows, spears, and shields were no match for the superior arms of the Spanish or the terrifying sight of their monstrous horses. In a series of two battles several days apart, the invaders defeated the K'iche' army and their allies without a

BELOW: Ceramic masks representing pre-Hispanic Maya dieties and warriors for sale in the Chichicastenango Market

single Spanish casualty, forcing the K'iche' to retreat in surrender.

In a few short years, Alvarado conquered the Maya nations of the western and central highlands, and plunged north and eastward to claim new territories and subjects for the Spanish Crown. During a very brief alliance of convenience with the Kaqchikel confederation, the Spanish headquartered at Tecpán, adjacent to the Kaqchikel citadel at Iximche'. When this alliance ruptured, the Spanish executed the Kaqchikel leaders, and relocated further east, in the valley of Alotenango. In 1525, while Alvarado was waging battles in Cuscatlán (El Salvador), an earthquake flooded their new capital (called *Cuidad Vieja* today), claiming Alvarado's wife and son among its many victims. Spanish conquistadors relocated their headquarters once again to the nearby Panchoy Valley. On December 13, 1543, Spain formally established the *Audiencia de Guatemala*, claiming the modern-day territories of Chiapas (Mexico), Guatemala, El Salvador, Honduras, Belize, Costa Rica, and Nicaragua. They christened their new capital, *Muy Leal y Muy Noble Ciudad de Santiago de los Caballeros de Goathemala* ("Very Loyal and Very Noble City of Saint James of the Knights of Guatemala"), which is the town of La Antigua today. Following extensive earthquake damage in 1717 and 1773, the Spanish abandoned this capital and moved to the location of present-day Guatemala City in 1776.

After conquest of the K'iche', Kaqchikel, Tz'utujil, and Mam confederations, Spanish generals moved to consolidate their control over peripheral areas in the western and central highlands of present-day Guatemala. Spanish military accounts of campaigns to subdue the indigenous communities of the eastern Cuchumatanes were preserved by the colonial historian, Francisco Antonio de Fuentes y Guzmán in the *Recordación Florida*, written in 1690 (and later transcibed in 1800 by Domingo Juarros, the Spanish priest in Nebaj).[21] According to these accounts, in December 1529, General Francisco Castellanos led a batallion of 40 cavalry, 32 infantry, and 400 mercenaries into the eastern Cuchumatánes. Upstream from Sacapulas, they constructed a log bridge to ford the river and began a steep ascent into the mountains. Near the first ridge, the invaders confronted an army of four to five thousand warriors from Nebaj and surrounding communities. According to Ixil oral history, indigenous warriors bombarded the advancing Spanish with tree trunks and rocks from the high ridges between Nebaj and Cunén; Ixil women joined in the defense by raining hot liquids and dry chili powder down on the enemy.[22] The Spanish cavalry managed to gain the advantage of the heights, and then pursued retreating indigenous warriors to a heavily fortified town of Nebaj, surrounded by steep ravines. The mercenaries scaled the perimeter embankment of this fortress and set the besieged town on fire. The Spanish subdued Nebaj and imprisoned its leaders. The following day the nearby population was shackled, forcing the leaders of Chajul to surrender. A parallel Spanish contingent commanded by Francisco de Orduña marched on Uspantán in 1529, but was repulsed by a fierce coalition of warriors from Uspantán and Cotzal; however, a second offensive in 1530 successfully brought these communities under Spanish control.[23]

COLONIAL RULE: POPULATION RESETTLEMENT, FORCED LABOR, AND CONVERSION TO CATHOLICISM

Once the major military campaigns had subdued the Maya, the Spanish Crown authorized Franciscan and Dominican clergy to administer large areas of the new empire. For the most part, Ixil communities shared the fate of other indigenous communities under colonial rule: forced resettlement, expropriation of indigenous land, harsh discipline of the Catholic clergy, and death in huge numbers. Historians and demographers estimate that the indigenous population of the Cuchumatanes numbered between 250,000 and 300,000 on the eve of the Spanish conquest. Over the next century and a half, a combined toll of warfare, forced labor, and relentless waves of European-imported diseases had thoroughly decimated the indigenous population, to as few as 16,000.[24]

By 1540, Dominican missionaries under Bishop Marroquín mapped out regional administrative centers and began conversion of the Maya. In the northwestern section of Guatemala, including the Ixil region, forty *congregaciónes* were established, grouped into eight parishes, each with an administrative and ecclesiastic center (*cabecera de doctrina*).

Colonial resettlement policy met with stiff resistance, as it was designed to undermine traditional communal authorities and distance the Ixil population from their ancestral lands and sacred sites. According to oral history, the Ixil evaded the Spanish by melting into the forests whenever soldiers came looking. In due course, however, the Spanish managed to corral, at least temporarily, much of the Ixil population into four major towns: Nebaj, Chajul, Cotzal, and Ilom. The Spanish abandoned Ilom after repeated raids of Lacandon tribes and relocated half of Ilom's population to Chajul and the rest to Santa Eulalia. A history of the early colonial period written in the early seventeenth century by Dominican monk, Andrés de Remesal, describes the colonial directives for resettlement in the Ixil-speaking region:

> *To Chaul [Chajul] in the sierra of Zacapulas were brought the settlements of Huyl, Boob, Yllom, Honcab, Chaxa, Aguaçaq, Huiz, and four others . . .*
>
> *To Aguacatlan [Aguacatán] and Nevá [Nebaj] were brought together the settlements of Vacá, Chel, Zalchil, Cuchil, and many others*

BELOW: Triple bell façade of the Catholic church in Chajul, built by Spanish Dominican priests and Ixil labor and artisans in the late 16th century.

upward of twelve in number. To Coçal [Cotzal] were brought together Namá, Chicui, Temal, Caquilax and many others . . . [25]

In remote colonial outposts like the Ixil townships, resettlement policies fell far short of their objectives. Implementation of Crown directives depended on the enlistment of indigenous leaders, referred to as *caciques*, or "work bosses," to communicate with and mobilize the local population. Thus, relocated communities managed to preserve and reinforce traditional authority structures within the new town centers. Further, the Spanish had limited power to police the population. As indigenous communities were reluctant to abandon their ancestral lands, many returned to their previous settlements, while others migrated seasonally to maintain their maize fields.[26]

The Spanish instituted systems for extracting free labor and taxes from the conquered population. In addition to the extensive powers granted to the Catholic Church to colonize, convert, and tax the indigenous population, Pedro de Alvarado rewarded his generals with private land grants, or *encomiendas*, which conferred a feudal right to exploit the land and labor for personal and commercial gain. A number of such grants were awarded in the Cuchumatán highlands, including several in the Ixil region.[27] The lavish revenue and excessive demands associated with such *encomiendas* provoked a number of bloody revolts and eventually forced the Crown to curtail the tenure of such grants. However, the *encomienda* experience established a precedent for the usurpation of indigenous lands. During the eighteenth century, the transfer of communal lands into private hands accelerated as Crown agents presided over the sale of state and former Church domains, as well as illegally contrived theft of other indigenous land.[28] Historians argue that the colonial pattern of large landed estates, *haciendas* or *fincas*, "played a significant role in the economic, political, and social development of Spanish America," and set the stage for the increasing marginalization of the indigenous population that has continued to the present day.[29]

Across the *Audiencia de Guatemala*, Franciscan and Dominican missionaries resorted to draconian measures to convert indigenous communities to Catholicism and obliterate ancient religious beliefs and rituals. They burned sacred Maya divinatory almanacs (codices) and destroyed ancestral altars and physical idols. The rhythm of the Gregorian calendar was superimposed on the sacred and solar calendars of the Maya; celebration of Catholic saints replaced homage to Maya daygods.[30] In every *cabecera*, missionaries mandated that all dwellings be located within a regulated radius from the Church. Attendance at daily Mass was obligatory; continued observance of traditional rites met with severe punishment. Missionaries recruited indigenous leaders for membership in religious brotherhoods—*cofradías* for men and *hermandades* for women—to raise money for the celebration of the saints and to support church operations. Catholic indoctrination and coercion forced the Ixil, like other Maya communities, to accept the religion of their conquerors and to find ways to accommodate traditional religion and its practice

ABOVE: Hand-dipped beeswax prayer candles lit in conjunction with Catholic prayer offerings and traditional Maya ceremonies.

within the rituals of the Catholic Church. The Ixil were not unique in forging a hybridized version of old and new, fusing the Maya concept of the Creator with the Spaniards' Almighty, and cloaking Catholic saints with the attributes and powers of Maya deities. Beyond the policing eye of the lone parish priest, Maya priests continued to observe their sacred calendar rhythms and to perform traditional prayer ceremonies at ancient mountain altars.

In 1754, the Spanish Crown ordered the secularization of parish control and expropriated Church-owned lands. In many remote areas of the empire, however, the Church continued to function as a Crown surrogate, but exercised diminished authority over Maya communities.[31] Catholic clergy considered the Ixil parishes a highly undesirable post. Although the lonely priest was nominally in charge of civil and religious affairs in the Ixil towns, surviving parish records voice their frustration with the population's disregard for Church decrees and retrenchment in former "heathen" ways.[32] Similarly, Cuchumatán communities remained completely peripheral to the emerging business and land-owning interests of Spanish descendants.

Independence to Civil War (1821–1960)

NATION BUILDING: SWEEPING POLITICAL AND ECONOMIC REFORM

The territories of colonial Guatemala declared independence from Spain in 1821 and formed a union with the Mexican Empire. By 1823, this restive union proved unworkable, and the United Provinces of Central America was created to include the areas of present-day Guatemala, Costa Rica, Honduras, Nicaragua, and El Salvador. Within a few short years, separatist revolts further splintered the confederation. Rafael Carrera, an uneducated but socially ambitious and charismatic Ladino,* led a revolt of nationalist landowners and conservatives against the federal government, resulting in a separate Republic of Guatemala in 1839. Rafael Carrera served two terms as president of the new Republic (1844–48 and 1851–65), presiding over efforts to stimulate the fledgling economy, including the modernization of land tenure. The State reclaimed all outstanding Church land, "vacant," and untitled lands, compelling indigenous communities to formally apply for title to their ancestral lands.[33]

ERA OF LIBERAL PARTY REFORMS: LADINOS, LABOR RECRUITERS, AND LAND-HUNGRY ARRIVE IN THE IXIL REGION (1870–1930)

The presidency of Justo Rufino Barrios (1873–85), followed by a series of other Liberal Party governments, marked the end of Ixil isolation and the beginning of new State control over indigenous communities. The new Republic's first constitution secured freedom of the press, limitation of Church powers, and the institution of public education. In the economic arena, Barrios intended to catapult Guatemala into the international market by ramping up agricultural exports, including coffee, and by offering generous incentives to Guatemalan businesses and foreign investors. The Liberals accelerated the land-titling process and issued mandatory municipal labor orders (*mandamientos*) for public infrastructure projects. Private labor contractors worked the rounds of indigenous communities, plying the population with liquor and easy loans. In this manner, labor contractors ensnared tens

---

* *In Guatemala, the term, Ladino, is used expansively, referring to a Spanish-speaking person of mixed descent and, commonly among indigenous communities, to describe any non-indigenous person or, in a derogatory sense, an indigenous person who abandons his or her customs for "western" or "outsider" ways.*

Anthropologist Jackson Steward Lincoln Opens a Window into Ixil Society and Culture (1930–40)

When Lincoln conducted his research in 1939–40, he found the Ixil region under siege. By this time, the Ladino population had grown to about 1,200, and the Ladino *fincas* commanded huge numbers of local laborers—2,000 alone on the Finca San Francisco in eastern Cotzal. The American anthropologist described the Ixil population's deep distrust and disdain for virtually all Ladinos and foreigners. Lincoln's generosity toward rural villagers and his knowledge of the ancient Maya calendar system earned him a degree of trust and access to traditional knowledge normally denied to outsiders. Through this anthropologist's keen observations and interviews, we have a rare window into Ixil society and culture at mid-century. Despite unprecedented incursions of Ladinos and central government authority in the region, Lincoln observed that Ixil culture remained deeply centered around pre-Hispanic traditions. He noted the persistence of ancient social caste distinctions, the centrality of the sacred maize crop, and a deeply religious practice tuned to an ancient Maya calendar system, which he described as a "working pagan-Christian religious compromise."[42]

Unfortunately, Lincoln contracted pneumonia and died in Guatemala City in late 1940 prior to finalizing his study. Such was the respect that his Ixil guides and

interpreters felt for Lincoln that a small delegation came down from Nebaj to speak with Lincoln's widow. Not knowing where she was lodging, they stationed themselves for several days in the main marketplace in Guatemala City in the hopes of seeing her. Indeed, they managed to find her in the crowd and to relay their condolences and ascertain that she, herself, was all right.

Lincoln's wife arranged for the final editing of her husband's manuscript. The Carnegie Institution published *An Ethnological Study on the Ixil Indians of the Guatemala Highlands* in 1945. This important work was never translated into Spanish. A microfilm copy is available through the archives at the University of Chicago. I consulted Lincoln's original typed and hand-noted manuscript in the Tozzer Library at Harvard University; my citations are from this original version.

of thousands of indigenous seasonal laborers in a system of perennial debt peonage, forcing debtors to work off their loans on distant plantations three to six months of every year. The Boston-based United Fruit Company launched its "Banana Republic" in Guatemala in 1904. The company extracted lucrative tax concessions and monopolies for construction and operation of a Pacific port, railroads, and energy production. Within a mere twenty years, the United Fruit Company and a conglomerate of American businesses would account for two-thirds of Guatemalan imports and 80 percent of exports.

The Ixil of Nebaj proudly memorialized the hamlet in Salquil Grande where the wounded war hero Barrios sought refuge in 1871. President Barrios turned a blind eye to illicit Ixil trade with Mexico, which initially augured well for continued Ixil autonomy. The lonely parish priest, who ministered penuriously to the entire territory of Nebaj, Chajul, and Cotzal, remained the only resident "outsider" in the region. Anthropologist Jackson Stewart Lincoln's 1939 interview with "Doña Juana B," a schoolteacher and the first Ladino woman to settle in Nebaj in 1887, paints a picture of early 20th century Ixil society still dominated by members of precolonial lineage elites, and daily life deeply rooted in ancestral traditions.

> *There was always a lot of praying and costumbre [spiritual practice and customs] by the zahorines [traditional Maya priests] at all the crosses and mounds in town, and especially at the great cross in front of the church...*
>
> *The cerbatana [blowgun for hunting birds] was constantly in use. In the houses, all of which were of the same, probably early Spanish type as today, meat hung drying over the fire and altars. There was no milk, but some cattle, sheep, and many pigs.*
>
> *In the government [of Nebaj] there were no Ladinos, only Indian alcaldes [elected "mayors" and assistant "mayors"], and the town was virtually ruled by the governor, assisted by his top-caste associates who were very ruthless with lower-caste or poor Indians. [Lincoln's note: It is still impossible to say how much was really caste and how much was economic status.]... One or two Indians could read or write Spanish as taught by the priest, but most could neither read, write, nor [speak] it, and they did not want to learn.*[34]

It was only a matter of years, however, before others would follow Doña Juana to Nebaj and into Chajul and Cotzal. The arduous access to the Ixil region no longer posed an insurmountable obstacle, but a golden opportunity to stake out early claims in uncharted territory. According to Doña Juana, the indigenous population met the first wave of outsiders with outright hostility. In Nebaj, the local population repeatedly burned the wood she had collected to construct her house, and told her to go back to where she had come from. They feared that "if she settled [there], other Ladinos would follow and spoil their life and interfere with their traditional spiritual practices (*costumbre*)."[35]

The 1893 census noted 98 Ladinos in the Ixil region.[36] In the vanguard came petty merchants, the rare teacher like Doña Juana, small farmers, and labor contractors, like the Italian-descendant, Pedro Brol, looking to fill their quota with Ixil laborers. Outsiders also brought the first cane liquor, *aguardiente*, to Nebaj, but this lucrative business quickly caught on among indigenous entrepreneurs.[37] By 1910, as annual Guatemalan coffee exports soared to 50,000 tons, dozens of liquor stores and saloons had sprung up in Nebaj. Cheap liquor and easy loans not only greased the "recruitment" of seasonal labor, but also rapidly "monetized a subsistence economy," according to anthropologist David Stoll. The effects were profound and irreversible for traditional Ixil society and culture.[38] A huge portion of Ixil families became trapped in a state of perpetual debt peonage: an estimated 6,000 Ixil—men, women, and children—made the annual three- to six-month trek to harvest coffee and sugar cane on the Pacific slopes and coastal plantations. Many lost land to liquor or debt. The failure of Ixil leaders to protect the interests of the local population undermined traditional community authority and cohesion.

For millennia, Ixil subsistence farmers had cleared and worked community lands to fulfill their basic needs through traditional *usufruct* practices, i.e., conferring a community-accepted right to exploit common or private land for personal gain, but not conferring permanent or legal ownership. Like other Maya communities, the Ixil maintained areas of open and forested lands strictly for common use, known as *ejidos*. In the five centuries since the Conquest, only the Catholic Church and a few of Alvarado's conquistadors had exercised certain land claims within Ixil territory. After independence, however, a series of new land-titling requirements challenged every indigenous community to defend and register their traditional land claims. This process exacerbated historical feuds among and within communities. Not surprisingly, Ladinos who controlled the land-surveying and registration process argued that lands in indigenous hands were "completely unproductive" and an obstacle to economic progress.³⁹ When the Ixil municipalities eventually received titles to their municipal lands between 1885 and 1903, all had lost portions of their ancestral lands to early claimants and to arbitrary State grants. Nebaj lost an estimated 7 percent of its original claims, Chajul, 5 percent, and Cotzal, 45 percent.⁴⁰ Outsiders controlled some of the most productive land in the region.

Up through the early decades of the 1900s, powerful Ixil individuals and descendants of former Ixil ruling elites occupied the municipal offices of mayor (*alcalde*) and councilmen (*regidores*). A Ladino usually held the important post of municipal secretary, whose job it was to negotiate mandatory government labor requirements, among other administrative responsibilities. These employees were frequently able to manipulate labor detachments or arbitrate local disputes for their own personal benefit. Several Ixil *alcaldes* also exploited their office in order to acquire additional personal lands. By 1924, there were more than 800 Ladinos living in the Ixil region.⁴¹ The government solidified central authority over indigenous communities by requiring that there be a Ladino counterpart for every indigenous officeholder. This measure further eviscerated traditional Ixil authorities and accelerated the transfer of Ixil lands into the hands of outsiders.

OPPRESSIVE LABOR LAWS AND EXTENSION OF STATE CONTROL PROVOKE OPPOSITION (1931–1944)

General Jorge Ubico Castañeda catapulted to power in 1931 on a single-candidate ballot after President Chacón suffered a stroke. The Great Depression and the collapse of world coffee prices wreaked economic havoc and political unrest in Guatemala, and Ubico seized the mandate to revive the leading agricultural-export sector and to centralize presidential power. Among his early decisions was to grant the United Fruit Company a monopoly over the railroads and the seaport of Puerto Barrios. He strengthened military capability to quell any opposition, and enforced his agenda by instituting a new post of military *commandante* at the municipal level. With his power base assured, Ubico moved to guarantee agricultural export producers, mainly large plantation owners, with reliable sources of cheap labor. With one hand, Ubico abolished the controversial practice of private debt peonage, leading to widespread celebration among indigenous communities and consternation among the dreaded labor contractors and their patrons. With the other hand, he imposed a new regime of national labor conscription. The new Vagrancy Law (*Ley contra La Vagancia*) and Validity Law (*Ley de Vialidad*) required all non–wage earners (mostly indigenous subsistence farmers) to provide 12 days of free labor per year for public infrastructure projects and 150 days of low-wage labor on private farms or plantations. Everyone subject to the labor requirement carried a personal "passbook" (*boletos de vialidad*), in which government authorities and private employers recorded the individual's fulfillment of their labor quota.

The new labor laws incited opposition throughout rural communities. In Nebaj, a delegation of Ixil community leaders converged on the municipal offices to demand an explanation. Summoned by the Ladino *commandante* for an explanation of the new laws, the local populace gathered on the town plaza.

Summoned by the Ladino *commandante* for an explanation of the new laws, the local populace gathered on the town plaza. According to Lincoln's second-hand account, a careless insult by the *commandante* ignited a highly combustible situation, and a skirmish erupted. The *commandante* was knocked down and the crowd hastily disarmed his seven-member garrison. Although no shots were fired and the confiscated rifles were voluntarily returned, the army chief in Santa Cruz del Quiché dispatched troops to Nebaj. The army summarily executed seven [later versions note six leaders] Ixil leaders in the central plaza as a warning against further insurrection.

Ubico's heavy-handed presidency climaxed in widespread opposition and forced his resignation in 1944. In the ensuing political chaos, Ubico loyalist, General Frederico Ponce Vaídes, made a bid for power. Young reformist military officers, Captain Jacobo Árbenz Guzmán and Major Francisco Javier Arana succeeded in rallying anti-Ponce military officers and forcing Ubico and Ponce into exile. Árbenz and Arana joined with progressive businessman, Jorge Toriello, to form a provisional military junta and announced national elections. Their actions cleared the way for Juan José Arévalo, a philosophy professor teaching in Argentina, to win the presidency with 85 percent of the vote and a popular mandate for democratic reforms.

GUATEMALA'S "DECADE OF SPRING" (1944–1954)

The presidencies of Juan José Arévalo (1945–51) and Jacobo Árbenz Guzmán (1951–54) came to be known as "The October Revolution" and the "Decade of Spring." Arévalo swiftly annulled the Vagrancy Laws and presided over a revamping of the constitution; among the most popular reforms: legalization of labor unions and cooperatives, passage of minimum wage and social security laws, extension of public education in rural areas, and an expansion of the political party system. Against a backdrop of increased regional polarization between hard-line right-wing regimes and growing socialist movements, Arévalo trod a middle ground. On the one hand, he refused to legalize the Communist Party and pressed forward with the modernization of capitalism. On the other, Arévalo expanded opportunities for the middle class, wage laborers, and small landowners by curtailing abusive labor practices and by requiring large landowners to rent unused acreage at accessible rates. For the first time in Guatemala's history, Arévalo's government raised the possibility of unseating entrenched power elites. Not surprisingly, opposition by old-guard conservatives, large landholders, and U.S.-backed businesses was shrill, fomenting fears about "Indian"

BELOW: Printed back of a Q100 currency bill issued in 1985, portraying a Guerrilla Army of the Poor (EGP) fighter trading in his weapon to an Army soldier for cash. The Guatemalan ruling military junta employed such propaganda tools to convince opposition fighters and sympathizers to abandon their cause.

uprisings and a "communist" dictatorship.

Jacobo Árbenz won the 1950 elections with 65 percent of the vote. He pressed vigorously ahead to solidify legislative progress on both economic and political fronts. Land redistribution and breaking the monopoly of the United Fruit Company over the country's ports and rail system were central to the president's agenda. According to the 1950 Land Census, a handful of wealthy owners controlled 40 percent of the best agricultural land in Guatemala, while small farmers owned only 14 percent. The *Agrarian Reform Law* of 1952, known also as *Decree 900*, mandated a formula for expropriation of uncultivated acreage on estates greater than 90 hectares, and compensation at the registered land value. Landless rural families could apply to receive land grants through local Agrarian Councils. By June 1954, the Árbenz government had expropriated approximately 521,000 hectares from 800 private farms and awarded land to 100,000 rural families.[43]

National reforms permeated deep into the Cuchumatanes.[44] Electoral reforms returned municipal offices to local control. In Chajul and Cotzal, Ixil candidates prevailed in the mayoral elections; in Nebaj, two ardent Ladino reformers served as mayor in 1947 and 1949. Decree 900 raised hopes of redressing the rising anger of many Ixil community leaders and small farmers toward large plantation owners in the region. Local claims against undeveloped acreage at Finca La Perla in Chajul and Finca San Francisco in Cotzal were prepared, expropriated, and slated for redistribution.[45]

COUP AND COUNTERREVOLUTION (1954–1960)

President Árbenz's actions to nationalize land of the United Fruit Company in March 1953 solidified landed and business opposition to the reform government. John Foster Dulles, U.S. Secretary of State and an investor in the United Fruit Company, urged President Eisenhower to squash Árbenz and "communism" in Central America. Together with Guatemalan-exile Lieutenant Colonel Carlos Castillo Armas, the CIA hatched a plot to overthrow Árbenz. In June 1954, the "National Liberation Army" invaded Guatemala from Nicaragua, forcing Árbenz into exile in Mexico. On July 2, the CIA flew General Armas into Guatemala City as figurehead of the counterrevolutionary forces.

The "springtime of reform" came to a screeching halt. Land expropriation was canceled and reversed; ultimately, only 500 out of the 10,000 rural families awarded land under this program were able to stay on their new land. The right-wing group, calling themselves the National Committee of Defense Against Communism, created a blacklist of Árbenz supporters to be summarily "eliminated": reformist students and university professors, union and cooperative leaders, rural local agrarian committees, progressive-minded teachers, and community leaders.

Arbitrary arrests, torture, and death-squad activity intensified after the National Liberation Movement's right-wing coup. Ensuing power skirmishes resulted in the 1957 assassination of Colonel Armas, whereupon successive military juntas propelled the country into a full-scale attack on any and all left-leaning and socially progressive elements of Guatemala's Ladino and indigenous population.

Civil War (1960–1996)
"La Violencia"

The brutality and scope of the counterrevolution campaign alarmed and polarized communities across Guatemala, setting the stage for deepening and widespread civil war. Then, and even now, Guatemalans speak about this horrific period simply as *La Violencia,* speaking as though the country had been possessed and devoured by a hideous demon.

For the next three decades, the country spiraled into an increasingly violent and bitter struggle that fractured both urban and rural communities along shifting and complex political, economic, ethnic, and class lines.

Opposition to the right-wing governments coalesced around four main insurgency groups, including the Guerrilla Army of the Poor (EGP), the Revolutionary Organization of People in Arms (ORPA), the Rebel Armed Forces (FAR), and the National Directing Nucleus of the Guatemalan Labor Party (PGT-NDN).

By 1982, leaders from these groups came together to create the Guatemalan National Revolutionary Unity (URNG), which would increasingly serve as the national voice of the opposition. The ten years from 1975 to 1986, coinciding with the presidency of General Romeo Lucas García (July 1978–March 1982) and the military juntas led by General Efraín Ríos Montt (March 1982–August 1983) and subsequently General Oscar Mejía Victores (August 1983–January 1986), witnessed the greatest violence and human rights violations. Incidents of "arbitrary execution" spiked to over 10,000 per year between 1980 and 1982.[46]

By the late 1960s, *La Violencia* had crept in to the Ixil region, as a vanguard of opposition forces moved stealthily into northern Quiché and Huehuetenango to galvanize a rural insurgency movement. Spearheaded by young, university-educated, and mostly Ladino opponents of the right-wing government, the Guerrilla Army of the Poor (EGP) organized and trained for several years in Ixcán camps before moving south into Ixil territory with a small band of recruits. Rodrigo Asturias, son of the Guatemalan writer, diplomat, and civil war exile, Miguel Angel Asturias, cofounded another rebel group, the Revolutionary Organization of People in Arms (ORPA), operating to the west in Huehuetenango and San Marcos. To demonstrate his solidarity with the cause of indigenous repression and rebellion, Rodrigo chose Gaspar Ilom as his *nom de guerre*, from the protagonist in his father's epic novel, *Hombres de Maíz* (*Men of Maize*).[47] In June 1969, Jorge Brol was gunned down on the road to the family's Finca San Francisco in Cotzal. Although his murderer turned out to be a disgruntled labor contractor with unproven ties to guerrilla forces, the brazen attack on a Ladino landowner and its equally brutal aftermath (the contractor was apparently thrown into the coffee-drying ovens at the Finca) jarred the local community, stirring up old feuds and new unrest.

A few years later, in June 1975, the EGP assassinated Luis Arenas, the controversial land baron of Finca La Perla near Ilom, in front of plantation workers on payday. In 1979, the guerrillas shot Enrique Brol, a former Mayor of Cotzal and part-owner of the extensive wealth and territory of Finca San Francisco in eastern Cotzal. Enrique was widely disliked for his callous treatment of indigenous plantation workers (and their wives), and feared for his brutal reproach of anyone who crossed his path. While these specific "grenades" failed to spark a spontaneous uprising of indigenous support, the insurgents' call to overthrow entrenched land-holding elites resonated in many quarters. Unresolved land disputes, feudal labor conditions for indigenous workers on Ladino plantations, and abrupt reversals of highly anticipated land reform caused many among the Ixil population to be susceptible, if not sympathetic, to the revolutionary message.

When the army moved into the Ixil municipalities in 1979 to squash incipient guerrilla support, however, the ferocity of its death-squad activity produced just the opposite effect. Army brutality galvanized

> *I learned from* La Violencia *in Guatemala how quickly one can sink beneath the anger and outrage that is translatable into purposeful energy, the will to act. I learned also that such stock phrases as "police state," "totalitarian repression," and "systematic genocide" can be blunted by premature and inappropriate use, so that when the real thing looms in the doorway, all their energy is spent and there are no words left. There is only exhaustion, deadness of spirit, and paralyzed acquiescence.*
>
> —Victor Perera, *Unfinished Conquest: The Guatemalan Tragedy* (1993), pp. 50–51.

ABOVE: One of a series of wall paintings in Chichicastenango town center, remembering the horrors of civil war violence in El Quiché.

local material support and an unknown number of indigenous recruits for the insurgency, although postwar accounts suggest that the ranks of the EGP, which began as fifteen guerrillas in the mid-1970s, may have swelled to three to five thousand enlistees at the peak of the conflict in the early to mid-1980s. Guerrilla forces materialized briefly in Ixil towns and villages to urge uprising and gather supplies, but just as quickly, they melted into forest cover following brazen attacks on symbolic targets, army units, and those considered traitors to their cause.

The government mobilized the army and paramilitary groups in a twofold *Operación Ixil* strategy: destroy the EGP and paralyze their base of support. Army units patrolled the streets of the Ixil municipal capitals, leading house-by-house searches for suspected rebels and laying ambushes for the EGP. Between 1978 and 1982, the counterinsurgency

> *It was very hard. But at the same time, the formation of the Communities of Population in Resistance was an important moment in our lives. We were in solidarity, organized, and united to defend ourselves. We were discovering the value of life. Even though we suffered from hunger, and in spite of the scarcity, in spite of everything, we wanted to live. We learned how to defend ourselves, how to organize ourselves, and how to survive on nothing.*
>
> —Gaspar, member of a Community of Population in Resistance (CPR)
> (*Our Culture is Our Resistance: Repression, Refuge, and Healing in Guatemala,* by Jonathan Moller and Ricardo Falla, et al.)

efforts escalated in intensity, scope, and brutality. Army and paramilitary forces carried out more than a hundred massacres in Ixil communities, destroying scores of villages in a systematic "scorched earth" campaign. Unofficial estimates put the toll of dead and "disappeared" (unaccounted-for) at greater than 20,000—roughly equivalent to one out of every three people (including men, women, and children) recorded in the census data for 1973. The army torched the houses and fields of indigenous families, poisoned wells with decaying bodies, and destroyed maize fields and livestock. Persons suspected of working with or for the guerrilla forces suffered gruesome torture, disfigurement, and often public execution.

For most of two decades, a majority of the rural Ixil population was displaced from their homes and fields. A small contingent joined the guerrilla forces. Thousands fled to refugee camps in Chiapas, Mexico; others found refuge in the dense forests of northern Chajul and lowland jungles of the Ixcán and Petén, evading detection and forging Communities of Population in Resistance (CPRs). By 1985, the army had corralled over 10,000 Ixil villagers into "poles of development," also fallaciously called "model villages," to control population movements and to strangle supply and communication lines with guerrillas.[48] The three Ixil *cabeceras* became virtual military garrisons, where routine arrests, interrogations, torture, and public executions kept a terrorized populace in check. The army occupied the Catholic churches, viewed as sympathetic to the opposition; colonial bell towers served as military lookouts and bristled with automatic weapons. An estimated 80 percent of Ixil men and youth were conscripted into civilian patrols (PAC) to "defend" towns from attack and deter local contact with guerrillas.[49]

With minimal resources and increasingly on the defensive, the EGP proved incapable of arming or protecting their supporters against the swift and punishing reprisals of government counterinsurgency forces. After an initial groundswell of popular support and recruitment for the opposition cause, Ixil villagers found themselves increasingly vulnerable and paying the ultimate price for their revolutionary struggle. The army's strategy ultimately prevailed: trauma, fear, and desperation gradually muted and then choked off Ixil villagers' support for the revolutionary struggle. The grim choice between survival and death turned the deadly tide, forcing many Ixil to cooperate with the army in further isolating the EGP. Anthropologist David Stoll describes this predicament, and its fatal consequences for many Ixil townspeople and villagers, in his study of this bitter period, *Between Two Armies in the Ixil Towns of Guatemala* (1993).

Ladinos in Nebaj, Chajul, and Cotzal, who had grown in numbers, land holdings, and influence since 1900, also suffered marked reversals and losses during the civil war, according to David Stoll.[50] The EGP kidnapped and killed prominent Ladino plantation owners in Chajul and Cotzal, terrifying other Ladinos into temporarily abandoning their land and businesses and fleeing the region. Guerrilla forces similarly targeted notorious "Ladinoized" Ixil, who had too often wielded power to benefit local elites. Contrary to expectations, the military governments running Guatemala at this time did little to defend Ladino assets. Army commanders in the Ixil requisitioned plantations to stage new offensives, but left no reinforcements when they moved on. Some landowners came under assault from the government's National Institute for Agrarian Reform, charged with recouping land abandoned during the civil war or erroneously titled. Before the war, Roberto Herrera Ibárgüen was the second-largest landholder in Cotzal. Kidnapped by the EGP in 1977, Herrera relinquished his entire Ixil land holdings to the government shortly after his family was forced to pay a royal ransom for his release. When the worst of the violence was over, Ixil individuals had recouped control of municipal affairs and replaced many Ladino shopkeepers in the major towns. A number of Ladino plantation owners had permanently abandoned their claims; others,

Nebaj municipal cemetary: final burial for exhumed remains of civil war victims.

> **Excerpt from the "Agreement on Identity and Rights of Indigenous Peoples," signed in Mexico City, on March 31, 1995:**
>
> 1. Recognition of the identity of the indigenous peoples is fundamental to the construction of a national unity based on respect for and the exercise of political, cultural, economic, and spiritual rights of all Guatemalans.
>
> 2. The identity of the peoples is a set of elements, which define them and, in turn, ensure their self-recognition. In the case of the Mayan identity, which has shown an age-old capacity for resistance to assimilation, those fundamental elements are as follows:
>
> Direct descent from the ancient Mayas;
>
> Languages deriving from a common Mayan root;
>
> A view of the world based on the harmonious relationship of all elements of the universe, in which the human being is only one additional element, in which the earth is the mother who gives life and maize is a sacred symbol around which Mayan culture revolves. This view of the world has been handed down from generation to generation through material and written artifacts and by an oral tradition in which women have played a determining role;
>
> A common culture based on the principles and structures of Mayan thought, a philosophy, a legacy of scientific and technical knowledge, artistic and aesthetic values of their own, a collective historical memory, a community organization based on solidarity and respect for one's peers, and a concept of authority based on ethical and moral values; and
>
> A sense of their own identity.[51]

seeing the political tide turning against their interests, sold off part or all of their holdings.

PEACE NEGOTIATIONS

The first opening for peace came in 1986, with the election of Vinicio Cerezo Arévalo, ratification of a new constitution, and congressional appointment of a human rights ombudsman. In 1987, the government and a united opposition represented by the URNG held initial discussions in Spain, all the while continuing their military offenses. The peace process gained new impetus in 1992, when the Nobel Peace Prize Committee named a young Maya woman and indigenous rights advocate, Rigoberta Menchú Tum, for the prestigious award. In 1993, right-wing president Jorge Serrano Elías attempted to suspend constitutional rights, but this effort backfired and he was forced to resign. The National Congress appointed Ramiro de León Carpio, serving as human rights ombudsman, to forge a path toward peace. On June 23, 1994, the government and URNG agreed to initial terms of peace in the Oslo Accords. Two more years of tough negotiations led to the Peace Accords of 1996, signed by URNG leaders and President Álvaro Arzú Irigoyen. The Peace Accords articulated a legal framework for national reconciliation and recovery: broad in their implications for redressing overarching issues of historical social injustice and state abuse of power, and detailed enough to direct legal and institutional measures necessary to rebuild the war-torn society.

WAR'S AFTERMATH: FACTS, TESTIMONY, AND THE CHALLENGE OF RECONCILIATION

The civil war exacted a gruesome toll: an estimated 200,000 Guatemalans killed or forcibly "disappeared"; 658 documented massacres; and 360 indigenous villages destroyed.[52] One million persons were displaced from their homes, internally or in exile; an estimated 150,000 fled to Mexico, of which 45,000 occupied refugee camps in southern Mexico, some for as long as fifteen years. In sum, one out of every five Guatemalans was victimized in some form or another by the violence; in the Ixil region, one in five Ixiles was killed, and all were victimized in some form. When the fighting was over, Guatemalan society and its landscape were deeply scarred. Grief and fear of

> *The eyes of the buried will close together on the day of justice, or they will never close.*
>
> —Miguel Angel Asturias, Guatemalan Nobel Laureate for Literature; Prologue, *Guatemala: Memory of Silence* (Commission for Historical Clarification)

reprisals left many unable or unwilling to speak about the horrors of *La Violencia*.

The 1994 Oslo Accords called for a Commission for Historical Clarification (CEH), "to clarify with all objectivity, equity and impartiality" the human rights violations and violent acts of the civil war. The process of uncovering the facts of the war and its violence would consume the next five years in intensive investigations. In a parallel inquiry aimed at national reconciliation, the Catholic Archdiocese of Guatemala launched the Recovery of Historical Memory Project (REMHI), and issued its own report, "Guatemala: Never Again" (*Guatemala, Nunca Más*), on April 24, 1998. In his speech that day, from the Cathedral of Guatemala City, Bishop Juan Gerardi Conedera declared,

> *As a church, we collectively and responsibly took on the task of breaking the silence that thousands of war victims have kept for years. We opened up the possibility for them to speak and have their say, to tell their stories of suffering and pain, so they might feel liberated from the burden that has weighed them down for so many years . . . To open ourselves to truth and face our personal and collective reality are not options that can be accepted or rejected. They are indispensable requirements for all people and societies that seek to humanize themselves and to be free.*[53]

Two days after his speech, Bishop Gerardi was bludgeoned to death—a stark reminder of the divisions and bitterness that would continue to threaten a fragile peace and future reconciliation. Three army officers were eventually convicted and sentenced for the murder.[54] A year later, on February 25, 1999, members of the CEH submitted their findings in a report entitled *Guatemala: Memory of Silence* (*Memoria Del Silencio*). The Commission's conclusions about the historical roots of the conflict and recommendations for reparation and reconciliation are available online (see bibliography). On the basis of extensive fact-finding and testimony, the CEH determined that the army, together with civil patrols, military commissioners, and other right-wing death squads, were responsible for the vast majority—93 percent—of all incidents of torture, death, and forced disappearances. The Commission assigned 3 percent of human rights violations to guerrilla forces, and the remainder to "other unidentified groups." Of the 658 documented massacres (defined as "the collective killing of more than 5 members of a defenseless population"), 626 were attributed to State forces and 32 to guerrilla forces. Of the war's confirmed dead, indigenous Maya accounted for 83 percent; Ladinos, 17 percent. The Commission concluded that the majority of human rights violations and acts of violence had been carried out "with the knowledge or by order of the highest authorities of the State." Further, the CEH declared that State-directed operations in certain indigenous communities constituted acts of "genocide" as defined by the UN Convention on the Prevention and Punishment of the Crime of Genocide:

> *[T]he CEH concludes that agents of the State of Guatemala, within the framework of counterinsurgency operations carried out between 1981 and 1983, committed acts of genocide against groups of Mayan people which lived in the four regions analysed. This conclusion is based on the evidence that, in light of Article II of the Convention on the Prevention and Punishment of the Crime of Genocide, the killing of members of Mayan groups occurred (Article II.a), serious bodily or mental harm was inflicted (Article II.b) and the group was deliberately subjected to living*

conditions calculated to bring about its physical destruction in whole or in part (Article II.c). The conclusion is also based on the evidence that all these acts were committed "with intent to destroy, in whole or in part" groups identified by their common ethnicity, by reason thereof, whatever the cause, motive or final objective of these acts may have been (Article II, first paragraph).[55]

The affected Maya communities cited by the CEH included the Maya-K'anjob'al and Maya-Chuj in Barillas; Nentón and San Mateo Ixtatán in northern Huehuetenango; the Maya Ixil of Nebaj, Cotzal, and Chajul; the Maya K'iche' in Joyabaj and Zacualpa of Quiché; and the Maya-Achi in Rabinal of Baja Verapaz.

The Ixil region suffered 114 documented massacres during the civil war: 54 in Nebaj municipality, 38 in Chajul, and 22 in Cotzal.[56] One in six Ixil children lost a parent. A 1989 census of the three Ixil municipalities counted 2,642 widows and 4,186 orphans; more in hiding or refugee camps were unaccounted for. The vast majority of rural villages had been burned to the ground. Farmer cooperatives were shuttered; seed corn and livestock were gone. Everyone was hungry. Well into the 1990s, tens of thousands remained in refugee camps in Chiapas and in the isolated Communities of Population in Resistance (CPRs). When war survivors returned home, many found that strangers had taken over their property.

The CEH called for formal apologies by the government and the URNG to the Guatemalan people; systematic searches for the dead and missing; honor for the victims; restoration of land and economic assets of the victimized; programs for social rehabilitation; and mechanisms to protect human rights and strengthen instruments of law. The Commission also demanded the prosecution of crimes of genocide, torture and forced disappearance, and other violations of domestic and international law.

On March 10, 1999, President Bill Clinton apologized for the U.S. role in supporting State military repression and violence during the civil war: "It is important that I state clearly that support for military forces and intelligence units which engaged in violence and widespread repression was wrong, and the United States must not repeat that mistake."

On March 13, 1999, URNG leaders issued an unconditional apology to the Guatemalan people and embraced the Commission's recommendations. At the time, government response was viewed as muted, if not equivocal. In an earlier speech of December 1998 in Santa Cruz del Quiché, President Arzú had apologized on behalf of the government for "acts or omissions, for what we did do and what we didn't do." The government issued an initial response to the CEH, stating that the report was a "contribution to a task that has just barely begun." The armed conflict was over, but reconciliation would prove elusive.

Postwar Challenges for the Ixil Region

The business of implementing the Peace Accords began slowly. Guerrilla forces were formally reintegrated into civilian life, and the dreaded rural civil patrols, disbanded. Government decommissioned two-thirds of its wartime military forces. Nevertheless, tension and uncertainty lingered. Neighbors who had experienced the conflict from different camps remained wary. Every Ixil family mourned a relative or neighbor. With the assistance of the Guatemalan Forensic Anthropology Foundation (Fundación de Antropología Forense de Guatemala), survivors began to exhume the dead from mass graves and to give their loved ones proper burials. Most of the "disappeared" were still unaccounted for. Women from Chajul shared their experience of *La Violencia* and hopes for peace in a collection of photo essays published in 2000 as *Voices and Images: Maya Ixil Women of Chajul*.

> *At present we are in the peace process and now that the people are rebuilding their spiritual and material lives, we are fighting so that this peace will continue and grow within each one of us. Perhaps what was lost before is being rebuilt anew, although with a lot of suffering and scars in our hearts, because after so much destruction, a huge wound remains.*[57]

In 2005, when I visited this region for the first time, peace felt fresh and fragile. In most conversations, someone would mention an irreplaceable loss or burst into tears. The plazas in the municipal capitals of Nebaj, Chajul, and Cotzal were all under renovation in a unified effort to pave over memories of terror, but tension and uncertainty lingered in the faces of weary survivors. The bonds of former Ixil community cohesion were frayed, if not permanently fractured.

On a hillside near Nebaj, scores of blue tarp tents marked the most recent resettlement of returning

BELOW: Chajul's municipal plaza underwent complete reconstruction to help expunge horrific memories of torture and executions carried out here during the 36-year civil war.

refugees, named *Nueva Esperanza* ("New Hope"). Local headquarters for the National Program of Compensation were freshly painted, but the budget fell woefully short of promises. CONTIERRA, the government institution appointed to adjudicate land disputes, was mired in paperwork and had settled few cases. A postwar influx of relief aid and reconstruction projects had stimulated a burst of economic activity in the town centers of Nebaj and Cotzal, but the majority of Ixil families struggled to put tortillas and beans on the table.

Many fathers and sons—even some daughters, I learned—had gone "north" to find work. Among those who were now landless and widowed, some had relocated to the urban slums of Guatemala City. As a volunteer for the nonprofit organization, Safe Passage, I encountered a contingent of Ixil widows and children recycling cans and bottles for a few Quetzals a day in the municipal garbage dump. One of these women told me her story: "We lost everything—my husband and son, our house, our cow. Here, we are far from the cruel reminders; I can work each day for myself and my children's future."

Today, fifteen years after the signing of the Peace Accords, daily life in the Ixil region has resumed many of its familiar rhythms. Maize is sown in the family *milpa,* wood is gathered and chopped, the loom is warped, a piglet is fattened for market, and women rise with the dawn to prepare tortillas for the family. However, much in the Ixil region and the daily lives of the Ixil people has changed forever, due not only to the recent war devastation, but also to national and global currents of economic, social, and political change surging up and over the southern ridges of the Cuchumatanes.

Ixil families face a period of unprecedented transition, with daunting challenges as well as new and exciting opportunities. The road system to and within the region has been improved and extended; each year brings more traffic, commerce, and communication between Nebaj, Santa Cruz del Quiché, and Guatemala City. The ethnic makeup of Ixil mountain valleys and hilltops is becoming more diverse: While a majority of the population still speaks Ixil, other ethnic Maya—primarily K'iche' and K'anjob'al—now represent 20 percent of the area's population; Ladinos account for another 20 percent. With these changes, many aspects of traditional Ixil culture are fading; some will disappear when the current elders pass on. The voices of new Ixil economic, political, and professional elites speak more loudly in community affairs than those of traditional authorities. A conflagration of evangelical faith groups continues to erode both Catholic and traditional Maya spirituality, dividing old communities and forging new ones.

Population in the Ixil region has fully recuperated since the war, intensifying pressure on land resources. Indeed, since 1950, the region has witnessed more than a fourfold increase in population. Children and youth under fifteen years old now account for 50 percent of the population. Ixil elders over sixty-five years old, guardians of the culture's stories and customs, represent less than 5 percent. An eighty-year-old grandmother from Chajul worries that the younger generation will not know how to bury her in the hallowed traditions of her Ixil ancestors.

Poverty maintains a merciless grip on the majority of Ixil families. The average land holding per family is declining; a land use survey in 2008 showed that 70 percent of registered land holdings in Cotzal, which has the highest population density among the Ixil municipalities, were smaller than one manzana (0.7 hectares, or 1.74 acres). An estimated 30 percent of Ixil families no longer produce enough maize to feed their family year-round, and most family budgets are increasingly vulnerable to escalating food prices and international market trends. According to a 2006 survey by the National Institute of Statistics of Guatemala (INE) on poverty and basic living conditions, 51 percent of Guatemala's population was living at or below the poverty line, with 15 percent of the poor living in "extreme" poverty, subsisting on

ABOVE: Photo by Juan Clemente Raymundo Velasco. Ixil elders share soup during interview about the community's future promises and challenges.

Q8.8 (US $1.17) or less per person per day in 2006 prices. As the table below illustrates, the vast majority of indigenous families in the Department of Quiché, 84 percent, were considered poor, with a quarter of the poor living in "extreme" poverty. Nebaj, Chajul, and Cotzal count among the poorest municipalities in Quiché, and in all of Guatemala.

While these statistics reveal troubling challenges for Ixil families, I see strong signs of cultural resilience and adaptation across the region. The Ixil people have faced adversity before and possess an enormous capacity for endurance and hard work. For the first time in Guatemala's history, the affirmation of Ixil identity in civic, political, social, and economic affairs is recognized as a fundamental and constitutional right of indigenous people in accordance with the 1996 Peace Accords. In Nebaj, Chajul, and Cotzal, I sense a palpable resurgence of Ixil identity and cultural pride. New road signs and radio programs broadcast information in both Ixil and Spanish. Young Ixil women

POPULATION OF IXIL MUNICIPALITIES

	NEBAJ	**CHAJUL**	**COTZAL**	**TOTALS**
1893 National Census	5,945	3,329	2,825	12,099
1950 National Census	13,253	8,258	9,244	30,755
1973 National Census *(1)*	27,259	18,092	12,698	58,049
1981 National Census *(1)*	18,134	15,713	10,944	44,791
2002 National Census	53,612	31,780	20,050	105,442
2012 estimate *(2)*	75,056	44,492	28,070	147,618

NOTES: *(1)* Census data likely compromised by ongoing civil war. *(2)* Estimates are based on population growth rates for the Department of Quiché, issued by National Institute of Statistics of Guatemala (INE).

POVERTY IN GUATEMALA AND THE DEPARTMENT OF QUICHÉ (2006)

	POPULATION	**POOR**		**NOT POOR**
		Extreme	Non-Extreme	
National total	12,987,829	15%	36%	49%
Indigenous	4,907,693	27%	48%	25%
Non-indigenous	8,056,261	8%	29%	64%
Dept of Quiché	769,364	26%	55%	19%
Indigenous	90%	27%	57%	16%
Non-indigenous	10%	12%	39%	49%

Extreme poverty: Consumption at or below Q8.8/person/day (US $1.17)
Non-extreme poverty: Consumption at or below Q6,574/person/day (US $2.40)
Q7.5 = US $1 (2006)
Source: National Institute of Statistics of Guatemala (INE), *Encuesta Nacional de Condiciones de Vida*, 2006.

BELOW LEFT: The majority of Ixil families still plant a variety of indigenous maize adapted to local conditions over centuries of careful selection and preservation. **CENTER:** Painted on a school wall in Pulay, Nebaj: "Education is the vaccination against violence." **BELOW RIGHT:** Nebaj civil war memorial painting portrays a brighter future for Ixil children and communities.

parade the streets in stunning traditional woven blouses (*huipiles*). Ixil children are attending school in record numbers. Each year, a growing number of Ixil university graduates return home, ready to contribute their knowledge and skills to social programs and income generation in the region.

Summoning a deep reservoir of determination, Ixil families have managed to rebuild war-ravaged homes, villages, and towns. Farmers, entrepreneurs, cooperatives, and women's groups are embracing change and new technology. Ixil teenagers and grandmothers alike now carry cell phones, texting local friends and family, as well as those far from home, in Guatemala City, Los Angeles, and Boston. Farmers are planting new vegetables, some for export; slowly, they are adapting intensified production methods. Rural entrepreneurs gather villagers to demonstrate the economic and financial returns of new wood-saving stoves, water purifiers, and solar lights, and Ixil cooperatives reap premium prices for their organic mountain coffee.

The lessons of history, both defeats and victories, are not lost on the Ixil community. Civil war survivors understand the importance of community cohesion and organization. More Ixil women are taking active leadership roles in their communities. More Ixil students are attending political rallies to ask candidates for transparency and answers. Traditional community leaders and modern Ixil professionals are advocating together for a stronger voice in the economic and social future of the region.

On this optimistic note, I conclude this brief chronology of Ixil history. Along the route to learning about the past, I have discovered many interesting facets and tangents to this long and winding story, each deserving more depth and detail than are possible here. Therefore, I strongly encourage readers and travelers to consult the bibliography for further references.

OPPOSITE: Photo by Chris Percival. Clear road markers along the new highway from Sacapulas to Nebaj.
ABOVE LEFT: Bus transport is easy and inexpensive, but frequently overcrowded.
ABOVE RIGHT: Chajul friends review topographic map with author.

CHAPTER 3

Planning the Journey

During a recent foray to the Chichicastenango market, I struck up a conversation with a tourist bent over the map of Guatemala. "What's beyond Chichi?" he asked, pointing to the vast territory of the Department of Quiché, stretching due north 130 kilometers (about 80 miles) to the Mexican border.

"Breathtaking landscapes, unforgettable experiences, wonderful people," I jumped in. "Are you traveling by foot, bus, or rented car? How much time do you have? Do you have a sleeping bag, warm clothing, a raincoat?" I do not know whether this tourist ever made it to Ixil country. Perhaps he was worried about road conditions, a language barrier, accommodations, or personal safety. Most tourists do not travel beyond "Chichi" because there are too many unknowns; it is simply beyond their comfort zone.

The purpose of this guide is to render Ixil country more accessible to international and Guatemalan visitors. The distance from Guatemala City to the town of Nebaj is about 230 kilometers (126 miles), just 106 kilometers (66 miles) beyond Chichicastenango. Within the last few years, the major roads to and within the region have been vastly improved for year-round travel. What used to be an arduous and unpredictable daylong road trip can be accomplished in half that time today. Visitor accommodations and services are good and expanding every year.

But beyond the logistics of travel, this guide also offers other important ingredients of accessibility: insight into the region's history and culture; detailed explorations of its villages, markets, schools, enterprises, sacred sites, and natural wonders; and suggestions for conversations and experiences with the region's people that transcend language barriers (I should know!). This guide is also an unabashed appeal for visitors to get involved and support a culturally, environmentally, and economically sustainable future for the Ixil population and their majestic mountain homeland.

Although spontaneity works for seasoned adventurers, most travelers can benefit from some advance planning. Depending on traffic and road conditions, the direct drive from Guatemala City to Nebaj is at least six hours, but with add-ons for rest stops, photo opportunities, and a generous allowance for the unexpected road delay, deluge, or detour. It is virtually impossible to visit the region in one weekend, or to "swing through" en route to somewhere else. Ixil country is a destination that draws one in and requires a commitment of time in order to truly explore and appreciate it—my kind of travel! I recommend that visitors spend a minimum of four to five days in the region, and I hope that this guide will give them reasons to stay longer and return again.

Maps and Guides

MAPS

The small-scale tourist maps of Guatemala that are readily available in bookstores and online show the principal population centers and highways, but lack detail and topography that are essential for exploration at the local level. As I have discovered, distances can be deceptive without the reality check of a topographic map, if not a knowledgable local guide. The *Instituto Geográfico Nacional de Guatemala* (ING) produces a series of large-scale topographic maps (1:50,000) covering every section of the country; they are accurate as to geography, but sorely out of date (many from the 1960s), and cannot be used as road maps or to reliably locate small towns. An updated series is eagerly anticipated. Travelers should purchase these sectional maps directly from the ING headquarters in Guatemala City: Avenida Las Americans, 5-76, zone 13, Guatemala City. Phone: (502) 2248-8100. The cost per map is Q55 (about US $7).

Google digital satellite maps provide remarkable clarity for some, but not all, areas of the Ixil region.

To create the maps for this guidebook, I drew on a combination of sources, including schematic maps from the municipal offices of Nebaj, Chajul, and Cotzal, Google Earth images, academic and NGO publications, and local knowledge.

GUIDES

REGIÓN IXIL GUÍA DE SENDERISMO (Guide to Ixil Region Hiking), published in 2005 by Solidarity International, provides thirty guided treks with elevations and detailed maps. Unfortunately, copies are scarce. Hikers can ask for this guide at Popi's Restaurant or El Librito store in Nebaj.

THE GUÍAS IXILES, the Rural Tourism Project, launched by Community Enterprise Solutions in Nebaj (www.nebaj.info/index.html). Phone: (502) 5847-4747 or 5749-7450. For Spanish speakers, contact miguelbrito8@gmail.com; for English-only speakers, contact turismonebaj@gmail.com.

LAVAL IQ', Community Network for the Environmental and Cultural Development of the Ixil Region, formed by leaders of nineteen Ixil

Travel by rented vehicle provides latitude for endless roadside photo opportunities and for detours off the main roads.

communities to promote local ecological and cultural tourism. Contact: redlavaliiq@gmail.com or call (502) 7755-8337.

See also chapters on Nebaj, Chajul, and Cotzal for suggestions of guides within each municipality.

Transportation

There are as many modes of transport as there are appetites, budgets, and schedules. I have met hikers traveling by bus and foot, carrying their own tents and backpacks; bicyclists who peddled over the Cuchumatanes from Tierra del Fuego to San Francisco; extreme kayakers navigating the Xak'b'al River; and students and volunteers hitchhiking from village to village. My dream is to ride on horseback over the mountain trails, but up until now, I have traveled primarily by rented pickup. Four-wheel-drive is preferred for any weather, all terrain, and disorganized gear, and offers room to pick up passengers ("*¿Quiere jalón?*").

BUS

All buses to and from the Ixil region begin, end, or transfer at the bus terminal in Santa Cruz del Quiché. Thanks to recent road improvements, what used to be a teeth-rattling, dust-choking, half-day trip to Nebaj now takes about three hours on a paved road all the way. Count on an extra thirty to forty minutes if you are heading to either Cotzal or Chajul. The three major Ixil towns have their own bus company, but if you are hopping on at Santa Cruz with Nebaj as your destination, taking any of the three will get you there for about Q30. The bus attendant loads bags on the top of the bus, along with baskets of produce, chickens, bundles of firewood, and anything else that won't fit in an overhead bin. Count on three to a seat and standing room only at the busiest times. The Veloz Nebajense bus line ends in Nebaj; Blanca Estella travels to the town of Cotzal and beyond, to the Finca San Francisco; San Juanera travels to the municipal capitals of both Cotzal and Chajul.

MINIVAN SHUTTLE

Private minivan service now challenges buses for business all over the country. They hover around the market or main entrance to town, and passengers hop on and off all along the route. Vans leave Santa Cruz del Quiché every hour and cost only Q25. From Nebaj to Chajul, the price is Q10, from Nebaj to San Francisco in eastern Cotzal, Q15.

CAR RENTAL

Car rentals are available in Guatemala City or in Antigua from a number of vendors. I favor renting in Antigua, where it is convenient to load up on supplies and easy to join the Inter-American Highway. Here are a couple of websites to get you started:

www.guatemalarentacar.com
www.tabarini.com

When to Travel

Every month offers something special in the Ixil region, whether it's the bright green of the new maize shoots after planting, the fireworks and parades of local fiestas, or the community mobilization for the coffee or maize harvest. The rainy season, also the warmest time of the year, lasts from mid-May to mid-October, and features daily downpours, spectacular rainbows, and occasional mudslides that may require delays or detours. The dry season, from about mid-October into May, is cool until March, with a strong possibility of rain or foggy mornings at the highest altitudes until March. October through February, temperatures range from 40 to 70 degrees Fahrenheit—chilly in the early morning, pleasant by midday, and downright cold at night. From March through September, expect higher temperatures in the 60 to 85 degrees Fahrenheit range. All year, the many microclimates between peaks and valleys of the Cuchumatanes offer delightful variation (see Appendix 1: Calendar of Fiestas in the Ixil Region).

PRINCIPAL MARKET DAYS IN THE IXIL MUNICIPAL CAPITALS

Nebaj	Thursday	Sunday
Chajul	Tuesday	Friday
Cotzal	Wednesday	Saturday

Travel Tips

CELL PHONES AND INTERNET

Technology has leapfrogged landlines all over the world. Guatemala is no exception. I am no longer surprised when young and old pause from their homework or their harvest to whip out a cell phone. The major wireless companies include Tigo, Movistar, and Claro. I have had no problems with local or international calling when traveling as far as the Ixil region, and one can replenish cell minutes even in the most remote aldeas. The country code for Guatemala is 502, and all phones in country have eight digits. Landline phones in Guatemala City begin with a "2," and for the rest of the country, a "7"; cell-phone numbers generally begin with a "5" or a "4." Visitors can now find Internet cafés in almost every medium-size town.

MONEY AND CURRENCY CONVERSION

Outside of the most modern shops, hotels, and restaurants, the Guatemalan economy runs on cash transactions. Visitors should expect to exchange foreign currrency or traveler's checks only in major banks in Guatemala City, Antigua, Quetzaltenango, and Huehuetenango. There are freestanding ATM machines in the most major towns. It is always safest to change money in a bank or use an ATM that is located in the lobby or interior of a bank. I encourage visitors to follow the example of Guatemalans, who carry minimal amounts of cash and distribute this discreetly among several deep, buttoned pockets and a pouch under one's clothing.

SAFETY PRECAUTIONS

According to GlobalPost.com, 1.8 million people visited Guatemala in 2011, double the number in 2000. At least half were foreign tourists. The U.S. Department of State issues warnings about the risks of travel in Guatemala, and these are not to be ignored, but there have been no reported incidents involving tourists or foreigners in the Ixil region. When people ask me whether I feel safe traveling in the Ixil region, my answer is an unqualified "yes." I have traveled extensively through the region since 2004, with only positive experiences, encountering friendly assistance and ready hospitality everywhere. The Ixil are proud of their cultural heritage and rich natural resources, and they welcome respectful cultural and ecotourism. For emergencies, I always carry the twenty-four-hour hotline number to our embassy and a Xerox copy of my passport. I suggest that all foreign nationals traveling in Guatemala consult the advisories provided by their governments prior to travel.

International travelers should check in with their respective state departments and local embassies for updated emergency contact information and other travel advisories.

TIPS FOR STAYING HEALTHY

- Bring your own essential medicines for colds, sore throat, upset stomach, and aches and pains.
- Drink bottled water.
- Eat only sanitized and peeled fruits and vegetables.
- Choose hot meals in *comedores* or restaurants.
- Avoid eating in the market.
- Wash hands compulsively.
- Stay warm and dry.

PACKING CHECKLIST

- Waterproof sandals
- Sneakers and/or hiking boots
- Quick-drying clothes and a dozen clothespins
- Warm jacket and rain poncho
- Flashlight and batteries
- Mosquito repellent
- Mosquito net (optional for rainy season and lowland areas)
- Gifts for hosts (school supplies, solar flashlights, etc.)
- Swiss Army knife (to peel fruit, open bottles, sharpen pencils)
- Basic first-aid kit, plus Imodium, Cipro, sunscreen
- Tin bowl and utensils (to avoid stomach issues, eat *only* piping-hot food in local markets)
- Vegetable/fruit sanitizer
- Sleeping bag
- Quick-drying towel and antibacterial soap
- Extra duffel bag
- Camera and binoculars
- Passport (Xerox copy)
- Guatemalan cell phone (inexpensive, indispensable)
- Cell-phone-minute cards (available everywhere)
- Funds (Quetzales) in small denominations (ATM machines in Nebaj)

Electric current in Guatemala is 110v. Outlets couple with the flat two-prong adaptor (like in the United States), but only the most modern outlets feature the third, ground prong. If traveling with a laptop or other electronic devices, visitors should bring appropriate adaptors and surge protector.

Route to Nebaj

The principal access to the Ixil region in northern Quiché is from the south, through Santa Cruz del Quiché, Sacapulas on the Rio Negro River, and up the sheer face of the Cuchumatán Mountains in a series of dizzying switchbacks and stunning views to the municipality of Nebaj. Sacapulas is located at the intersection of well-traveled roads from Santa Cruz del Quiché and Huehuetenango to the west.

From the east, Uspantán or Cobán in the Department of Alta Verapz, a good road joins the route to the Ixil region at Cunén, roughly halfway between Sacapulas and Nebaj. There is poor road access to the Ixil municipalities from the northern sections of Huehuetenango or Alta Verapaz departments. However, recent road construction from the municipal capital of Chajul north to the new hydroelectric dam at Jua' and beyond to Ilom and Chel has now made it possible to visit the incredibly beautiful cloud forest of the Visis Cabá National Reserve. Similarly, there is now a good road to the northeastern boundary of Cotzal municipality, along the Rio Cotzal to the Finca San Francisco. Every year sees new roads carved into the once-impenetrable Ixil country.

For the purposes of this guide, I have described my customary route to the Ixil region.

I normally set out from Antigua, 28 kilometers west of Guatemala City (one-hour drive) and travel the most direct route west via the Pan-American Highway to Los Encuentros, and then due north through the Department of Quiché.

ANTIGUA TO LOS ENCUENTROS (80 KILOMETERS)

My starting point is Antigua—the capital of colonial Guatemala from 1543 to 1773, when a devastating earthquake forced the governor to move to the present-day site of Guatemala City. Antigua is stunningly beautiful, historical, walkable, and most deserving of its distinction as a UNESCO world-heritage cultural treasure—sure to be on the itinerary of most foreign tourists. Here, I shake off travel fatigue, get acclimatized to the mile-high altitude and a slower pace of life, enjoy the color, art, wonderful food, and great Guatemalan coffee, repack, and rent a pickup for the Ixil journey. I time my departure from Antigua to coincide with the biweekly market in Chichicastenango, Thursdays and Sundays year-round.

From the center of Antigua, our access to the Inter-American Highway, CA#1, is a ten-minute drive through picturesque **JOCOTENANGO**, with its ornate orange-and-white Catholic church, a clearly marked

---

Anthropologist Jackson Steward Lincoln's Travel Checklist for his Ixil field research, 1939–40

Canvas boots
Gun for hunting
Dogs
Lamps
Flashes
Mosquito bars
Tent
Presents for Lacandones
Knives
Mirrors
Colored handkerchiefs
Shells
Tin boxes for matches
Snake-anti-toxin
Quinine
Sulfanilamide

Halazone
Anti-mosquito
Flint
Food for a month
Blanket
Poncho
Comfortable mattress
Mexican tourist card (permit to leave and reenter Guat)
Carnegie cards to Intendentes
Horses and pack mules to headwaters
Boats further on to Tzendalis
Boats down either Rio Ixcán or Xaclal to Lacantun

ABOVE: Antigua's colonial architecture, cobblestone streets, color, and convivial climate make this walkable town a popular destination for Guatemalans and international visitors and students.

right turn and steep climb out of the Panchoy Valley toward **EL TEJAR** and **CHIMALTENANGO,** along the north side of the Volcano Acatenango. The drive west to the first major waypoint, Los Encuentros, is an easy drive of about two hours. Climbing west along the rising ridges of the Sierra Madres, the beauty of highland Guatemala unfolds with each bend in the highway. The intensely cultivated family fields, burgeoning hillside towns, enterprising roadside businesses, even the political billboards, add to the composite picture of Guatemala today.

This leg of the trip takes us through the industrial center of **CHIMALTENANGO**, the country's third most populous city, the extensive market gardens of **PATZICÍA**, and into the forested valleys and productive fields of **TECPÁN,** where the Spanish conquistadors established their first headquarters near the Kaqchikel Maya capital of **IXIMCHE'**. From Tecpán, the road climbs to the crest of the Sierra Madres, offering dramatic vistas to the west, of Lake Atitlán and the three volcanoes that rim this ancient sacred lake of the Maya. Off to the north, the undulating Quiché plateau comes into view, with the dark and imposing wall of the Cuchumatán Mountains beyond.

LOS ENCUENTROS TO SANTO TOMÁS CHICHICASTENANGO (20 KILOMETERS)

At the bustling transport hub of Los Encuentros ("the meeting" of four major roads from four cardinal directions), we turn north onto Route #15 and head into the heartland of Quiché, bound for

ABOVE: The ancient crater lake, Atitlán, is rimmed by volcanoes and Kaqchikel or Tz'utuhil communities. The principal town of Panajachel and/or lakeside villages offer a wonderful stopover coming or going to the Ixil Region.

Chichicastenango. For the first 10 kilometers, the road winds by maize fields and orchards of apples, plums, and peaches (new varieties introduced by early U.S. Peace Corps in the 1960s and '70s) and lurches over speed bumps (*tumulos*) as it traverses the tiny towns that hug this well-traveled road. The last 10 kilometers is a veritable hair-raising roller-coaster ride into and out of two deep ravines (*barrancos*). Tackling this section requires brawny courage, good brakes, and even better gears, to navigate quickly and safely through the hairpin curves while negotiating with oncoming and tailing traffic.

Over the crest of the second ravine, the road careens into this ancient highland market, christened Santo Tomás Chichicastenango by the Spanish in the sixteenth century, with sweeping views north to the heartland and ancient capital of the K'iche', at Gumarcaah (Utatlán). This site was formerly an important Kaqchikel center, but was abandoned after war broke out between the Kaqchikel and K'iche' nations in the late fifteenth century. The K'iche', who later occupied this site, called it *Tziguan Tinamit* ("surrounded by canyons") and *Chugüilá* ("above the nettles"). When the Nahuatl-speaking mercenaries who accompanied Pedro de Alvarado arrived at this site, they called it "city of the nettles," *Tzitzicaztenanco*—hence, "Chichicastenango."

OVERNIGHT IN CHICHICASTENANGO TO ENJOY MARKET DAY

My usual plan is to arrive in "Chichi" the afternoon before market day, no later than 3:00 or 4:00 in the afternoon. This is the time when indigenous vendors from the surrounding western highlands set up their tiny stalls in their well-rehearsed tradition. In these relatively tranquil hours before dusk, visitors can calmly enjoy the earnest ambiance of this historic Maya town, as well as an advance showing of the incredible variety and vitality of local produce and artisanal skills that will be on display the following morning. There are guides for hire that roam the downtown area, or one can explore more informally, poking into the permanent shops, the two historic churches on the central plaza, and the tiny municipal museum.

I always make time to take the pulse of the economy: talking with vendors, checking out the price of corn seed and skirt (*corte*) cloth, and to buy at least Q1 worth of piping-hot tortillas off the griddle (*comal*). As the evening wood fires and incense swirl with the mountain mists, I climb the circular steps of Santo Tomás Church, erected 400 years ago by the Spanish missionaries on the ramparts of an ancient K'iche' Maya temple, and watch the scene below, as Maya families put the finishing touches on their preparations for the following market day.

Chichi offers a number of small inns and bed-and-breakfasts, although most tourists blitz in by bus and van early on market day and desert the town by midafternoon. My favorite places to stay include the lovely colonial-style **MAYAN INN** (info@mayaninn.com.gt, (502) 7756-1176 or the hotel offices in Guatemala City (502) 2470-3710) and the home-style **POSADA EL ARCO** run by Pedro Mercario (502) 7756-1255. A number of family restaurants around the periphery of the market offer simple, hot meals,

ABOVE: Chichicastenango, preparations for the ritual procession of the Santo Tomás cofradia (religious brotherhood) honoring this ancient highland market town's patron saint.

and often the aroma of the tiny *comedores* in the interior of the market lures me, with my cup and spoon, for a steaming bowl of traditional meat and vegetable soup. The Restaurant San Juan offers an artistic and airy second-floor dining area, overlooking the market, with reliable and delicious fare.

Long before the sun rises, but not before the first crazy rooster sets off a cacophony of all the other feathered and furry creatures in town, Chichicastenango is awake and bustling. Jam-packed buses, minivans, and pickups clog all the arteries into this town, disgorging bundles of all shapes and sizes, as thousands of people, many selling and all buying something, converge on the central marketplace. The transformation of the marketplace from the night before is unbelievable, and the crowds are intense. The stalls along the outside periphery of the plaza cater mostly to visitors and foreign tourists with an inexhaustible inventory of home-crafted, handwoven, traditional and modern clothing, real and fake jade necklaces, blankets, hammocks, and museum-quality copies of ancient Maya ceramics.

In the interior maze of narrow aisles and market stalls, vendors offer everyday necessities to mostly indigenous buyers, from hardware, thread, weaving implements, shoes, baskets and rope, to fruits and vegetables, spices, candles, maize and rock lime, live turkeys and baby chicks, flowers, and more. In the congested corridors of the interior market, I once discovered a forlorn traditional bulbous guitar (*guitaron*) and purchased it for Q100; the instrument provided for lively conversation and entertainment for the duration of my trip. The vitality, creativity, diversity, and industriousness of Guatemalans on display in the Chichi market never cease to astound me.

CHICHICASTENANGO TO SANTA CRUZ DEL QUICHÉ (20 KILOMETERS)

By late morning, as the market throngs rethread their journeys home and the narrow streets of Chichicastenango open slowly for traffic, it's time to get back on the road north. With great patience and a plenty of *gracias*, it is possible to coax the clutch of the car into the mainstream of vehicles jostling for pavement and make one's way under the grand concrete archway at the north side of town, marking Route #15 to Santa Cruz del Quiché. After a quick coast downhill from the town center, there are two more ravines to negotiate before the road levels off for an easy thirty-minute drive to the sprawling departmental capital.

The quickest way through Santa Cruz del Quiché is via a right-hand turn at the southern entrance of town, passing the main bus terminal on the left and the municipal soccer stadium on the right. From the bus station, continue around the eastern periphery of the city, looking for 1ª avenida ("*¿La salida para Sacapulas?*"), which will rejoin Route #15 to Sacapulas.

VISIT TO GUMARCAAH (UTATLÁN), A FIVE-MINUTE DRIVE TO THE WEST OF SANTA CRUZ DEL QUICHÉ

I highly recommend a short detour to the ancient capital of the K'iche', Gumarcaah (later named Utatlán), which is located on a wooded promontory, 2 to 3 kilometers west of Santa Cruz. The turnoff is not well marked, so you may need to ask for directions. At the entrance to the ancient site, the visitor center displays a scale model of the former citadel, built in the mid-twelfth century during the reign of Lord Gucumatz, called "the Creator." The K'iche' nation consolidated its power over other Maya kingdoms in the western highlands in the early decades of the fifteenth century. Gucumatz's heir and successor, Kikab' (AD 1425–75), faced growing strife among the formerly allied nations, including the Tz'utujil, Kaqchikel, and Rabinal, as well as insurrection amid the ranks of restless K'iche' princes and warriors. By the end of fifteenth century – on the eve of the Spanish Conquest – the former K'iche'-dominated empire was on the verge of collapse.

Gumarcaah is strategically sited on three hills, surrounded by ravines, and reinforced with massive stonewalls and a single entrance rampart. Within the citadel, the families of the principle K'iche' nobility lived in distinct residences in each of four corners of the town, while a central plaza hosted four sacred temples set at the cardinal directions. On the eastern side, toward the rising sun, was the temple of *Toh'il* (God of the Sky and Sun), the supreme god of K'iche',

BELOW: Traditional Maya prayer ceremonies continue to be held among the impressive ruins of the ancient capital of the K'iche' Empire, Gumarcaah.

which originally stood 33 feet high and 66 feet on each side. When explorers Stephens and Catherwood visited this site in the 1830s, this temple was described to them as *El Sacrificatorio*, the "place of the sacrifice," where K'iche' rulers sacrificed their victims on an altar at the top of the temple, offering the pulsating heart to the god of the sun.[58]

Opposite, on the western side, was the pyramidal temple to *Awil'ix* ("Goddess of the Moon"). To the north, a round temple was dedicated to *Gucumatz* ("The Creator"), and on the south side, another round temple to *Jakawitz* ("God of the Mountains"). The plaza also held a ceremonial ballcourt, representing the entrance to the Underworld and the realm of the gods, where K'iche' spectators gathered for the ritual ball game and the reenactment of the mythical struggles between the Maize Twins, their progeny— The Hero Twins— and the Lords of the Underworld.

The last great ruler of the K'iche', *Tecún Umán*, was slain by Pedro de Alvarado on February 20, 1524, during the battle at Olintepeque, near modern-day Quetzaltenango. Alvarado pursued the retreating warriors to Gumarcaah, where two surviving K'iche' princes schemed to lure the Spaniards into a trap. The Spanish got word of this plot at the last moment and stormed the defenses of the K'iche' fortress, whereupon they proceeded to summarily burn the K'iche' leaders at the stake and set fire to the residences and buildings within the citadel. Gumarcaah was abandoned.

According to the garrulous Spanish *padre* who accompanied Stephens and Catherwood to this site, the former K'iche' palace had remained virtually intact until around 1800, when the discovery of a small gold image at Gumarcaah led to its further destruction by treasure hunters dispatched by the president of Guatemala. Today, the ruins of Gumarcaah have been documented but not restored. The great temples lie in a state of collapse, and what remains of their massive stepped ramparts, now shrouded in grass and weeds, continue to crumble with each rainy season.

At the center of the plaza, in a smoke-blackened opening at the base of *Toh'il*'s temple, Maya priests (*sacerdotes Mayas*) still conduct prayer ceremonies for petitioners. During one visit here, I had the opportunity to observe such a prayer ritual from a respectful distance, as a young couple knelt with an offering of flowers, incense (*pom*), and candles, and the traditional priest intoned prayers to the gods for insight and intercession on behalf of the supplicants. Several tunnels burrow from the perimeter of Gumarcaah to smoky ceremonial altars under the ruins of the great pyramids. Being somewhat claustrophobic, I have ventured only a few meters into this underworld, but intrepid companions have confirmed that the inner chambers are still used today by Maya priests for traditional prayer ceremonites.

SANTA CRUZ DEL QUICHÉ TO SACAPULAS (46 KILOMETERS)

From the center of Santa Cruz, the newly paved Route #15 winds north, a trip of about an hour, to Sacapulas. The Sierra Madres recede from view to the south, and one travels through an increasingly arid landscape into the valley of the Rio Negro. The imposing and sheer Cuchumatán Mountains loom up ahead, their ragged peaks frequently shrouded in heavy cloud cover. Sacapulas lies just east of the confluence of the Rio Negro and Rio Blanco rivers, which water its rich alluvial soils and give it the reputation of a desert oasis. This valley receives less than 10 inches of rain a year, as the majority of seasonal precipitation falls on the cooler mountain peaks to the north. Due to its favorable year-round climate and the presence of black salt deposits on the river flats, the Spanish chose Sacapulas as the administrative headquarters for the surrounding region. By 1530, the Dominican order had launched the construction of a large church and monastery on the banks of the river, from which to direct Christianization, taxation, and trade for Spain. Today, Sacapulas retains a predominantly Ladino population and character.

In 2005, heavy flooding washed out the major bridge over the Rio Negro at Sacapulas, halting all north-south traffic in and out of the Cuchumatanes. If I had not seen the headline news as I departed from Antigua, I would have been waylaid in Sacapulas. Thanks to the tip, I took the detour west as afar as Huehuetenango, and doubled back south through Aguacatán, where I crossed over the Rio Negro and followed the road on the north side of the river to Sacapulas.

Now a new bridge crosses the Rio Negro several miles upstream from Sacapulas center. When approaching Sacapulas from Santa Cruz, take a left on the paved road down toward the river, across the new bridge. On the opposite bank, turn right, and follow the river downstream to the juncture with Sacapulas center. The single-lane, suspended cable bridge temporarily installed after the 2005 flood is still in use today. Quite rickety and unreliable now, I recommend crossing only by foot.

SACAPULAS TO NEBAJ (40 KILOMETERS)

From Sacapulas, improved roads into the Cuchumatanes have reduced a three-hour "extreme driving" adventure to Nebaj to just one hour, opening access to isolated communities in these mountains as never before. I am cautiously optimistic that this is a positive development, even though some features of "national integration" and globalization have adversely affected indigenous culture and livelihoods.

Having fueled up in Sacapulas, follow Route #7 north, zigzagging up the formidable face of the mountains, from 1,200 meters (3,900 feet) at the Rio Negro, to 2,400 meters (7,880 feet) at the top of first ridge.

Reflections of Scott Stoll, U.S. Peace Corps volunteer posted to Sacapulas in the 1970s

Two giant Ceiba trees, a Maya symbol of the Universe, stand in the central plaza of Sacapulas. Their ancient and powerful buttress roots have evolved to provide stability and capture nutrients from the rugged environment. For centuries, these very trees have cast welcome shade over the town center and the biweekly market spread out under their gracious canopy. Unfortunately, even in this small town, the pressures of urbanization and modernization appear to be stressing, if not overwhelming, the noble Ceibas. Three decades ago, when I was a young Peace Corps volunteer here, these great trees flourished with minimal restraint. Today, when I stop here on my way to the Ixil region, lingering on the central plaza to take the pulse of Sacapulas, I am struck by the sorry state of these ancient Ceibas. Their extensive drip line is now paved over; concrete benches collar their roots; and many of the embracing branches are cracking and leafless. I wonder how much more "progress" the Ceibas can endure, and how deep the roots must penetrate to find sustenance. I wonder if anyone here worries about these trees and what will happen when they fall.

Perhaps people's hearts have hardened or are indifferent to the sacred aspects of these sturdy trunks and soaring branches. During the civil war, within reach of the Ceibas' shadows, the Guatemalan army set up camp in the maize field next to the one-room house where I lived. A sign outside the army compound read only those who fight deserve to live. From here, the army carried out their campaign against Maya communities, not only smoking out sympathy and support for opposition guerrilla forces, but also choking indigenous leadership and the economic lifeblood of ancient communities.

Today, the war is long since over, and during this visit, I see that my old house now serves as a storefront for seed corn and fertilizer. As children frolic and elders rest in the shade on the plaza, I can't help but wonder how much longer these weary Ceibas will endure, and whether indigenous traditions, similarly rooted deep in the land and in the arching cosmos, can survive the inevitable march of modern forces.

Heading north from Santa Cruz del Quiché, the Sierra de los Cuchumatanes loom up ahead and indicate the ardous climb to Nebaj ahead.

While I admit to some nostalgia for the washboard and single-lane road cuts of the old passage, I am reassured that the new guardrails and storm runoff gutters will reduce fatalities along this route. I used to stop at each switchback to admire a new aspect of the breathtaking views, but more traffic and the guardrails make it harder to pull over at whim. Visitors should take advantage of scenic pull-offs (*mirador*) and share spectacular vistas with the buzzards and raptors that glide effortlessly by on a steady updraft from the valley floor.

After climbing steadily through the villages (*aldeas*) of Chiorno, Chibuc, and El Rancho, to the top of the first ridge, a prominent sign indicates that you take a left to reach Nebaj, Chajul, and Cotzal, and a right to get to Cunén. Take the left fork onto Route Quiché #3. The road winds continuously uphill, navigating rocky ridges and valleys cloaked in a dense patchwork of maize fields, occasional plots of hearty wheat and oats, and scrubby pasture for nimble sheep and scrawny cattle. At the windy, ridge-hugging town of Chiul, vehicles must take a detour (*viraje obligado*) on Wednesday and Saturday mornings around the town market. Beyond Chiul, the road ascends for another 5 kilometers to 2,600 meters (8,500 feet) to the last ridge before entering Ixil country.

Bienvenidos announces a sign at the summit of this ridge. Clouds permitting, the view into Nebaj's fertile cauldron below is stunning. Arriving at this gateway to the Ixil in 1939, anthropologist Jackson Steward Lincoln also marveled at this sight:

> *To arrive for the first time at the top of the second mountain pass 8,000 feet high on the way over from Sacapulas and look down from the strip of tropical cloud forest, occasionally filled with the roars of howling monkeys, into the beautiful open*

valley with the town of Nebaj 3,000 feet below is an unforgettable experience. Guarding this pass is a shrine in a grotto containing two crosses, strewn with rose leaves and the ashes of pom incense.[59]

In Ixil, the name *Nebaj,* formerly *Naab'a,* means "birthplace of water." Even at the height of the dry season, it is easy to see why the Ixil chose this name. Within these sacred mountains, the rivers run year-round, gushing at full strength over cliffs in spectacular waterfalls during the rainy season and meandering tamely through shallows and around sandbars by the end of the dry season. From this mountaintop, the road winds precipitously to the valley floor to the largest town in the Ixil region, Nebaj, our gateway to the Ixil homeland.

CHAPTER 4
Nebaj

OPPOSITE: In 1529, Spanish conquerors vanquished Ixil Maya warriors on this fortified site, raising the Catholic Church and municipal headquarters to consolidate their rule and convert the Maya to Christianity. **ABOVE LEFT:** Mythical creatures and sacred symbols populate weaving from Nebaj. **ABOVE RIGHT:** The older Nebaj architecture of adobe brick and clay roof tiles is fast disappearing and being replaced by modern, reinforced concrete structures.

Overview - At the end of a long day's drive through the historic and arduous landscape of Quiché, it is a relief to downgrade to a crawl and appreciate the spectacular setting of Nebaj, the capital, or *cabecera*, of Nebaj municipality. The town sits on an elevated promontory in a broad river basin surrounded by soaring mountains. The former washboard road is now wider

and paved. There is even a new gas station at the periphery of town for those who coasted downhill on diesel fumes from the escarpment above! Within a kilometer of town, however, the daily Ixil tread reasserts its right-of-way, and a steady stream of people and domestic animals returning from surrounding fields and forests spills into the roadway. Young boys follow in their fathers' footsteps, carrying sacks of maize or bundles of firewood, axes, and hoes; the ubiquitous machete dangles from every belt, swinging like a Maya pendulum with each stride. Heavily loaded horses and mules follow the path they know by heart; the family dog trots, panting, alongside. Women wend their way home from the market

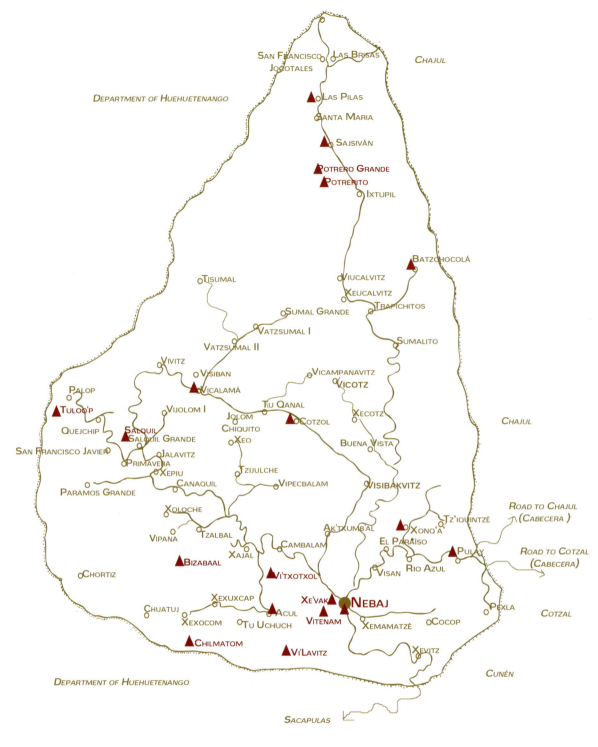

or the maize mill, balancing containers of ground maize (*masa*) or baskets of greens on their heads, and sleeping infants slung in woven shawls (*rebozos*) across their backs. Clusters of teenagers, some with school backpacks, amble toward the town center.

In the sixteenth century, the Spanish christened this new parish "Santa María Nebaj," but today everyone refers to the municpality and its capital, *or cabecera*, simply as "Nebaj." The statue of Santa María de La Asunción, however, is still reverently paraded through the streets for the annual patron-day fiesta, on August 15, and during Easter Week (*Semana Santa*). The municipality of Nebaj covers an area of 608 square kilometers (235 square miles); its population of about 75,000[60] is dispersed among eighteen districts (*aldeas*), and scores of small hillside or valley settlements (*caserios*). A quarter of the municipality's population lives in and around the town of Nebaj. According to the most recent official census (2002), Ixil-speaking residents represented 72 percent of the population of Nebaj; K'iche', 16 percent; and Ladinos, 12 percent.

The distinctive regional dress, or *traje*, still worn by the majority of women, is the telltale sign that we have finally arrived in the Nebaj. Their regal *huipiles* feature a dense collage of natural and human figures; age-old symbols mirror Ixil reverence for the gods, the mystical power of the mountains, and man's humble place within the Maya "cosmovision," or world vision. Older women crown their heads with elegant twirls of glossy hair and geometrically patterned sashes (*cinta*), knotted with the flourish of silky iridescent pom-poms.

ABOVE: Photo by Michel de la Sabelier, The majority of women in Nebaj woman continue to weave and wear regal traditional dress (*traje*).

Aside from indigenous dress, little else in the town's physical aspect appears traditional. Upon first impression, Nebaj center seems like a frontier boomtown. A resurgence of economic activity and population growth since the end of the civil war has completely transformed the town's former colonial character. Most of the older adobe and tile-roof homes and shops have now been replaced by earthquake-resistant, concrete-block constructions. The urban core consists of a tight grid of about six north-south streets and ten east-west streets, mostly paved, radiating from the central plaza. Spilling off this promontory, narrow roads and footpaths fan organically into surrounding rural neighborhoods (*cantóns*) and a patchwork of densely cultivated parcels.

The town is a fascinating fusion of old and new. Shops lining the major streets offer modern goods and services—corrugated metal, pharmaceuticals, school supplies, shoes, lightbulbs, and cell phones. The traditional market, a maze of tarps, tables, and vendor stalls spread over several blocks to the east of the plaza, carries the basic necessities: vegetables, maize, herbs and spices, rope, baskets, cotton and textiles, and machetes. Ladinos used to dominate the formal business sector in Nebaj, but today, Ixil entrepreneurs run most of the commerce in town. Competition is lively; new services, products, and stores pop up each year. With increasing access to higher education, women are fast making inroads into formal-sector jobs previously dominated by men. Electronics stores, cell phones, and Internet cafes, along with pirated CDs and DVDs, attest to the arrival of the newest technology. The vitality is particularly evident in the late afternoon, when schools let out and fieldwork is finished. Everyone is out, buying produce, strolling through the plaza, heading to evangelical services, or just navigating their way home, mostly by foot, although an increasing number of motorcycles and three-wheeled taxis (*tuk-tuks*) stir up their share of dust and noise in the softening light as the sun dips below the rim of surrounding mountains.

Visitor Services in Nebaj

Overnight lodging options are excellent, ranging from several modern hotels to family-style guesthouses (*hospedajes*) and backpackers' hostels. Except for major fiesta days (see Appendix 1: Calendar of Fiestas in the Ixil Region), rooms do not need to be booked

My wife, Irma, and I, Juan Clemente Raymundo Velasco, welcome you to the Ixil region. We invite you to visit the homeland of the Ixil, to appreciate its physical beauty, indigenous customs, and the current realities of our people. Like our parents and ancestors, we were born and raised in the municipality of Nebaj. Irma is a social worker, trained at the Universidad Rafael Landívar, and I graduated from the University of San Carlos as an engineer. Our academic accomplishments and current professions reflect the constant struggle and sacrifice of our parents, to whom we dedicate our eternal gratitude. We are bringing up our own children today to honor and respect the harmony between nature, man, and God, who is at the center of all our relationships, projects, and dreams. The survival of the Ixil depends on our commitment to preserve the indigenous culture and the wealth of nature that surrounds and nourishes us in so many ways.

We encourage you to share in our rich traditions and to understand our aspirations and endeavors to build a promising future for our children and this region. We are confident that this exploration of the Ixil region will be an unforgettable experience, offering you a chance to participate in our culture and to understand how our people view the physical world and its hidden mysteries. You will discover a world of wonderful sites, thoughts, and customs, adorned with centuries of history and steeped in ancient culture and modern challenges.

We welcome visitors as friends and family. As our grandparents say, "Once someone has felt the deep bonds that unite this land and people, it is impossible to say good-bye." Enjoy your explorations and return to Ixil country often.

—JUAN CLEMENTE RAYMUNDO VELASCO

RIGHT: Hotel Santa María de Nebaj with modern rooms and internet service.
FAR RIGHT: Popi's Restaurant doubles as a popular eatery and hub of non-profit activity. **BELOW:** Gran Hotel Ixil offers simple rooms and a great balcony view.
BELOW LEFT: Count on Comedor Elsim's hot lunch or dinner of local, inexpensive fare.

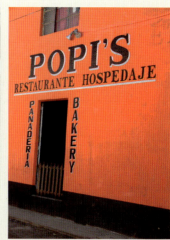

in advance. Most hotels provide off-street parking, although none serve breakfast. It's easy enough to trot the few short blocks to El Descanso or explore the downtown area for other busy eateries (*comedores*).

LODGING

- *Villa Nebaj:* Large, multistory Western-style hotel in town center with conventional comforts. Q135/single, Q200/double; Calzada 15 de Septiembre 2-37. Telephone: (502) 7756-0005; Email: contact@villanebaj.com.
- *Hotel Santa María:* A delightful small hotel offers a dozen brightly decorated rooms with comfortable beds and private bathrooms, free wireless, and ample parking. Cantón Batzbaca, 2 blocks north of Central Park. Q150/single, Q200/double. Telephone: (502) 4212-7927, 4621-9890; Email: hsmnebaj@gmail.com; www.HotelSantaMariaNebaj.com.
- *Hotel Utz'la ja' (Casa Bonita):* A multistory hotel located downhill (east) from the market and bus terminal. Q75 single, Q140 double; Cantón Tu Salina; Telephone: (502) 7756-0231.
- *Hotel Ilebal Tenam* ("Your Place of Rest"): Older hotel located near Triángulo gas station; quieter rooms in rear with pleasant garden courtyard. Q120/double; Calzada 15 de Septiembre. Telephone: (502) 7755-8039.

ABOVE: Beautiful older adobe and tiled roof houses in Nebaj are gradually being replaced by cement block construction.

- *Hotel Turansa:* Clean, unadorned rooms looking onto interior courtyard. Q60/single. 5a Calle y 6a Avenida. Telephone: (502) 7755-8219 or (502) 7755-8483.
- *Gran Hotel Ixil:* A small family-style accommodation, with ten simple bedrooms looking out on sunny courtyard. Q120/double room. 2nd Avenue and 9a calle; Telephone: (502) 7756-0036.
- *Hotel Shalom:* Older two-story accommodation with bright balconies, simple rooms. Calzada 15 Septiembre and 4a Calle; Telephone: (502) 7755-8028.
- *Popi's Hospedaje:* Backpackers' hostel and restaurant, offering dorm-style rooms run by NGO Mayan Hope. Gringo owner Don offers a sitting area with cable TV, a "gringo" menu, and a bakery with fresh banana bread, cookies, and rolls; Q25/single; Email: admin@mayanhope.org.
- *Media Luna, Medio Sol:* Backpackers' hostel run by the NGO, Community Enterprise Solutions; offers a "campers' kitchen" equipped with pots and dishes, rustic Ping-Pong table, cable TV; Q30 for a dormitory bunk bed or

> A word of caution about the typical hot-wired showerhead, better known and respected as the "suicide shower"—*No toque!* Do not touch the tangle of wires overhead in an effort to improve your shower experience. The key to coaxing hot water to come out is to run the water at a trickle through the hot coils of the showerhead. Temperature and flow are inversely proportional; the lights dim as the coil kicks in with a promise of warmth to come.

Q50 for a private room. Two-minute walk from El Descanso restaurant. Telephone: (502) 5749-7450.

FOOD

Nebaj offers a number of eateries, bakeries, and mini-stores (*tiendas*). *Comedores* serve a limited menu with two or three daily offerings: eggs, beans, and tortillas for breakfast; soup (*caldo*), rice, beans, and tortillas for lunch; and a variety of grilled meats accompanied again by beans and tortillas for supper. The daily special is always the safest and best option, as it is also the freshest. Expect to pay Q10 to Q20 in a *comedor*, or Q25 to Q50 in restaurants.

- The popular *Comedor Elsim*, located on the northeast corner of the central park, serves a savory hot meal for lunch or dinner.
- *Comedor El Buen Apetito*, located across from the Nebaj bus terminal, is popular with Peace Corps types for the chocolate-covered banana or ice cream for dessert.
- *Restaurante Popi's* offers a menu of "American-style" dishes and daily baked goods (cookies, rolls, banana bread), "to go" (*para llevar*). On holidays, the American owner and founder of Mayan Hope, Don, has been known to prepare "comfort food for foreign volunteers," such as turkey and stuffing for Thanksgiving and ham for New Year's Day.
- *Restaurante El Descanso*, run by the nonprofit Community Enterprise Solutions, serves meals all day, as well as snacks and their own version of chocolate chip cookies. Menu includes local specialties, pasta, sandwiches, grilled burgers, chicken, and *quesadillas*. Visitors can relax with board games, magazines, and cable TV in the restaurant's lounge. Patrons can check their email at the adjoining Internet café, called *La Red* ("the Net"), or look into guided tours to Nebaj sites with Ixil Guide Services.
- *Asados Pasabien* restaurant is a good choice for grilled steaks, chicken, and pork chops. It is located close to the Hotel Gran Ixil on the main road from Sacapulas.
- *Restaurante Maya Inca* offers a menu of "Peruvian" and local fare.

GUIDE SERVICES

Guías Ixiles

This office is part of the Rural Tourism Project started by Community Enterprise Solutions, and is located under the same roof as El Descanso restaurant. Working with a half-dozen local Ixil guides, they offer explorations ranging from a few hours to ten days. The excursions are extremely reasonable: half-day tours cost under Q100 per person, and three-day treks, including accommodations and meals with Ixil families, can be arranged for about Q500 per person. Telephone: (502) 5847-4747 or 5749-7450. Website: www.nebaj.info/home.html; Email: miguelbrito@solucionescomunitarias.com. For English-only speakers, contact turismonebaj@gmail.com.

Región Ixil Guía de Senderismo (Guide to Ixil Region Hiking)

Published in 2005 by Solidarity International and Spain's Oficina Técnica de Cooperacíon, this compendium of fifty hikes in the region includes topographic maps. Although one may have to hike all over Nebaj to find a copy of this guide, it is well worth it. Inquire for the trekking guide in Popi's Restaurant or El Librito school-supply store.

Giant's Tours

Advertises day and overnight tours, plus horseback treks. Telephone: (502) 4928-6878.
Email: giantstours@hotmail.com.

Laval Iq' Community

Community Network for the Environmental and Cultural Development of the Ixil Region, formed by leaders of nineteen Ixil communities to promote local ecological and cultural tourism. Telephone: (502) 7755-8337. Email: redlavaliiq@gmail.com.

HEALTH SERVICES

Outside the major cities in Guatemala, health services range from being stretched to virtually nonexistent. The only hospital in the region is in the town of Nebaj. Staffed by Cuban and Guatemalan doctors and surgeons, it has a good reputation. My advice to travelers:

- Bring your own essential medicines for colds, sore throat, upset stomach, and aches and pains.
- Drink bottled water.
- Eat only sanitized and peeled fruits and vegetables.
- Choose hot meals in *comedores* or restaurants.
- Avoid eating in the market.
- Wash hands compulsively.
- Stay warm and dry.

Medicines can be purchased without a prescription from numerous small pharmacies. Traditional Maya herbal remedies are widely used by the community, and several "naturalist" pharmacies dispense standardized packages of dried herbs with instructions. Among the most commonly used herbs: chamomile (*manzanilla*) for stomach pains, menstrual cramps, cough and flu, anise (*anís silvestre*) for intestinal gas, garlic (*ajo*) for high blood pressure and intestinal worms, amargo or dandelian greens

BELOW: Photo by Scott Stoll. Lively activity day and night on Nebaj's newly renovated central plaza.

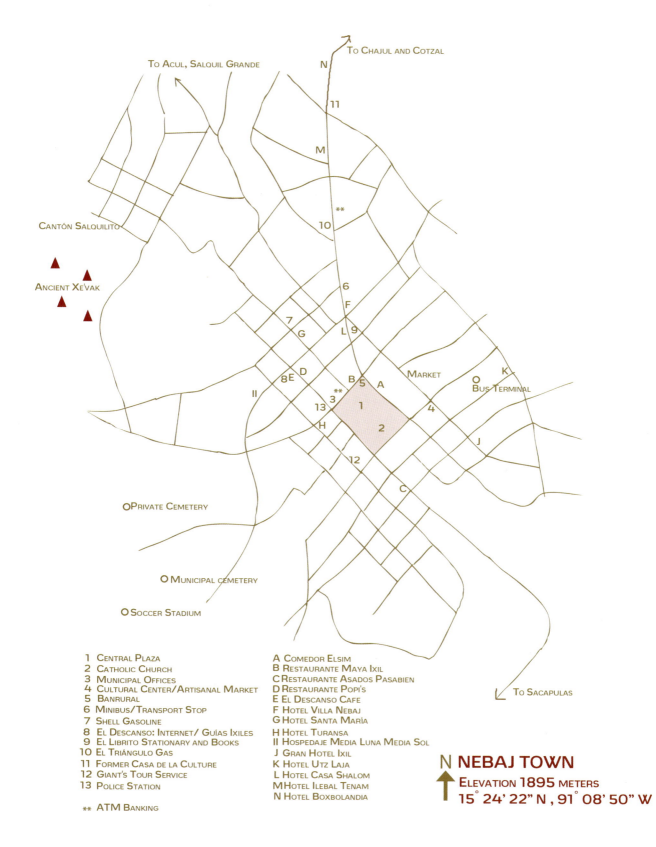

(*amargon*) for anemia, eucalyptus (*eucalipto*) for chest and nasal congestion, plantain leaf (*llantén*) for diarrhrea, and nettle (*ortiga*) as a blood purifier, also, as I learned, when applied ot he scalp, prevents one's hair from falling out!

BANKING

This is strictly a cash economy. Use one of the ATM machines in downtown Nebaj to replenish your cash, but be aware that these machines run out of cash on the weekends, major market days, fiesta days, and sometimes even shortly after breakfast. There are three banks in town, but count on a long wait and endless paperwork to cash a traveler's check. Small bills and coins are essential for purchases in the open market.

INTERNET AND CELL PHONES

Internet cafés are sprouting up all over Nebaj center. Cell phone service works flawlessly in almost every corner of the Ixil region. You can readily buy additional cell-phone minutes in every town and hamlet by buying a phone card in denominations of Q25, Q50, or Q100, or by paying a cell-phone-minute vendor to dial in your purchase from their phone franchise.

ABOVE: Painful memories of Nebaj's civil war dead and "disappeared" live on; forensic teams continue to exhume victims of war massacres throughout the Ixil region.

Explorations in Nebaj

HISTORY OF THE CATHOLIC CHURCH AND THE CENTRAL PLAZA

Between 2005 and 2007, the municipality of Nebaj renovated the central plaza to erase the memories of terror, executions, and intimidation witnessed here in previous epochs. Architects and stonemasons removed the plaza's former austerity by adding a gazebo, fountain, sculpted seating arrangements, flowerbeds, and trees. Beneath the plaza lies the region's first subterranean parking garage and shopping arcade, including a branch of the national bank, BanRural. The Catholic church dominates the south side of the plaza, facing a row of municipal offices on the north side.

Although obscured today by urban sprawl, Nebaj's town center is situated on a defensible plateau in this broad mountain valley. On this spot, Ixil warriors from the surrounding region took their final stand in 1529 against the approaching Spanish forces. According to colonial accounts, nimble mercenaries scaled the fortifications and set fire to the walled city. Ixil leaders succumbed to superior Spanish firearms and cavalry and were branded and chained by their conquerors.

Within a few years, the Spanish returned to round up and resettle the dispersed indigenous population, convert the Maya to Christianity, and devise systems for extracting taxes and wealth for the Crown. Dominican missionaries christened this parish Santa María Nebaj, and imposed a colonial grid on the smoldering ruins of the former Ixil center. The first Catholic church and plaza were built with forced labor crews between 1540 and 1580, directly on top of an Ixil ceremonial center. This church was no mere rural chapel, but an indisputable cathedral to the Christian god of the conquerors. It measured 17 meters high, 18 meters wide, and 45 meters from the altar to the front entrance. The massive wooden beams for the rafters were cut and hauled into town from the surrounding mountains, requiring 100 porters each. According to an Ixil legend, "a spirit-figure appeared astride the wooden beams, magically lightening the load." The original church was fashioned in a classic Renaissance style, crowned with three bell towers. By church edict, all residents of the parish had to live within a prescribed distance from the church and plaza in order to be readily summoned for daily Mass and colonial service.

Following Guatemala's Independence in 1821, a combination of natural forces and shifting political powers altered the church on numerous occasions. State authorities routinely commandeered the central plaza for announcements, organization of forced labor, and public displays of discipline. When General Justo Rufino Barrios came to power in 1871, the church façade was reworked in a more imperialistic style; however, perhaps in a premonition of the general's imminent death, the new façade collapsed in an earthquake just prior to its completion. Half a century later, in 1936, six Ixil leaders were publicly executed on the central plaza for their supposed role in instigating protests against General Jorge Ubico's "vagrancy laws."

Over the three decades of the civil war, the plaza and church in Nebaj mirrored national and local violence. The earthquake of 1976, which caused widespread devastation throughout Guatemala, crumbled the church façade once more and damaged much of the interior. Reconstruction was delayed until the mid-1980s, as civil war raged in the region. The army requisitioned the church grounds for its headquarters; guns bristled from the bell towers, and troops set up barracks and detention cells to the rear of the church. Church archives were burned, along with portions of the colonial rectory. At the height of the counter-insurgency campaign, the army dragged suspected guerrillas and sympathizers into the plaza, where they were tortured and frequently executed. Refugees fleeing violence in the countryside were funneled through temporary camps near the plaza and hastily resettled in army-controlled population encampments, termed *polos de desarrollo* ("poles of development"). After 1996, the fact-finding commissions mandated by the Peace Accords, including extensive eyewitness interviews and exhumations of mass graves of war victims, perpetuated tensions in Nebaj. In February

BELOW: Nebaj's newly renovated plaza is a crossroad as well as destination for the town's residents and visitors.

of 2002, the Catholic priest in Nebaj received death threats for his collaboration with forensic teams, and arsonists destroyed his offices.

Today, the church bells peal freely once more, but they represent a mere shadow of the Catholic Church's former power and reach. This whitewashed monument belies a somber interior, reflected in the paucity of salvaged ornamentation. In an alcove near the entrance, parishioners erected a shrine to local victims of the civil war, sharing flickering candlelight with a crucified Christ figure. Since the 1980s, evangelical congregations have mushroomed in many communities throughout the Ixil region, fast eclipsing Catholicism as the dominant institutional religion in the region. On the opposite side of the plaza, the municipal offices are once again in the hands of elected Ixil officials. On weekdays, petitioners queue on the portico for an appointment or signature.

Today, Nebaj's central plaza looks and feels, perhaps for the first time in its history, like a space for everyone. All day long and into the early evening, young and old congregate here: elders take a respite from errands, mothers chat as they watch their frolicking children nearby, knots of teenagers gather and set off together, young couples rendezvous for courtship and a memorable photo. Visitors like me enjoy a chance to rest their feet, observe the tableau of Ixil daily life, and scribble in their journals.

MARKET DAY IN NEBAJ AND BASIC IXIL FOODS

A morning in the traditional market is not to be missed. Most towns in Guatemala hold an open market twice a week, staggering the days within a region to accommodate vendors who move from one to another. Official market days are Thursday and Sunday, but Friday and Saturday seem just as busy. The market is in full swing by seven in the morning and occupies

RIGHT: Nebaj market offers fresh produce, imported and local housewares, electronics, shoe repair, rope, machetes, modern and traditional clothing.

every square meter of four blocks between Hotel Villa Nebaj and the Cultural Center. Vendors and buyers come from all over the region and from other nearby municipalities, such as Cunén, Chiul, Uspantán, Aguacatán, and as far away as Cobán and Sacapulas.

During peak hours, be prepared for shoulder-to-shoulder crowds. Watch your step; yield the right-of-way to those laden with large bundles and baskets. If you plan to shop, bring small change and your own basket or backpack.

For the locals, the market is an opportunity to purchase essentials, as well as for socializing. For visitors, it presents a great opportunity to survey the regional produce, culture, and economy. I like to see what's new and to take the pulse of the local economy. Women make up the majority of produce vendors and consumers. Men trade in tools, machetes, hardware, electronics, saddles and bridles, and the butchered meats. From the time they can carry or count, young children assist their parents with weighing, bagging, and selling snacks of freshly cut fruit and chips. Ixil women wear some of their best *huipiles* to market; older men don the traditional palm hat. The parade of produce and people is a veritable feast for the eyes, showcasing Ixil industriousness, cultural pride, and the region's agricultural abundance. The dominant colors in the market—greens, reds, yellows, and purples in every hue and pattern—match those of traditional Nebaj dress.

Basket of Ixil Basic Foods

The Ixil basic diet consists of maize (mainly in the form of tortillas, tamalitos, and tamales), beans, chili peppers, spices, salt, and squash, along with seasonal greens and meat (chicken, pork, or beef) on special occasions. Food is still prepared on an open hearth in most homes. Although a European Union–financed project in the Ixil region (2004) estimated that about three-quarters of Ixil families were still largely self-sufficient in maize, an increasing proportion of families must buy maize during some part of the year. The following table provides a snapshot of the cost of basic commodities in 2011. A handful (*mano*) indicates five items.

TABLE: THE COST OF IXIL STAPLES	Q	US $
5 lbs. of dried maize (daily)	2	0.25
1 lb. of rock lime (every 2 weeks)	1.5	0.20
1 lb. of black beans (daily)	5	0.65
1 oz. of dried chili pepper (daily)	3	0.40
1 oz. green chili pepper	1	0.13
1 green squash	1.5	0.20
1 handful of onions	0.75	0.10
1 handful of carrots	5	0.65
1 lb. of tomatoes	2	0.25
1 head of cabbage	2	0.25
1 lb. of beef	20	2.50
1 lb. of beef bones	10	1.30
1 lb. chicken breast	8	1.00
1 lb. chicken feet	3	0.40
1 melon	4	0.50
1 handful of mangoes	3	0.40
1 bundle of wood (every 2–3 days)	25	3.00

WEAVING TRADITIONS IN NEBAJ

The ancient art of backstrap weaving continues to thrive in Nebaj, passed down through generations from mother to daughter and protected by the Maya goddess, *Ixchel*, patron of weaving, fertility, and birth. Most Ixil women still weave their own blouse (*huipil*), shawl (*rebozo*), belt (*faja*), and hair tie (*cinta*), as well as clothing for their children and other decorative and utilitarian textiles for the home. A local cottage industry of treadle, or foot-loom, weavers supplies the dark-red-and-brown-striped cloth for the ankle-length wrap-skirt (*corte*). Despite the apparent vibrancy of Ixil textile traditions, Western styles and clothing are becoming more common with each passing year. Men and boys today dress almost entirely in Western-style jeans and T-shirts. A few older men still wear a long woven belt to secure their pants, and special occasions like fiestas, weddings, and funerals bring out the traditional men's outfit of white trousers and red-striped jacket with black embroidery. Also likely to prevail a while longer are the men's distinctive palm fiber hats and the male custom of carrying a woven, over-the-shoulder bag (*morral*).

Women say that they weave every day, even for a few minutes, between other chores. *Our hands are always busy* is the way one woman described the tapestry of her daily work. The traditional loom is perfectly portable, so women weave at home, in the corner of a lazy afternoon market, or under a shade tree as they keep one eye on their children or a grazing flock. As there are no written patterns to follow, weavers learn designs by heart, patience, and practice. Apprenticeship for girls begins at an early age, working alongside their mother or grandmother. Toddlers wind balls of thread; young girls thread the warping board and work on their first belt or small cloth (*manta* or *tzute*); teenage girls study each other's *huipiles* to borrow a design and calculate the cost of thread. Completing an intricate *huipil* of their own is like a rite of passage for young women. By the time she is a proficient weaver, a young Ixil woman has acquired her own set of wooden loom pieces—shed rods, a batten, shuttles, and picks—which she will maintain for life, smoothing dents or sharpening picks with fine sandpaper.

Photo by Michel de la Sabelier. While a majority of Ixil men sport the palm fiber hat, the bright red embroidered jacket is increasingly reserved for special occasions.

The Market Value of Traditional Weaving

Despite rising costs of cotton and a limited market for their textiles, weaving remains one of the few sources of cash income for rural Ixil women. The material costs of a *huipil* have jumped 100 percent within the last decade alone. Women told me that the cotton and specialty threads to make an adult-sized huipil costs a minimum of Q200 (US $25); however, they rarely keep track of or assign a value to the hours they spend warping the loom, weaving, and embroidering finishing touches. Most manage to put in two to three hours of weaving a day, sandwiched in between all the other demands on their time. At this rate, Ixil women say it takes between two to four months to complete a traditionally intricate blouse or shawl.

On the back of an envelope, I try to calculate the real economic value of a new *huipil*. Cotton for the warp threads, or solid background, costs about Q100, and a dozen small balls of colored threads for the weft-face design add another Q100 (minimum), for a raw material cost of Q200. Monetizing the weaver's skill and labor is more difficult, and there is no doubt that an accomplished weaver works an intricate design from memory and with greater fluidity. Applying the Guatemalan minimum wage for agricultural and nonagricultural laborers (in 2011) of Q8/hour, or about US $1/hour, I arrive at an average labor cost of about Q336 (three hours per day for four months). Raw materials plus labor come to about Q540 (US $70).

BELOW: Weaving styles in Nebaj have evolved rapidly in the last 50 years due to greater social change and cross-cultural communication, an expanded market for new threads and colors, and the economics of back-strap loom weaving.

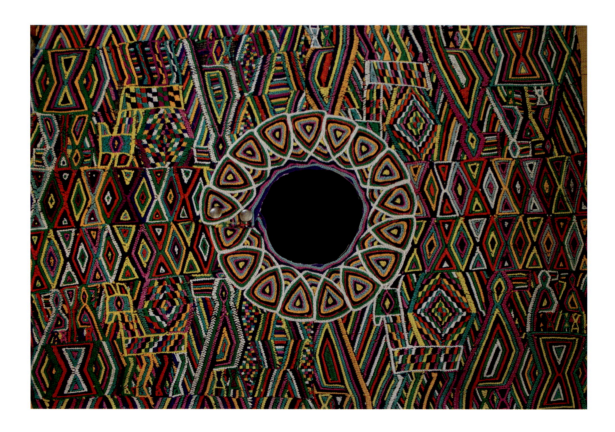

BELOW RIGHT: Author gladly trades US baseball cap for regal Nebaj hair tie (cinta). **CENTER:** Nebaj weavers share their life stories and dazzling weaving skills and products with visitors. **BELOW LEFT:** Nebaj's Cultural Center and Artisanal Market, open 7 days a week, and not to be missed by visitors.

As I survey the price of readymade *huipiles* in the Nebaj market, I realize that my calculations are probably not too far off. Professional Ixil women, like teachers and store owners who have little time to weave for themselves, tell me that they can buy or commission a new *huipil* for everyday wear for between Q700 and Q800 (US $90–100); a more-elaborate *huipil* or shawl for a wedding or special celebration can command Q1,000 to Q4,000 (US $125-$500), as it requires more thread and more time. By my calculations, the weaver's potential "profit" from selling a lovely, "everyday" *huipil* comes to between Q160–260 (US $20–40) for four months of part-time work. For the buyer, the new *huipil* is a real investment; indigenous women expect to wear it for many years. It is common to see women wearing their *huipiles* inside out to protect the blouse from daily wear and tear and from bleaching the bold colors in the sun.

Such are the economics for a handful of the most accomplished and sought-after weavers in Nebaj.

The majority of Ixil women weave principally for themselves and their family; any extra production is for pure speculation. When they succeed in selling a new or used weaving, the price rarely covers the cost of their labor. Why is this? Indigenous weavers face a national and global market oversupplied with colorful textiles: masterful, traditional weavings compete with mass-produced, "made for export" pieces. Few buyers understand the difference. Ixil weavers live far from the major tourist markets, and visitors to the region are too few. Eager to redeem some cash for their labor, Ixil weavers must contract with itinerant middlemen who buy at wholesale prices and resell the textiles for artsy purses and eyeglass cases sold in Chichicastenango, Panajachel, and the duty-free shops at the airport.

Only on rare occasions do Ixil weavers have the opportunity to meet potential customers face-to-face. As I have discovered, such an occasion is a real treat for both. Ixil weavers take great pains to showcase their intricate designs to would-be buyers, explaining the cultural significance of each color and icon, pointing out the evenness of the weave and the dense embroidery at the collar. Indeed, this is their best chance to sell a piece of fine art for close to its real value. I encourage visitors to relish such an opportunity to buy a lovely souvenir of Ixil weaving, and to negotiate a price that honors the cultural heritage, skill, and time invested in the piece. Weavers sell surplus or used *huipiles* and other *traje* at a discount.

NEBAJ'S CULTURAL CENTER AND ARTISANAL MARKET

Visitors to Nebaj will have no trouble locating the two-story, salmon-colored Cultural Center, located at the southern end of the market street. It is open seven days a week, from about 10:00 a.m. to 4:00 p.m., but closes most Sundays at noon. A dozen individual and cooperative vendors staff small booths within the center's interior courtyard, weaving quietly on their backstrap looms as they wait for customers. The second story was conceived as a cultural museum, but progress has been slow on getting this launched. For traditional textile enthusiasts and weavers, an afternoon at the Cultural Center is akin to a personal primer on the history, symbolism, and technique of backstrap loom weaving in Nebaj. Several Nebaj weavers offer private weaving lessons (Q20 per hour) at the Center or in their homes.

No two *huipiles*, even by the same weaver, are exactly alike, but all reflect the central spiritual elements of the Ixil cosmovision—portraying harmony and balance within the Maya universe. The common Nebaj blouse and shawl are woven with double-strand thread for extra insulation in the cool mountain climate. Woven in two complimentary, rectangular pieces, the boxy blouse is tucked into a wrap-skirt and secured with a wide, brocaded belt. Rarely seen today is the longer, three-panel ceremonial *huipil*, worn by new brides, women members of the religious *cofradía*, and others for special occasions.

A century ago, before commercially dyed cotton became available in rural communities, the Nebaj *huipil* was principally white; weavers relied on natural dyes to create the weft-faced design. Within the recent memory of Nebaj's elderly weavers, *huipil* colors and styles have been evolving rapidly with the proliferation of imported colored cotton and synthetic threads and the increased mobility and interregional contact among women. Today, weavers design their *huipiles* with a dark background, often green, red, or maroon. Compared with even forty years ago, weft-faced designs today cover more of the surface of the blouse. Hierarchical ranges of stylized humanity, animal, and plant figures encoded with mythical and spiritual significance decorate both front and back of the *huipil*. Intensely colored zigzags, chevron, and diamond patterns symbolize supernatural and sacred powers of the mountains and natural forces, such as wind, rainbows, and lightning bolts. By opening the side seams and laying the *huipil* flat, one can read the spiritual narrative of its elaborate iconography. The circle of the collar represents the sacred sun and Creator, the "Heart of the Sky and Earth" (*El Corazón del Cielo y de la Tierra*). Four heraldic medallions, arranged at the collar center front, back, and at the shoulders, symbolize the four cardinal directions and corners of the Maya universe.

An elaborately woven hair tie (*cinta*), 2 to 3 meters long, crowns Nebaj *traje* in the colors of quetzal tail feathers. Women twist this green-and-red-striped tie around their long black hair, wind the luxurious swirl around their head, and knot it with six silky pom-poms just above the forehead. A versatile, elaborately patterned shawl (*rebozo*) completes a woman's outfit, worn across the chest for warmth or folded on top of the head against the harsh sun.

To appreciate regional dress and the skills with which it is painstakingly woven and worn, it is worth having expert and patient hands at the Cultural Center select and dress you in full complement from head to toe. The experience of twisting, knotting, tucking, and tying is one that you can bring home in your suitcase.

RIGHT: Nebaj is teeming with new businesses, sandwiched along side traditional artisans and vendors.

POSTWAR POVERTY AND RECOVERY

The protracted civil war took a devastating toll on the Ixil region. In addition to the enormous loss of life and psychological trauma, the majority of families here lost all of their property—land, maize, animals, dwellings.

An eighty-five-year-old man living in the Cantón Vitzal of Nebaj spoke of his losses:

My wife and I had accumulated different kinds of property, including horses, cows, pigs, chickens, goats, and a number of small parcels of land. We had worked very hard for these things, but when the war came and my wife and three sons were killed, we lost everything. Over the next eighteen years, little by little, I have been recuperating some of what I lost.

Another Ixil elder and farmer talked about lingering fear and sadness:

Now, we are much poorer and often we dream that we are still living the war and our heads are full of fear; we still haven't recovered from the hurt and fear we suffered.

An Ixil woman from Juil, just ten years old at the height of the civil war, recounted her story:

I was born in Chacalté, we were all born there, and my parents had their land and animals there. Before the war, it was all so beautiful. I remember going into the mountains to work and look for animals and to play. With the war, everything changed . . . We sought refuge in a cave, but could hear the screams of people and the yelp of dogs as the village was attacked and burned. Afterwards, my mother and my siblings escaped into the forested mountains looking for refuge.

These accounts are the rule, not the exception. Since the civil war, Ixil families have scrambled to legitimize their land claims, assisted in great part by the earnings of family members who left the region to find work in urban areas of Guatemala or outside the country. The number and percentage of *microfincas* smaller than 1 *manzana* (equivalent to 0.7 hectares, or 1.74 acres) have steadily increased, as land is continually subdivided among new family members. In 2003, 88 percent of registered land holdings in Nebaj fell into this category, accounting for 60 percent of registered land area. *Microfincas* are considered marginal to sustain the typical family of seven to nine members. Concurrently, the number of large land holdings, termed *multifamiliares,* with a minimum of 64 *manzanas* (45 hectares, or 112 acres) has also declined since 1979, from 31 (representing 29 percent of total registered land) to 15 as of 2003, accounting for 15 percent of registered land area in Nebaj.[61]

The majority of Ixil families engaged in subsistence agriculture are experiencing decreasing soil fertility. Where their grandfathers had enough land to leave certain lands fallow, farmers today are forced to plant their fields every year, buying fertilizer when they can afford it. Maize yields vary between 15 and 20 *quintales* (about 100 pounds) per hectare (or 1,500 to 2,000 pounds) with fertilizer. Where annual rainfall and temperatures permit, farmers might eke out a small second crop of maize annually. The average family consumes at least 50 pounds of maize every ten days, thus about 1,800 to 2,000 pounds per year. Even under the most advantageous conditions, an increasing number of farming families can no longer grow sufficient quantities to meet their total consumption needs.

ABOVE: Many Ixil families use herbal and other natural remedies passed down from generation to generation; modern pharmaceuticals are expensive and still poorly understood among illiterate parents.

The options to supplement food and income needs are limited and difficult. An increasing number of Ixil men look for daily agricultural wages on others' land, including the few large coffee plantations in the region, farms and ranches in the Ixcán territories to the north of Chajul, and sugar and coffee plantations on the Pacific Coast. Many are forced to migrate to Guatemala City or other urban centers, resigning themselves to great risks and long periods of cultural and economic deprivation. The clandestine routes to reach *El Norte* are increasingly dangerous and expensive; people will pay or pledge several thousand dollars to hire border-crossing guides (*coyotes*) to help them navigate the riskiest sections of the journey north. When and if they return to Guatemala, many confront fractured marriages and families.

Economic Activity

Against this backdrop of pervasive poverty, there is a defiant and hopeful crescendo of economic activity in

ABOVE: Wood saving stove: Community Enterprise Solutions tailors appropriate technology to the needs and budgets of rural families.

the town of Nebaj. Cell phones and radios, students and backpacks, and stacks of new laminated roofing material and rebar in pickups are signs of recovery. Dust and grit swirls in the morning traffic. The gas stations hum with trucks and minivans headed north to Cotzal and Chajul, and south to Santa Cruz del Quiché and beyond.

As a small business advisor with the U.S. Peace Corps in the 1970s and a former project analyst with the World Bank, I carry a notebook and sharp pencil (and pen knife) everywhere I go. I am curious about what is driving economic activity here, about prices in the market, and whether what is happening today represents sustained recovery for region. The most obvious engines of growth include top world prices for Ixil organic coffee and strong demand for Ixil natural and agricultural resources, such as maize, wood, livestock, and export-oriented vegetables. There is a visible increase in local consumer demand from the exploding population and the remittance checks of Ixil men and women working outside the region. A gradual improvement in the economic and social infrastructure—roads, schools, and health clinics—also supports this recovery. However, many of the same factors propelling current growth also contribute to the region's vulnerability: fluctuating world coffee prices, competition for land resources and gradual soil depletion, population growth, and family dispersion.

Each time I visit the town of Nebaj, I walk the main streets to see which stores are still in business, to note changes and new developments. There is a palpable dynamism here, a curiosity and openness in the townspeople, a vibrant NGO community, a steady trickle of international volunteers, and a growing activism among Ixil community groups. I sense a hunger for education and communication among the younger, postwar generation. In 2005, there was only one Internet café; today, half a dozen vie for burgeoning demand. Young people gather in the plaza and in several new cafes to exchange ideas and foster new networks. Time will tell which ideas and businesses will take root, but the economic growth I witness gives me reason for cautious optimism.

EL LIBRITO

Nebaj's leading store for school supplies is a testament to surging school enrollment in this region. President Álvaro Colom (2008–12) championed public education by abolishing school fees and launching an ambitious program to construct more schools in rural areas. Irma and Juan Clemente Raymundo Velesco, both university graduates, own and run this busy store opposite Hotel Villa Nebaj on the main road to Cotzal and Chajul. It is crammed with notebooks, maps, dictionaries, calculators, reference materials, Guatemala's legal codes, puzzles, brainteasers, and a dizzying selection of colored papers and markers to liven up any classroom or assignment. One can also get documents copied here and accessories for phones and computers. E-mail: librito@gmail.com

CENTRO NATURISTA "LA SALUD"

Due to the high cost of manufactured and imported pharmaceutical products, many Guatemalans continue to use traditional remedies, including a variety of herbal medicines. In recent years, the University of San Carlos in the capital collaborated with traditional healers to test and standardize dosages, and to establish a training certificate to dispense natural medicine. Stop in for a lesson on natural teas and salves for various ailments.

COMMUNITY ENTERPRISE SOLUTIONS

In 2003 two ex–Peace Corps volunteers, Greg Van Kirk and Bucky Glickley, launched this nonprofit organization to extend their commitment to the Ixil region. Their goal: to create an "incubator" for indigenous business. *Changing obstacles into solutions* became their motto. In 2009, Greg received

ABOVE: Radio is the major source of local and national news in rural areas; only the wealthiest families can afford a TV and antenna.

international accolades for their successful "micro-consignment" model of enterprise development, and was selected as one of the leading Ashoka Fellows in social entrepreneurship.

Their first investment consisted of a hub of rural tourism enterprises to welcome Guatemalan and international visitors and volunteers to the region: El Descanso Restaurant, La Red Internet café, Guias Ixiles guide service, and the Escuela de Idiomas, offering Spanish and Ixil lessons. They have now added the Medio Luna Medio Sol hostel. The restaurant and Internet café attract Ixil professionals, volunteers, and visitors. In the cool months of December through February, the place generates its own heat with conversation and connections. After eight years of operation and an approach that the founders have coined "interdisciplinary, intuitive and nonlinear, whereby all stakeholders add value," this cluster of services is a true success story in Nebaj. It is run at a profit and managed entirely by Ixil staff. As many of El Descanso's staff come from the nearby *aldea* of La Pista, their enthusiasm and earnings have had a ripple effect, resulting in a new library and after-school program in La Pista.

Greg and Bucky tested small-business ideas and recruited Ixil collaborators, international volunteers, and Ixil men and women eager to learn and launch micro-businesses with social impact. El Descanso provided the forum for people to exchange ideas, conduct research, make connections, and mull over feasibility studies—each with an Ixil chocolate chip cookie. Ixil entrepreneurs received training, an initial inventory of the product on a consignment basis, and follow-up support with marketing, financial, and technical advice. Entrepreneurs invest part of their profit into paying off the consigned products and expanding their inventory and outreach.

SCOJO Reading Glasses
One of the first enterprises launched was the SCOJO Reading Glasses initiative. Community Enterprise Solutions teamed up with the international SCOJO Foundation to teach enterprising women in Nebaj to conduct basic vision tests and sell appropriate-strength reading glasses. "Vision advisors" sell glasses for about Q40 (US $5.15), and earn Q10 per pair. The happy owner gains a new lease on productivity. By mid-2010, Community Enterprise Solutions' vision advisors had sold over 22,000 pairs of eyeglasses in Guatemala!

Ixil Stove Project (Estufas Ixiles)
Another successful business partnership has been the Ixil Stove Project, Estufas Ixiles, focused on replacing the traditional open hearths with fuel-efficient and health-promoting stoves. I met with Ixil entrepreneur, Agustín, who explained how the new stoves work. We visited a traditional adobe house where Agustín had installed a stove the previous year. We found a mother and daughter at home who proudly explained that the new stove uses only half the wood of an open hearth, yielding a savings of Q50 or more per month. The stove chimney vents stinging smoke that used to make the family cough and that previously coated the walls with creosote. Its raised flat cooking surface reduces accidents and discourages insects. The family paid off this improvement over six months. Agustín estimates that he earns about Q50 for every day he spends constructing the new stoves. Since the project's inception, Agustín and other trained "stove entrepreneurs" have installed over 2,000 stoves. Everyone benefits, and the Ixil forests are saved as well.

With a modest annual budget, Community Enterprise Solutions tackles Ixil poverty with common sense, appropriate technology, and local entrepreneurship. The enterprise incubator is humming: New micro-consignment projects include water purification filters, vegetable seeds packets, energy-efficient lightbulbs, and recently, solar lights. Community Enterprise Solutions has expanded its entrepreneurship training and micro-consignment model to other regions of Guatemala. They also offer intensive on-the-job field courses for American college students, and hope that tourists to Nebaj will volunteer for community development and empowerment activities. (www.CESolutions.org)

MAYAN HOPE
Started in 2003, Mayan Hope is another service-oriented NGO in Nebaj, run by founder Don Langley's sheer energy, insight, and compassion. You can usually find Don at the bright orange–painted Popi's Restaurant/Bakery and Hostel, which serves as headquarters for a variety of local initiatives spawned by Don and fellow volunteers and Ixil partners. The organization runs a small day-care center for children with disabilities, providing prosthetics and wheelchairs. It promotes local, environmentally friendly products.

Don launched the beekeeping cooperative, Ta'l Ka'b ("Honey Bee"), which boasts 450 hives and 8 tons of honey per year. He is working with Ixil partners to mold paper bricks from recycled trash, solar ovens, and a composting toilet. Don is a genius at mobilizing volunteers, networking, and stretching a shoestring budget. Dinner at Popi's is usually an opportunity to meet activists and to learn about the latest news and developments in the Ixil region. (www.MayanHope.org)

INDIGENOUS REGION COMMUNITY RADIO
News in the Ixil is disseminated almost exclusively person to person via cell phone—and via radio. You still cannot buy a national newspaper in Nebaj, and there is no local or regional newspaper. I kept the November 2004 inaugural and only edition of an Ixil start-up venture, La Region Ixil (*Tetz Lochb'al Tenam* in Ixil). The headlines read communication is the key to development. Unfortunately, this noble enterprise failed to attract enough literate customers to pay for the news. In 2006, the Department of El Quiché had the highest rates of illiteracy in Guatemala: 46 percent (combined indigenous and Ladino), almost twice the national average of 24 percent. With growing school attendance, however, functional literacy for the majority is attainable within another generation.

Cell-phone and radio towers have sprouted up all over Guatemala, and across this region's rugged terrain. Almost every family owns a small radio; the cheapest new transistor sells for Q80 in the market. I can usually pick up one or two of the commercial stations in Guatemala, as well as one of the local radio stations. The Catholic Church supports Radio La Voz de Nebaj (AM 907) and Chajul's Solo Voz (AM 1500); an evangelical foundation supports Radio Ixil (AM 1010) in Nebaj.

Radio Ixil (AM 1010)
This station provides cultural, educational, and Christian programming in Spanish and Ixil. The offices and transmitter are located in central Nebaj. I had an opportunity to be interviewed on the radio about this guidebook with the charismatic station manager, Diego Velasco. I asked him about the role of radio in Ixil communities:

Q: *Don Diego, tell me about the origins of Radio Ixil and how you got involved?*
A: The radio station was started in 1991, after the major conflicts of the civil war, to help people recover in their everyday lives. The goal was to reduce distance between people, transmit music, news, and education in the Ixil language. Fifteen years ago, when I was a young teenager, I began working as a volunteer for the Christian Fundación Emmanuel; I discovered that one of my strengths was talking into the microphone. Little by little, I improved enough to announce programs in Ixil, and eventually I became the director.
Q: *What do you think is the main importance of Radio Ixil?*
A: In the smallest and poorest outposts of the Ixil region, people can receive education and information about development: health and hygiene, mental health, advice about protecting the natural

environment, programs about conserving our culture, as well as spiritual themes to guide the general population. We broadcast our own programs during peak time from 4:00 a.m. to 10:00 p.m., followed by U.S. news and religious programming from 10:00 p.m. to 4:00 a.m.

Q: *How do you get audience feedback and know that Radio Ixil is heard and accepted?*

A: In almost all of our programs, we have time for listeners to communicate directly on air via telephone, including listeners from the United States who call to say *hola* to their families here. When we organize campaigns for donations, people respond to our appeals.

BELOW: Local radio stations broadcast in Ixil and Spanish: news, music, announcements of community events, and educational programming.

Q: *Who works here in the station?*

A: We have men and women from different villages who help us run the station. They don't earn very much, but they participate in an initial orientation course, learn on the job, and ultimately receive more formal instruction on strengthening their programs. The majority speaks Ixil, and we have several women who transmit programs directed toward women in the region.

An exciting new development in recent years is the network of community-supported radio stations in many towns and rural areas across Guatemala. As of 2010, there were 140 such stations nationwide, with several in the planning stages in the Ixil region. These stations are not-for-profit and guarantee access to all voices within the community. Partnering with Cultural Survival (www.CulturalSurvival.org) for

technical and networking support, they broadcast within the geographic range limited by their power and antenna. The typical monthly operating budget of about Q1,500, is funded entirely by the contributions of listeners, local businesses, and community organizations. Community radios broadcast in both Spanish and the local language, providing news, discussion of local affairs, and cultural and educational programming on such subjects as coffee production, environmental conservation, health, and nutrition.

DOCTORING IN THE IXIL REGION

Extreme poverty and a severe shortage of medical resources make the health and nutritional challenges in this country daunting. Across leading health indicators, Guatemala ranks toward the bottom of countries in Latin America. Average life expectancy is seventy years, but is three to five years lower among the indigenous women and men, respectively. Infant mortality has inched lower in recent years, to 29 per 1,000, but 35 of every 1,000 children die before they reach their fifth birthday.[62] Forty-four percent of children suffer from chronic malnutrition, the highest rate in all of Latin America.[63]

Dr. José Manuel Cochoy quoted a survey by the Cuban doctors in Nebaj, citing the main causes of infant mortality in the Ixil region as common infections, parasites, anemia, and respiratory illnesses.[64] The structural causes of death, he explained, are entrenched poverty, low levels of education, and inadequate public health programs. Most rural families here still live in precarious health conditions that leave them vulnerable to basic diseases. The doctor listed common factors that undermine basic health: lack of household sanitation, contamination of drinking water, inhalation of smoke from open hearths inside the home, insufficient clothing for the mountain climate, difficult working conditions, and insufficient calories and nutrition.

Medical services within the region are stretched thin. Several times a year, Ministry of Health medical teams sweep through all towns and villages to vaccinate children against the major infectious and childhood diseases. For all other health issues, from broken bones to pneumonia to problematic pregnancies, families line up at one of the forty public health clinics (*Puesto de Salud*) in the region, or seek the advice and care of a traditional healer. Rural health clinics are routinely short-staffed and underfunded. Few have a trained nurse on staff; a "health promoter" staffs most of these rural clinics. Health centers stock only the most basic medicines and experience chronic shortages. Although common medicines are available from pharmacies in the major towns here, their cost can be prohibitive for poor families. It is not surprising that many families apply traditional herbal treatments and healing practices first, and may seek out a shaman to conduct special prayer ceremonies, before resorting to modern medicine. For serious injuries and illnesses, families must travel to the hospital in Nebaj, and sometimes all the way to Santa Cruz del Quiché for specialty care. A medical condition that is readily treated in the U.S. is frequently life threatening in Guatemala.

It is heartbreaking, Dr. Cochoy acknowledged, that so many women continue to die in childbirth. According to the World Health Organization, the maternal mortality ratio for Guatemala was 110 deaths per 100,000 live births in 2008, compared to an average ratio of 85 for all Latin American and Caribbean countries.[65] In remote rural areas like the Ixil region, maternal deaths are much higher than the national average. Except for the occasional consultation with a local midwife, women receive no special prenatal care or vitamins. Pregnant women are unlikely to alter their diet and tend to continue strenuous daily routines right up to their delivery date. When complications arise during pregnancy or delivery, it is often a difficult trip to the Puesto de Salud, sometimes too late to save the life of the mother and/or the child.

When Ixil women learn that I have *only* two children, they often engage me in conversation about

Dr. José Manuel Cochoy arrived for our rendezvous on a mud-stained motorcycle in scrubs and a backpack. He had come from attending a difficult, breech delivery in a nearby village, and offered his assessment of the major health issues he confronts in the Ixil region on a daily basis. In the process, I also learned some things about José Manuel's background and training that have contributed to his remarkable dedication.

José Manuel grew up in a small village near Lake Atitlán, one of eleven children of Kaqchikel-speaking parents. In the 1970s, a young Maryknoll missionary from Oregon helped to organize an agricultural cooperative in his community, building the first primary school for indigenous children. José Manuel's father was emboldened by the young priest's teachings—that "education was a basic human right"—and sold parcels of the family land to ensure that José Manuel and his siblings could go to school. During the 1980s, when the Guatemalan army arrested local cooperative leaders on suspicion of being counterinsurgents, José

Manuel's uncle and many other villagers were killed, or "disappeared." Although the American priest was forced to flee the country, he maintained strong ties to the village, raising funds in the U.S. to help many young Maya pursue their dreams of an education. Every one of José Manuel's three sisters and seven brothers completed a university education; three are now medical doctors, one, an economist, and another, a midwife and shaman.

José Manuel attended medical school in Cuba. Although his contract with the Guatemalan Ministry of Health stipulated that he work in rural areas, he acknowledges that he embraced his assignment in the Ixil region as a matter of personal conscience and a desire to work in underserved communities. He was one of ten Guatemalan primary-care doctors caring for the region's 150,000 inhabitants (a ratio of one doctor per 15,000 people); an additional fourteen Cuban specialists staff the region's only hospital in Nebaj. After spending a year posted to Ilom in northern Chajul, followed by six months in Cotzal, José Manuel completed his public service commitment in Nebaj.

José Manuel has recently married a young Ixil woman and is planning to open a Pediatric Clinic in Nebaj.

Photo by Scott Stoll. Even though the scenery from the roadside is spectacular, I encourage travelers to walk the footpaths with a local friend or guide to experience other features of the Ixil history and culture.

family planning. Amid crushing poverty, strained land resources, and limited employment prospects, women, in particular, are seriously beginning to rethink family size. The pregnancy rate among Ixil women is extremely high—an average of seven pregnancies per woman. According to WINGS (www.WingsGuate.org), an NGO partnering with Guatemala's leading family planning services provider, APROFAM, only a third of reproductive age women use birth control. There is a growing, unmet demand for reliable methods to delay and to space out childbirth; however, some women have admitted to me that they are scared by rumors that contraceptives have adverse side effects and can cause infertility. Women's fears tend to be assuaged when they have access to professional medical consultations and the support of a peer group. Guatemala has the highest fertility rate, 4.4 percent, in Latin America, with an official population growth rate of 2.5 percent per year (3.4 percent per year in the Department of El Quiché).[66] After much controversy, the national Congress passed a law in 2005 supporting "Universal and Equitable Access to Family Planning Services." Hopefully, this law will spur the extension of reliable information and improved access to family planning services in areas like the Ixil region, where population pressure on diminishing land resources is exacerbating extreme poverty.

TREKKING AND TOURING IN NEBAJ'S ALDEAS

This region offers almost unlimited options for hiking or exploring in a four-wheel-drive vehicle. The key to a rewarding visit is adequate time for the unexpected and an ability to enjoy the journey as much as the destination. Although distances appear short on a map, experience has taught me to make generous allowances for rigorous topography, rough roads, and even rougher off-road paths, and the unpredictable. If you are traveling by car, it is a good idea to confirm directions frequently—local information can help one skirt a recent landslide (*derrumbé*) or a bridge repair. If you are hiking, it is prudent—and pleasant—to hire a guide service or local villager as a guide. They will keep you on the right path, but can also provide the respectful introductions to surprised villagers you will undoubtedly meet en route. By vehicle or foot, leave extra time for bird-watching, hidden waterfalls, coffee beans drying in the middle of the road, a local festival or market, and conversation.

Acul

Acul is wedged into the beautiful mountain valley watered by Rio Acul. Remnants of ancient ruins in the vicinity, dating from the Classic and Postclassic Period, indicate that the Ixil have inhabited this dramatic valley for over a thousand years. A few

BELOW: Finca San Antonio: a verdant pocket of dairy farming and cheese production in Nebaj and lovely bed and breakfast.

guidebooks note Acul for the picturesque Finca San Antonio, which produces the Gouda-like brand of cheese, *Queso Chancol*. Unfortunately, most visitors have largely overlooked the struggling village nearby, which was devastated during the civil war. Acul provides a quiet interlude for a trek further west to Xexocom, to the higher altitudes of Chortiz and Paramos Grande, or north to the *aldea* of Salquil Grande. The haunting beauty and contrasts of this verdant valley make for a thought-provoking visit.

There is a choice of routes to get to Acul from the town of Nebaj: a 4-kilometer hike through the mountains, or a 12-kilometer drive. Neither route is well marked, so the prudent course is to ask, and keep asking. Everyone will point the right way, but you want to be sure not to miss a critical turn. The footpath leads through the Cantón of Salquilito, northwest of Nebaj center. By car, bear left in front of El Triángulo gas station in downtown Nebaj; take your next left, and then a quick right down off the plateau. At the bottom of the hill, bear right at the fork and follow the bumpy road west. After passing through the hamlet of Cambalam, a pitted sign indicates a left turn into the valley of Acul.

The present-day town of Acul is planted on a rocky hillside. It shows signs of overgrazing from the gradual expansion of the dairy industry, which competes with traditional maize cultivation. Acul's dense core of grid-like streets is probably much the same as it was in the 1980s, when the Guatemalan army confined the local population to a "model village" they hastily erected in this location. Basic "lock and key" board (*tabla*) houses line the footpaths that branch off the main street. Fortunately, time and lush growth of family gardens have softened its wartime austerity. During the civil war, the army tortured and executed thirty villagers suspected of being guerrilla sympathizers.

Mental health issues continue to plague a generation of survivors in communities like Acul. In 2003, a team of psychiatrists tried to help the residents of Acul open up and talk about brutal memories and long-held anguish. A psychologist who was interviewed about the widespread and unmet need for truth and reconciliation in Guatemala commented: "For the Maya, the [spoken] word is important . . . to say you repent, you are respected."[67] In Acul, as in many other villages across Guatemala, breaking the silence is a first step toward reconciliation. Economic recovery, which has been bitterly slow here, is also critical. I believe that, in a small way, respectful and friendly travelers who stop here to talk, purchase a snack, or rest their hiking feet can help communities like Acul with the healing process.

Across the river and fields from the town nestle two large dairy farms, Finca Mil Amores and Finca San Antonio, which offer overnight lodging and home-cooked meals. On one of my first trips to the Ixil region, I arrived at the rustic Finca San Antonio at dusk, just as thirty Holstein milk cows were heading for the barn, gently nudged by a spotted sheepdog. The tinkling of cowbells and whistling of the milking crew gave me the momentary impression that I was in the European Alps! We were the only visitors that night, and the owner, Don Hugo Azzari, invited us to eat in the farmhouse kitchen with him. Over stew and farm cheese *quesadillas*, Hugo regaled us with stories of his Italian grandfather, who had immigrated to Guatemala by way of the U.S. and purchased land for the farm in 1903. The milk production of small Acul farmers and the two larger dairy farms in the valley is processed into *Queso Chancol* and distributed as far as Guatemala City.

We examined the hunting trophies and faded photographs of the Azzari dynasty before piling on extra blankets for a cool night's sleep in a rustic, whitewashed farm bedroom. Hugo Azzari died in 2007 and joined his forbears in the family cemetery above the farmhouse. The farm has passed on to Hugo's son and the next generation. The delicious cheese, which can be purchased at the farm and in Nebaj, as well as the welcoming guest rooms and simple savory meals, are expected to continue. Reservations at Finca San Antonio: (502) 5305-6240.

Salquil Grande

The idea for a road trip to Salquil Grande, 23 kilometers (14 miles) from Nebaj center, began over soup in a crowded Nebaj *comedor* when Domingo Perez Bernal introduced himself to us in flawless English. Domingo is a young Ixil professional—a computer expert and community development organizer, with a college degree from the University of Kentucky. Our lunch encounter turned into a supper date and a stimulating discussion about the necessity of education for Ixil youth in order to meet the significant social and economic challenges ahead.

Domingo's life story is remarkable, and illustrates the huge commitment of hard work, family support, and personal perseverance that are required by Ixil youth to obtain an education. It also underscores the enormous contribution that young Ixil professionals like Domingo are making to the development of the region. Domingo urged me to visit the Tuesday-morning market in Salquil Grande. "You can visit my brother and meet my parents," he added. So, we set off early for Domingo's *aldea*, thinking this would be a quick run up the mountains by pickup. The excursion took most of the morning, navigating rough roads, but we enjoyed the unfolding views and small hamlets. Domingo's childhood shortcuts across timeworn paths enabled him to make the trip in less time.

The road from to Salquil Grande leads west from El Triángulo gas station in downtown Nebaj. On the outskirts of Nebaj, the road forks left to Acul and Salquil, and right to Ak'txumb'al. Beyond the turnoff to Acul, the road crosses the Rio Xak'b'al and climbs steadily through the small villages and maize fields of Tzalbal, Vatzsuchil, Canaquil, and Xepium. The final ascent, in low gear, to Salquil Grande, leads directly onto the town's windswept plaza of huddled kiosks and the offices of the local *alcalde,* with a sweeping view of Nebaj municipality from 2,500 meters (8,200

BELOW: Photo by Chris Percival. Windswept Salquil Grande, recovering from civil war devastation, surveys splendid sweep of the high Cuchumatanes.

Ancient temple mounds at Pulay.

feet). The largest of the Nebaj's eighteen districts (*aldeas*), Salquil Grande hosts the second-largest market in the municipality, located a short walk downhill from the plaza. A lively commerce in mostly regional products booms from 6:00 a.m. to midday. By the time my companions and I arrived in the late morning, it was already winding down. Nevertheless, vendors packing up their wares were surprised and pleased to see the *gringos* who had come all this way to sample the market. We inquired after Domingo's younger brother, Diego, and found him in his brand-new school-supply store, AlfaNegocios. He does a good business: 1,000 children attend the public primary school here, and 300 students are enrolled in the Christian middle school, Colégio Luz y Vida.

A forlorn Catholic church sits in the north corner of Salquil Grande's main plaza, its doors gaping in the wind. Its demise mirrors the common fate of most Catholic parishes, as well as many evangelical churches, during the civil war. In villages and towns of the Ixil region, army forces targeted the Catholic missionaries and their followers as suspected "leftist sympathizers," while guerrilla insurgent leaders, many espousing communist views, discredited and disrupted nascent evangelical churches as a threat to their authority in areas under guerrilla control. As a result, communities in remote mountain villages, like Salquil Grande, found themselves under attack from the right and the left, with no option to remain neutral or to flee. Such was the case in aldea of Salquil, as described in the riveting life story of the Ixil evangelical pastor, Tomás Guzaro, as transcribed by Terri Jacob McComb in *Escaping the Fire*.[68] Convinced that his family and fellow villagers would eventually be killed in the heightening crossfire, in August 1982, Tomás Guzaro led 227 men, women, and infants along trecherous mountain trails to escape guerrilla-controlled enclaves and seek a government offer of amnesty and army protection in Nebaj. Following this daring exodus, Guzman returned to Salquil with Army backing and enabled a further 2000 Ixil to come

A Calling to Help the Ixil

When I first met Domingo Bernal, he was coordinating integrated teen health and development programs called Healthy Teens (*Adolescentes Saludables*) and Friendly Spaces (*Espacios Amigables*). On a recent trip, I learned that Domingo now works as a regional coordinator for the American, Christian-based development organization, Food for the Hungry (www.fh.org/).

Domingo's home is in Salquil Grande, the largest *aldea* in the municipality of Nebaj. He grew up as the oldest of eleven brothers and sisters in the high mountain village, helping his father in their maize fields. After primary school in Salquil, Domingo persuaded his father to let him continue his studies. For the next three years, he walked each week to the middle school in the town of Nebaj. A teacher in Nebaj encouraged Domingo apply to high school in Quetzaltenango. Domingo turned down a scholarship in Guatemala City to attend the University of Kentucky. Domingo credits his success to four factors: his father's unswerving support, his belief in the power of education, his deep religious faith, and a calling to help the Ixil and Guatemala invest in its own people.

down from the mountains into Nebaj to seek refuge from the conflict. The army subsequently captured this strategic *aldea,* rounding its remaining families into a guarded settlement to prevent further contact with insurgency forces.

Pulay

The *aldea* of Pulay lies 11 kilometers north of Nebaj. The new headquarters of the *Comunidad Lingüística* Ixil, the Ixil regional branch of the Academy of Mayan Languages, is located in Pulay, at the juncture of the roads to Chajul and Cotzal. The center continues important research, documentation, and preservation of the Ixil language (and dialects) and culture.

On a recent trip, when new maize shoots were just poking through the hoe-furrowed fields, I went scouting for signs of a pre-Hispanic ceremonial center mentioned by archaeologists Smith and Kidder in the 1950s, and Becquelin's team in the 1960s. I did not have to look very far. As I approached Pulay from the south, the silhouette of an ancient temple mound caught my eye among the lightly greening hillsides to the west of the main road. The temple mound stands about 8 to 10 meters high (24 to 30 feet) next to a flat rectangular area that was once a ceremonial plaza. Like most of the ancient Ixil sites I have visited, this impressive vestige of cultural patrimony lies abandoned, if not forgotten, on private farmlands. With each passing season, farmers' hoes and pelting rains disperse and erode the ancient structures.

The tree-shrouded mountain beyond the temple ruins harbors a limestone cave, where Maya priests have conducted traditional prayer ceremonies for centuries and where the residents of Pulay hid from the Guatemalan army during the civil war. I suggest that travelers inquire with local residents for directions and permission to visit the sacred cave. The cave is a ten-minute walk from the primary school, and a new café advertising *fuego lento* ("slow-cooked") barbecue. The route to the cave winds through a narrow valley serving as pastureland, walled on the left-hand side by rocky outcroppings. A tangle of overhanging vines curtains the elevated cave entrance from viewers below. I scrambled up to the mouth of the cave with an Ixil friend, who explained how villagers huddled here, undetected, while army soldiers in the 1980s searched the nearby town. Our flashlights explored the natural cave interior, judging that it was large enough to shelter twenty families. Amid the stalagmite pillars and stone niches, are a number of Maya altars, encrusted with candle wax and the heavy aroma of incense. Right outside the cave entrance, sky-blue hydrangea bloom profusely. The *hortensia* flower symbolizes "survival" among the Maya.

IXIL RELIGION: A BLEND OF ANCIENT AND MODERN FAITHS

Five hundred years after the Spanish outlawed "pagan" rituals and forced Catholicism on the indigenous population, Maya priests (*sacerdotes Mayas*)—their ancient ranks thinned by natural and unnatural assaults—continue to guard the sacred spiritual knowledge of their ancestors in the Ixil region and across the modern world of the Maya.

Although it may be argued that the Spanish accomplished a profound transformation of Maya religion, the conversion was far from complete in remote communities where Church power remained weakest. Across the mountainous "parishes" of the Cuchumatanes, lonely Spanish clergy had to rely on leaders of ancient Ixil lineage groups, including traditional Maya priests, to staff Church offices and the religious brotherhoods (*cofradías*) charged with the care and celebration of the Christian saints. Under the new cloak and calendar of Christian rituals, as well as in clandestine ceremonies, Maya priests preserved and perpetuated many aspects of traditional spiritual practice and customs (*costumbre*). As late as the mid-twentieth century, American anthropologists Jackson Steward Lincoln (field research 1939–40)

> ### The Ancient Maya Calendar System Among the Ixil
>
> Lincoln's primary interest was the survival of the ancient Maya calendar system among the Ixil. He discovered that Maya priests, also called "calendar priests" and "daykeepers," still kept track of the 260-day sacred calendar and the 365-day solar year. He recorded the Ixil names for the thirteen sacred Maya daygods and twenty sacred number count that combined in interlocking twenty-day cycles. Every five days in this eternal count, Maya priests paid homage to the principal "Yearbearer" days of the sacred calendar year, also referred to as the *Alcaldes del Mundo*.
>
> *The calendar is not only an accurate measurer of annual solar time, with the exception of leap year calculations, but is a religious, ceremonial and divinatory director of man's destiny. It controls his daily life in the sphere of worship, agriculture, domestic and social life and influences his behavior in connection with birth, love, marriage, social etiquette, and earning his living from the earth, and death. The days, which are also divinities to whom he prays, exert favorable and unfavorable influences on all his activities. Although some of the features of this ancient calendar are beginning to be lost, it still endures in spite of some knowledge and use of the Gregorian calendar as well, after 400 years of Spanish and Christian influence and effort to suppress native custom.*[70]

and Benjamin and Lore Colby, with Pierre van den Berghe (field research 1960–70), confirmed the continuing practice of traditional Maya *costumbre*, including observance of the ancient sacred calendar among the Ixil.

As Spain's imperial power waned in the eighteenth century, the Catholic Church in Guatemala suffered loss of power and resources. By this time, Catholic parishes in the Ixil region existed at the will of indigenous community leaders. One beleaguered Spanish priest in Nebaj wrote his superiors that the "Indians" of Nebaj and Cotzal were "if not of a docile character, at least timid, and with scolding and a few remonstrations one can make them do things," but that those of Chajul were "indomitable and discourteous." Clergy notes from Chajul disparaged the rebellion and disrespect of the local population: "The Indians are in control of items of the church and the priest would provoke a fight and quarrel to reclaim them" (1833); "It is a continual task of the priests to order the mortal remains covered in the church, to find out, threaten, punish and admonish them, etc. . . . once the priest leaves they return to the same practice" (1846–65).[69]

When Lincoln trekked into the Ixil region for field research in 1939, he quickly became aware that the knowledge and practice of the ancient priestly cast had, in fact, survived in these remote mountain villages. The American anthropologist arrived with an extensive knowledge of the ancient Maya calendar and managed to gain the trust of his Ixil guides and interpreters to learn more about traditional *costumbre* and its links to the sacred calendar system.

What Lincoln observed was "a wonderful amalgam of Christian and pagan,"[71] illustrated by a prayer that was commonly recited by his Ixil companions at traditional mountain crosses:

> *The deities petitioned in it were the Dios Mundo, Jesus Christ, Saints, Angels, the yellow Corn, the White Corn, the Holy Earth, the Carpenter Bird, the Mountains around Zotzil [sic] by name, the previous 13 days of the calendar as Day-Lords and called the 13 Kings, the 20 days of the Calendar and the Sun.*[72]

The coexistence of Maya spiritual practices and Catholic rituals varied greatly by community, depending on its proximity to Nebaj and to the presence of the Catholic padre, who made the rounds of the major *aldeas* several times a year. Lincoln noted that Ixil villagers dutifully lined up for baptisms and communion when the priest was in town, but participated in a robust practice of traditional ceremonies behind

ABOVE: Nebaj: one of the remaining traditional Ixil Maya crosses that delineated the spatial and sacred boundaries of this ancient Ixil settlement.

the padre's back. Even the Spanish padre's "right-hand assistant," who could recite the Mass in Spanish and Latin, refused to give the priest any information about such *costumbre*: "Unless the Indians feel that a person is sympathetic towards their *costumbre,* they close up completely. All that can be got out of them is '*A saber, no se, no hay, quien sabe.*' Diego L. [the priest's assistant] knows that sacrifices of animals are made at the mountain crosses but tells the Padre that they are made no longer."[73]

Following in Lincoln's footsteps two decades later, anthropologists Benjamin and Lore Colby delved deeper into Ixil religious thought and practice, working extensively with an Ixil "daykeeper" by the name of Pap Shas Ko'w. The extraordinary life story, philosophy, and divinations of Pap Shas illustrates the unique Ixil blend of Christian and traditional spirituality that had evolved in this region. The folk narratives and prayers of this diviner invoked the power of "God," the "Eternal Father," and Jesus Christ, but placed these sacred figures within the context of a more-expansive Maya cosmovision, populated by a host of primordial and local deities, supernatural and earthly forces. In Pap Shas' prayers, "Our Father" is also *Kub'aal*, "God of the World," the god of the rising sun, and the Maize God; the places where the Ixil must give thanks for their sustenance and time on the earth are referred to as the *Alcalde* cross on the mountain.[74]

Lincoln and the Colbys used the term *syncretism* to describe the state of Ixil religious belief and ritual in the mid-twentieth century. In some communities, an "accommodation" within the formal institutional structures of Catholicism is an apt description. The Spanish built their churches over Ixil traditional altars, but the Catholic Mass shared floor space with Maya offerings of candles, incense, and flowers. The

Spanish superimposed the Gregorian calendar on the 360-plus-5-day Maya solar calendar, but observance of ancient sacred rhythms persisted in both spiritual and secular aspects of Ixil community life. Ixil children were baptized with Christian first names, but welcomed into the world by communal "godparents" and given ancestral Ixil names. Celebrations of Catholic saints' days took place with all the incense, fireworks, and beat of traditional instruments rooted in ancient ceremonies. Well into the twentieth century, Maya priests (*sacerdotes Mayas*) played a key role in both secular and ritual events in the region, although the increasing presence of Ladinos and social cleavages wrought by changes in land tenure and commerce raised new challenges to traditional Ixil authority.

Since the 1970s, another imported religion, evangelical Protestantism, has begun to change the spiritual landscape of Guatemala again. In Lincoln's day, the sole evangelical missionary in the Ixil struggled to attract a meager following. During the civil war, however, the evangelicals gained in popularity,

BELOW: The monument bears the dedication of the former Secretary-General of the URNG, Rolando Morán (whose nom de guerre was Ricardo Arnoldo Ramírez de León): Ahora como nunca, nuestro reconocimiento a los caidos, a los mejores de nosotros que dieron su vida para abrir las perspectivas que nos corresponde continuar. ("Now, more than ever, we give our gratitude to the fallen, to the best among us who gave their lives to create a future for others.")

ABOVE: Accomplished astronomers, the ancient Maya aligned earthly and sacred space along four cardinal axes, north, south, east, and west, represented by different gods, powers, attributes, and colors (white for north, yellow for south, red for east, and black for west).

particularly with the ascent of self-proclaimed evangelical minister and military general, General Efraín Ríos Montt, to the presidency in the early 1980s. As the Guatemalan army persecuted social activists among the Catholic clergy, forcing many to flee their rural parishes, evangelical missionaries moved into the spiritual breach of traumatized communities and frequently aligned themselves with the government forces to protect their congregations from divisive violence. They preached a "spiritual rebirth" through personal salvation and a direct relationship with Jesus Christ, a truly radical concept for Catholics and believers in the Maya cosmology. Even though Catholic clergy returned to rural parishes following the war, evangelical worship now dominates formal religious life in a majority of Ixil communities.

Ixil religion is in a state of flux today, fractured by vying faith communities and confused by irreverent invasions of the modern media. Social disintegration, globalized demigods, and pop versions of the daily Maya "horoscope" undermine the cultural values and traditional community authorities central to Ixil religion before and since the Spanish Conquest. What I have observed, however, is that the Ixil remain deeply reverent. Prayer and "cognizance of the greater cosmos" permeate the daily lives of subsistence farmers

Photo by Chris Percival, View east to Nebaj town center from the municipal cemetery.

as well as young professionals here. Within the more socially cohesive towns, traditional Ixil leaders and Maya priests continue to exercise a measure of authority in community civic and religious affairs. Despite differences in religious affiliation, most of my Ixil friends continue to observe some elements of traditional religion. I know families that pray for relief or fortune in church and also engage a Maya priest to offer prayers at a traditional altar. They follow the Gregorian calendar in their civic and business lives, but join celebrations of the Maya New Year or the first day of maize sowing prescribed by the ancient calendar. The Maya cosmology—a sacred web of relationships uniting humans with the spirits of the natural and supernatural worlds—continues to be skillfully and reverently woven into the *huipiles* of Ixil women.

A better assessment of contemporary Ixil religious beliefs must come from Ixil observers of their own community. While I do not know of any such studies currently, I have no doubt such commentary will be forthcoming.

SACRED SPACES IN NEBAJ

Lincoln mentioned the existence of 105 sacred crosses in the municipality of Nebaj where traditional ceremonies were still being performed in the 1940s. In the 1960s, Benjamin Colby attended a "dawning" ceremony of the Maya New Year at an ancient ceremonial site in Chajul.[75] After discovering an old Maya cross embedded in a sidewalk near the Cultural Center in downtown Nebaj, I was curious about the extent to which Ixil *costumbre* and sacred sites had survived the civil war. I hired a local guide through Guías Ixiles to explore sacred sites within walking distance of the central plaza. I was in luck. After a hearty breakfast at El Descanso, my traveling companions and I met Don Nicholas, a dignified, middle-aged Ixil gentleman who was to be our guide. We were treated to a four-hour tour of modern and ancient sacred sites around the town of Nebaj and learned more about the state of traditional *costumbre* in the Ixil today.

Modern Cemeteries

The first stop on the tour was Nebaj's central plaza. As mentioned earlier, the Catholic church was deliberately built in the sixteenth century on top of an ancient ceremonial center, and the Dominican monks raised a large wooden cross on the plaza. During the colonial period, Ixil residents of Nebaj buried their dead in the original cemetery (*calvario*) in back of the church. As the power of the Church waned in the eighteenth century, Maya priests conducted traditional prayer ceremonies on the plaza, lighting incense and candles at the foot of the cross located there. Such overt practices of traditional religion came to a halt in the twentieth century, after Ladinos settled in Nebaj and decried such "pagan" displays in the center of town. According to our guide, in 1913, when "ancient bones were beginning to show" in the colonial cemetery adjacent to the Church, the Ladino mayor and parish priest demanded that Ixil elders move the burial grounds out of the town center. In 1936, municipal authorities also uprooted the controversial cross on the plaza.

We followed the ancient bones to the "new" municipal cemetery, on an airy hilltop west of town, where Ixil commoners now bury their dead. Here, graves are marked with a simple cross or a small enclosure serving as an altar. Bouquets of calla lilies and offerings of pine needles adorn gravesites. Colorful tatters of kites, flown from the graveyard on November 1 for the Day of the Dead (*Día de los Muertos*), flutter in trees overhead.

Among the humble graves stands a recent monument dedicated by the Guillermo Toriello Foundation (www.fgtoriello.org.gt) in January 2006. The Foundation was created in 1996 as a condition of the Guatemalan National Revolutionary Unity (URNG) to honor indigenous victims of the war. Paintings on the monument depict four chapters in the historic struggles of the Ixil people: the Spanish conquest, forced labor during the colonial and postcolonial periods, the martyrdom of six Nebaj leaders in 1936, and massacres of Ixil villagers during the civil war. Pointing to the bold outline of the mountains in one scene, our guide explained, "This community owes a lot to the mountains; because clouds may prevent us from seeing them on some days, the Cuchumatanes are honored here for sheltering us, along with those who lost their lives for us." Entombed in this monument are the identified remains of three of the six martyrs of the 1936 Ixil uprising; three spaces remain empty for the others ... also a reminder that hundreds of civil war victims still lie in mass graves yet to be exhumed and documented.

From the municipal cemetery, we took a five-minute walk to the small private cemetery, where deceased relatives of affluent Ladino and Ixil families are entombed in large family vaults. Within this veritable maze of mausoleums stands a simple roofed structure, a Maya ceremonial center (*casa oratoria*). Inside, a traditional altar is crowded with a forest of wooden crosses; the smell of incense lingers in the cool air, and pine needles and flowers carpet the dirt floor. This traditional sanctuary was built in fulfillment of the *Agreement on the Identity and Rights of Indigenous Peoples*, as part of the 1996 Peace Accords, formally recognizing indigenous communities' rights to practice their spiritual and cultural traditions.

According to our guide, the crosses have been placed here "for safekeeping." He explained that up until the civil war, it was customary for Ixil families to maintain an altar in their homes, lighting candles and incense in prayer to an amalgam of Christian and Maya deities. During the war, when Catholic parishioners were often targeted as "guerrilla sympathizers," fearful Ixil families were forced to hide or abandon their crosses. Around Nebaj and at sacred sites in the mountains, the army destroyed many traditional crosses. Apparently, when this *casa oratoria* was completed a few years ago, Ixil families and Maya priests placed surviving crosses here for safekeeping.

Ancient Altars of Xe'vak

From the modern cemeteries and civil war memorials, we followed our guide to the ancient Ixil ceremonial center of Xe'vak in the cantón of Salquilito, northwest of Nebaj center. Xe'vak is the region's most extensive ancient site, and functioned as a ceremonial center and residency of Ixil ruling elites for a major portion of the Early to Late Classic Period (AD 200 to AD 909). In the 1950s, archaeologists Smith and Kidder worked for several seasons here to document the remains of seventeen major temples, in addition to plazas, raised platforms, and a sacred ballcourt. They unearthed elaborate burial chambers and finely crafted royal artifacts in their excavation of two prominent temple mounds; many of these artifacts are on display in the National Museum of Ethnology and Archaeology in Guatemala City (www.munae.gob.gt). On the basis of this evidence, they speculated that the Ixil kingdoms might have served as an important trading link between the great lowland Maya city-states of the Petén and other highland kingdoms. After the Toltec tribes swept southward from central coastal Mexico and conquered the scattered settlements of the Cuchumatanes between AD 1000 and AD 1250, Xe'vak was abandoned. Characteristic of other highland settlements in the Postclassic Period, the civic and ceremonial center in Nebaj was relocated to a more-defensible site, the elevated promontory where the town of Nebaj stands today.

Local historians say that the area around Xe'vak, known as Salquilito today, was settled during the first millennium and has been in continuous occupation since. It is the only remaining cantón around Nebaj center where many of the houses are still traditional adobe brick with clay-tile roofs. *Xo'l Salchi'l*, the original Ixil name for this cantón, translates as "in the middle" or "among the seeds" (*entre pepitas*). According to Ixil elders in this cantón, the name is an allusion to the center of a dispersed settlement, like the popular *chilacayote* squash that produces its *pepita* seeds to spawn new plants.

Where the ancient Xe'vak plazas were once filled with crowds and processions, the traditional hoe (*azadón*) now furrows among sacred stones.

RIGHT: Photos by Scott Stoll, In this hauntingly beautiful ancient Ixil civic and religious center of Xe'vak, old temple mounds still serve today as ceremonial prayer altars for Maya spiritual priests and traditional believers.

Today, the entire area of this ancient ceremonial center is carved into privately titled plots for maize cultivation and cattle grazing. If one is fortunate to visit Xe'vak between January and early May, when the fields lie bare, the outlines of the ancient site are unmistakable: temple mounds, revealing occasional ancient ranges of cut stonework, rise 10 to 25 meters above the surrounding valley to reign over open plazas, a ritual ballcourt, and areas that once held royal residences. Sadly, the ancient structures, once massive and precise, are now defaced and eroded. According to Kidder and Smith, much of the original stonework of these structures was already long gone by 1950, probably requisitioned by the Spanish for their building campaigns. Although there have been no other officially sanctioned excavations at Xe'vak since the 1950s, I was told that treasure hunters continue to scavenge among the ruins; within recent memory of our guide, a "foreigner" bought a tract of land within Xe'vak, leveling an ancient platform in search of artifacts. Unfortunately, national institutions with the mandate to protect historical patrimony, including the Ministry of Culture and the National Institute of Anthropology and History, have not taken any measures to protect this ancient Ixil Maya capital.

Despite degradation and sacrilege, Xe'vak continues to hold sacred power for traditional Ixil

The Cantón of Salquilito is the cradle of history and culture of the Ixil people, just a ten-minute walk from Nebaj's central plaza. Today, you still find shadows of our ancestors in the adobe and tile-roofed architecture of many old houses, ancient crosses marking sacred altars, and footpaths worn by this community for centuries. Salquilito is proud of its cultural heritage and heroes. At the cantón's center is the older "prayer house" (casa oratoria) in the traditional architectural style used by our ancestors, as well as Ixil today, for sacred prayer ceremonies. Adjoining this casa, Salquilito recently dedicated a new public park enclosed by traditional pillars and symbols of the ancient calendar that is open to all. Visitors can share in the rich customs and celebrations of Salquilito and learn about textile traditions, local food preparation, Maya spirituality, art, music, and local agriculture.

Salquilito, like many villages in the region, was greatly affected by the thirty-six-year armed conflict; everyone here has a personal story about loss and survival. In order to survive the hardships and atrocities of that time, many people of my generation had to migrate to the south coast to harvest sugarcane. I accompanied my father for many seasons and labored under harsh and unjust conditions. At other times of the year, I attended night classes to complete middle school. When the first high school opened in Nebaj after the war, I seized the chance to complete a degree in teaching, and received my first job with a French humanitarian organization. After six years with this group, I pursued a dream to attend university. My goal is to use my knowledge and experience to benefit future generations of the Ixi community.

Please honor us with a visit to Salquilito and the Ixil homeland.

—MIGUEL RAYMUNDO CETO AND MAGDELENA TERRAZA CHEL

believers. We visited four altars, three located at the summit of ancient temple mounds and one near the base of a temple mound, regularly frequented for traditional ceremonies. A wooden cross and a small circle of blackened stones mark each altar, where copal incense (*pom*), candles, and liquor (or water from sacred caves)—elements of air, earth, and water—fuse into the sacred smoke as offerings to the gods. The ancient altars within Xe'vak are each associated with different deities; Maya priests conduct prayer ceremonies at one or the other, depending upon the nature of their clients' petitions. According to local sources, many Ixil families, including practicing Catholics and evangelicals, continue to observe aspects of traditional Ixil religious beliefs and practices. The remains of ancient temple mounds here are referred to as *Vitz*, the Ixil word for "mountains."

Vi'Chapa Vitz ("Mountain Spirit of Chiapas") is associated with wisdom. Prospective parents commission a prayer ceremony here so that their children may be born with vitality and intelligence. According to legend, a "tree of knowledge" from the Mexican (and predominantly Maya) state of Chiapas grew on this site; every part of the huge trunk contained knowledge about the future. Unfortunately, the leaves were poisonous and spread disease and death. The Nebaj community finally decided to cut it down. When the men put down their axes for the night, they returned in the morning to discover that the tree had regenerated. After many attempts, they succeeded in destroying and burning the tree.

Vi'k'uyi ("Mountain Spirit of the *Comadrone,*" or midwife) is the spiritual provenance of traditional midwives, where pregnant women and their spouses petition for a healthy pregnancy and trouble-free delivery.

Vi' Puk'Xu'K ("Mountain Guardian of Sacred Maize") is the altar of the "principle judge—the one who delivers justice." To reach this altar, one has to climb about fifty steep stairs built into the side of the ancient temple. A simple roofed structure shelters this altar. Traditional believers petition the gods for a good harvest, a wife, healthy animals, a job, or a safe end to a perilous journey.

Xo'l chax B'aatz' ("In the presence of the diety, B'aatz") is referred to as the *Cuarto Alcalde,* or the "Fourth Leader," and one of the twenty daygods in the sacred Ixil calendar. The sign of B'aatz', which literally means monkey, symbolizes a planner and spiritual guide. This altar marks the western point in the sacred dimensions of the ancient Ixil capital in Nebaj. This altar is particularly associated with prayers to honor Ixil ancestors.

Three other *Alcalde* altars are located in the broad valley encompassing the center of the ancient Ixil kingdom, and mark the sacred eastern, northern, and southern borders of the valley of Nebaj's ancient kingdom. These sacred sites, and others in the region, are described in the recent monograph on the Ixil published by the Academy of Mayan Languages,[76] and can be visited with a guide and the community's permission.

Ti'Kajay, Kub'aal No'j is the "First Alcalde" (*No'j* is the symbol for god or judge), and represents the principal god of the Ixil, *Kub'aal Salmik* ("the Heart of the Sky and Earth"); this altar is located south of the town of Nebaj.

Ti'kuixaal, Kub'aal Iq' is the "Second Alcalde" (*Iq'* is the symbol for air and wind), and is located north of the town center, in the cantón of Simocol.

Vi'Kutxul Ch'im, Kub'aal Che is the "Third Alcalde" (*Che* is the symbol for deer, horse, and agility), and is found northeast of the town center, marking the eastern edge of the ancient kingdom.

The mark of a good tour, in my mind, is one that leaves me wanting to know more. On subsequent visits to this region, I have returned to Xe'vak's ancient altars and learned more about efforts to preserve sacred *costumbre* that have bound Ixil community together during centuries of strife and change. I have a date with an accomplished Ixil weaver, who is also a shaman, to visit a sacred cave near Nebaj on my next visit. With Lincoln's sketch of a "so-called sun observatory" used by Maya priests in the 1940s to predict the dawn of the sacred days for planting and harvesting maize, I have engaged Ixil colleagues to help reconstitute this instrument of the ancient calendar. My hope is that we might interest a history class of high school students from Nebaj to join us in plotting the GPS location of ancient markers and ruins in the municipality—using modern technology to confirm the astronomical knowledge that Ixil ancestors applied to delineate the sacred dimensions of this ancient capital.

CHAPTER 5
Chajul

OPPOSITE: Chajul municipality harbors one of the last pristine cloud forests in Guatemala, set aside by the Government in 1997 as the Visis Cabá Biosphere National Reserve. **ABOVE LEFT:** Every year, forest cover is diminishing, to extend maize fields and cut trees for construction and cooking fuel. **ABOVE RIGHT:** Woven maize plant, central to Maya spirituality and daily sustenance.

Overview - Chajul municipality is renowned for its magnificent cloud forests, deeply traditional culture, and rugged isolation. It is the largest of the three Ixil-speaking municipalities, about 1,524 square kilometers (580 square miles), sparsely populated, and until very recently, almost completely inaccessible by vehicle. At one time, the prized jaguar roamed the misty mountains and dense virgin forests of northern Chajul. This ancient symbol of sacred power has been hunted to near extinction, but these cloud forests still harbor enormous biodiversity, including howler monkeys, the elusive Resplendant Quetzal, exotic orchids, and towering hardwoods and conifers.

I have the impression that rhythms of daily life, as well as the stories retold around the evening hearth, have changed less in Chajul than in most rural communities in Guatemala. Subsistence maize cultivation still dominates the local economy. Families still sow the *milpas* together and de-grain dried ears of maize by hand. For me, the Ixil of Chajul represent the primordial gods' final creation of man from yellow and white *masa* and the mythical Maya hero, Gaspar Ilom, of 1967 Nobel Prize winner

Miguel Angel Asturias' *Men of Maize (Hombres de Maíz),* who summons the mountain spirits to defend an ancient culture and way of life.

According to linguists, the pre-Hispanic name for this area was *Txao jul,* which literally means "washing among the rocks" (*lavando entre las joyas o piedras*). Some suggest that the name refers to a past practice of early Ixil settlers descending from the high mountain villages to bathe ceremonially in the rocky, sun-drenched pools in the valleys south of the colonial and present municipal capital.

DIRECTIONS TO CHAJUL

The municipal capital (*cabecera*) of Chajul, also known as San Gaspar Chajul, is 21 kilometers (13 miles) from downtown Nebaj. Take the main road north from Nebaj's El Triángulo gas station. Within 5 kilometers, a major fork indicates a left to Chajul and a right to Cotzal. At this junction of the three Ixil municipalities is the headquarters of the Academy of Mayan Languages of Guatemala for the linguistic community of the Ixil.

The road winds consistently uphill, across broad valleys thick with maize fields and toward higher mountains blanketed in dense forests in the distance. Vehicle traffic is still light to nonexistent. The daily bus to Santa Cruz del Quiché plows the curves early in the morning and returns at the end of the day; in between, one can catch a ride with the occasional minivan taxi. Traffic picks up during the maize and coffee harvests (December through February) and for important traditional fiesta days. The annual festival of Chajul's patron saint, San Gaspar, is celebrated on

BELOW: Clutch of Chajul girls in traditional woven blouse and wrap-skirt.

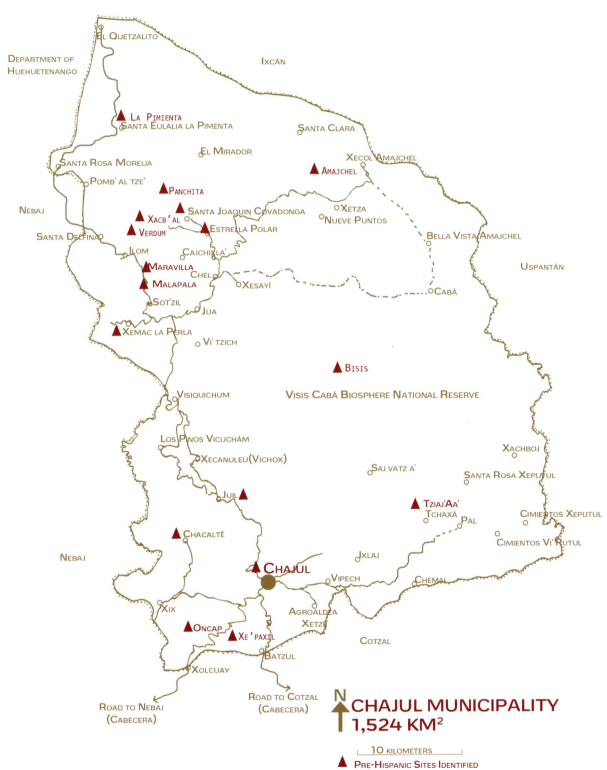

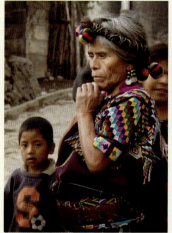

RIGHT: Street scenes in Chajul: modernity is definitely seeping into culturally conservative Chajul, but many wonderful old adobe homes and traditional pace of daily rhythms harkens back to an earlier era.

January 2. The next most important fiesta occurs on the second Friday of Lent, when religious pilgrims from across Guatemala stream into Chajul's Catholic church to petition the black Christ figure, *El Señor de Chajul,* for blessings and miracles.

Chajul's capital nestles at 1,980 meters (6,500 feet) in the protective foothills of the Cerro San Andrés (named for the senior mountain diety), commanding a sweeping southern vista across a broad, undulating valley. In stark contrast to the rapidly modernizing town of Nebaj, Chajul retains much of its eighteenth-century character. Most of the houses—old and new—are constructed in the adobe brick and tile roofs vernacular, oriented to the rising sun. For its tranquility, traditional character, and small-town feel, I frequently use Chajul as my base. With each successive visit, I notice the gradual inroads of rebar and concrete, corrugated roofing, and TV antennas. In the absence of a zoning or architectural commission to set building codes, I am hoping that the traditional aesthetic engrained in the amazing local craftsmen will preserve this town's distinctive beauty.

To the north of Chajul's *cabecera* lie the vast, tropical cloud forests of the municipality, 1,500 square kilometers in total, with mountain ridges rising to 2,700 meters (8,900 feet) and descending into the Ixcán lowlands to the north. The natural resources of this area are stupendous and beckoning to the ecologist in each of us. In 1997, the government set aside 450 square kilometers (175 square miles) of the Chajul municipality as the Visis Cabá Biosphere National Reserve, including a critical portion of the extensive watershed of the Xak'b'al River flowing northward through these mountains. The earliest known Ixil settlement was at Ilom, in the northern reaches of Chajul, perhaps as early as 500 BC. Since the Preclassic Period, indigenous hunters, traders, and warriors from lowland and highland city-states certainly navigated the Xak'b'al to supply their Maya rulers with the exotic resources of the northern Cuchumatán forests.

From colonial times until very recently, the town of Chajul was seen as the end of the road. The territory to the north remained inaccessible except by foot; rutted roads beyond were negotiable in dry weather only, by four-legged or four-wheel-drive transport. Few goods from the rest of Guatemala reached the more remote villages of Chajul; maize and lumber moved south via mules or strapped on men's backs by the ubiquitous *mecapal,* or leather strap across the forehead. The owners of Finca La Perla, the extensive coffee plantation carved out of northern Chajul between the 1880s and the 1920s, hacked a mule trail and eventually built a tiny airstrip to fly their coffee harvest down to Nebaj. During the civil war, the dense mountain forests sheltered Guatemalans escaping to refugee camps across the border in Mexico, displaced families who banned together in Communities of Popular Resistance (CPRs), as well as encampments of the Guerrilla Army of the Poor (EGP).

Today, one-third of Chajul's population, estimated at about 44,500 (as of 2012), is concentrated around the municipal capital. Another forty-eight small villages and hamlets are tucked into shadowed river valleys and perched on sunlit mountain slopes. The vast majority of Chajul's population is indigenous (70 percent Ixil, 17 percent K'iche', 13 percent Ladino). The average nuclear family size is seven; however, most rural Ixil homes accommodate several additional members of the extended family. Just as in the neighboring municipalities, the average land holding per family is decreasing rapidly as families divide their holdings among their grown children. A 2003 land survey revealed that about 85 percent of registered holdings (accounting for 36 percent of total registered area) were smaller than 10 *manzanas* (equivalent to about 7 hectares, or 17.4 acres); 28 percent of land titles were for parcels smaller than one *manzana* (0.7 hectares, or 1.74 acres).[77]

The vast majority of Chajul families are considered "poor" or "extremely poor," existing on less than Q18, or about US $2.40, of food per person per day.[78] In 2006, there were only ten medical doctors (two Guatemalan and eight Cuban) and thirty auxiliary medical staff to cover all of Chajul—one certified doctor to attend 5,400 men, women, and children. In 2002, adults over fourteen years of age had an average of only 3.3 years of formal education. Despite some progress in the expansion of social services in recent years, Chajul remains one of the poorest municipalities in Guatemala.

Visitor Services in Chajul

Accommodations and services for visitors are still limited in Chajul's capital, but what the town lacks in formal infrastructure, it makes up for in small-town friendliness, ease of finding one's way around, and people's eagerness to assist curious visitors. During my earliest visits, my companions and I were usually the only visitors in town. Once in a while, I would meet a foreigner working with the coffee cooperative or a missionary group in connection with the Protestant middle school. Chajul has recently embraced the young American and Guatemalan staff of Limitless Horizons, a nonprofit organization offering middle school scholarships, an inspiring after-school program, and a community library.

Photo by Chris Percival. Chajul's municipal capital, once christened "San Gaspar Chajul," retains the look and feel of an older colonial era.

LODGING

- *Posada Vetz K'aol:* Dormitory-style hostel run by the coffee cooperative, Asociación Chajulense; located near the southern entrance to town. Telephone: (502) 7775-7114.
- *Hotel El Descanso:* Small family hotel located on the lower road into town. Telephone: (502) 7755-4001 or 7755-4478.
- *Hotel Ixil:* Simple family-run guesthouse with three to four rooms, located several blocks to the east of the Catholic church.

For a stay of more than one night, I recommend Posada Vetz K'aol. I enjoy this lodging for its pastoral setting among the maize fields at the edge of town, the informal, cook-for-yourself kitchen, and the fact that visitors are supporting the work of the local coffee cooperative. Arriving in San Gaspar Chajul from Nebaj or Cotzal, a sign for the Posada directs visitors to take a right fork through the southern edge of town. If driving, have faith and heart as you negotiate a critically tight right turn at the top of a small ravine and lookout over town. A narrow dirt road leads through a maize field, past the front porticos of a busy and beautifully kept adobe compound, to another right into the parking area in front of the Posada.

In 2002 the Asociación Chajulense opened the Posada and training center to add economic diversity to their coffee business. It offers four to five bunk-bed-style rooms with shared bathrooms and showers, plus one private room with private bath. Ample wool blankets and towels come with the accommodations.

BELOW: Chajul, the rustic kitchen of Comedor Las Gemelas produces a daily hot soup from local market produce.

RIGHT: Reveling in beauty, resources, and friendliness of Chajul. New Zealand photographer, Mark Smith plays hopscotch with children; author maps out explorations with Ana and Ana.

There is a spacious kitchen, gas stove, fridge, cooking pots and plates, and utensils for thirty guests, and a sunny dining room with an idyllic view of the rolling valley to the south.

It is prudent to book ahead, as this lovely spot is best enjoyed when not being used for training sessions. The cost is Q50 per person in the dormitory-style rooms, or Q65 per person for the private bedroom. Posada: (502) 7775-7114, Asociación Chajulense: (502) 7755-1261.

FOOD

Comedor las Gemelas is located two blocks directly south of the main plaza. It is open only for a midday meal, closed on Sundays. The daily menu: a bubbling soup (*caldo*) or eggs any style, plus tortillas and a choice of soda. Cost: Q10–20.

Snacks of chips, crackers, and sodas are sold in the closet-size family stores (*tiendas*) on almost every street in town, as well as sugar cookies and rolls offered by several small bakeries (*panderías*).

If you are staying in Chajul for several days, other culinary adventures are available. I enjoy foraging in the municipal market for peelable fresh fruits and vegetables and other ingredients for a hot stir-fry

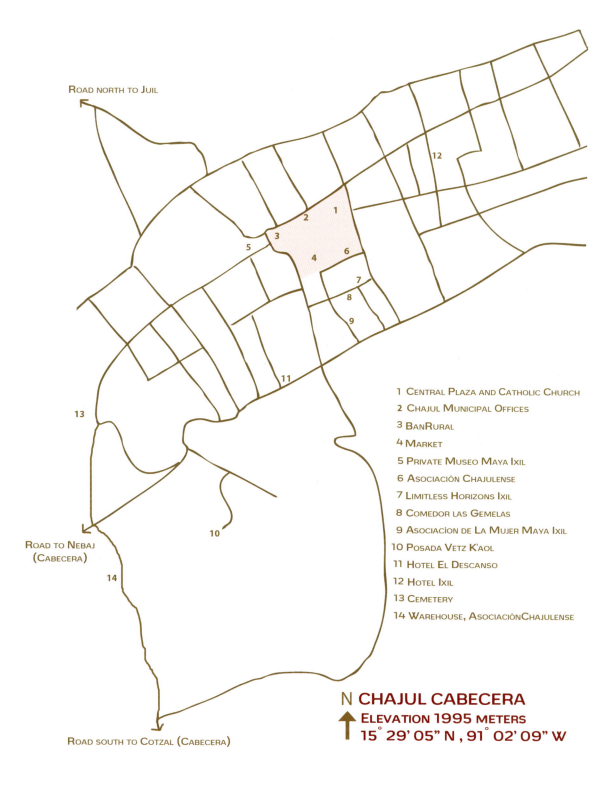

or soup I can cook up in the kitchen at Posada Vetz K'aol. Chajul's main market days are Tuesday and Friday, but most days, one can find a few other small stalls open with a limited choice of staples. With advance notice, one can commission tortillas or a freshly plucked chicken from the neighborhood. Best of all, visitors can arrange for a home-cooked meal or a culinary lesson in traditional Ixil specialties with the women's cooperatives, Asociación de la Mujer Maya Ixil. ADMI's office is located three blocks downhill from the plaza, just below Comedor las Gemelas.

GUIDE SERVICES

Inquiries can be made with the following:

- *ADMI—Asociación de La Mujer Maya Ixil* (Telephone: 502-5887-5797), with offices two blocks downhill from the marketplace.
- *Asociación Chajulense* (Telephone: 502-7755-1261), whose main office is one block downhill from the Catholic church, on the eastern end of the marketplace. www.asociacionchajulense.org
- *Felipe Rivera Caba* (Telephone: 502-4236-3149) is in the process of furnishing a small, private Museo Maya Ixil, located on the main street into town near the Central Plaza. Contact: MuseoMayaIxil@yahoo.es
- *Laval Iq',* Community Network for the Environmental and Cultural Development of the Ixil Region, formed by leaders of nineteen Ixil communities to promote local ecological and cultural tourism. Telephone: (502) 7755-8337. Email: redlavaliiq@gmail.com.

BANKING, INTERNET, PHONE SERVICE

Banco de Desarrollo Rural (BanRural) is located at the corner of the municipal plaza. As of 2012, there was still no ATM machine in Chajul. Chajul has two new Internet cafés. Guatemalan cell phones get good reception in most areas of the municipality, and minutes can be purchased in every town.

Explorations in Chajul

WALKING THROUGH HISTORY IN CHAJUL

Walking through the town of Chajul offers a fascinating view into Ixil history and culture, its local economy, traditions, and unfolding transitions. The barest threads of history, which I recount in this guide, come from a mere handful of written sources, oral history, and the conversations I've shared with my Ixil friends and several Ixil elders. The best way to see and absorb this history and culture lesson is to amble around town, one block at a time.

As in most colonial-era municipal capitals, the Spanish laid out Chajul's parish center in a tight geometric grid. Minimal concession was paid to topography. Three principal streets in the sixteenth-century colonial center hug the east-west contours of the mountainside. The middle, and primary, street in Chajul leads directly from the entrance of town to the central plaza and the huge Catholic church. A half-dozen north-south streets cope with uncompromisingly steep grades. Fortunately, most of the central streets have been paved in recent years; dirt roads degenerate quickly into muddy slides in the rainy season (May to November).

The Central Plaza

Brutal battles for the Ixil soul have been fought on the central plaza, just outside the huge double doors of the whitewashed façade and triple bell tower of the Catholic church. The plaza was the site of public floggings, forced labor gangs, and death by smallpox and other epidemics during the colonial period. Following independence in 1821, the plaza continued to serve as a locus for exploitation of the Ixil population, when labor-hungry Ladino landowners arrived with open cattle trucks to pack in men, women, and children for the twenty-four-hour trip to coastal sugar plantations and coffee fincas. During the recent civil war, especially at the height of the army's "scorched earth" rural campaigns in the early 1980s, the plaza was once again the center of torture and death in Chajul, as recounted by witnesses:

> *They sent word to her mother, informing her that her daughter had been captured by the (civil patrol), So her mother went running to help her daughter and she said, "This is my daughter. She's not a guerrilla." Even so . . . no one would listen to her at all . . . The next day she heard the sound of the bell being rung. That sounding of the bell signified death according to army tradition. If they sound the bell it's to gather the people of the town. Just at that moment, they came to inform the woman that they were going to execute her*

OPPOSITE: A real icebreaker on my first trip to Chajul was the copy of *Voices and Images: Maya Ixil Women of Chajul* (*Voces e Imágenes: Mujeres Maya Ixiles de Chajul*) (2000), which I carried with me from Boston. This portrait of life in Chajul after the civil war was a collaboration between ADMI—Asociación de La Mujer Maya Ixil; M. Brinton Lykes, professor of psychology at Boston College; and Juana Utuy Itzep, the Guatemalan coordinator of the nonprofit organization, PhotoVoice. The book literally served as my first map to the town, when I recruited a young schoolgirl to lead me to the homes of several of the remarkable women portrayed in its pages (www2.bc.edu/~lykes/voices_book.htm).

daughter by hanging. She was filled with sadness for her daughter's fate because the hour of her death had arrived and there was no reason for it.

The daughter was hung in front of the municipal building with all the people looking on because they were forced to watch the soldiers carry out their justice. But this was not justice, because they killed honorable people, people who were without blame.[79]

The municipal government recently completed a major public works project to transform the plaza from a place of death into a space for happy social gatherings. Thousands of cobblestones were skillfully laid in a pattern, along with decorative benches, and a new fountain, crowned with a rather incongruous cement duck.

Chajul's Catholic Church

A gracious sweep of twenty contoured steps rises from the plaza to the doors of the Catholic church in Chajul, the largest in the Ixil region. It comes as little surprise that Spanish missionaries selected the site of San Gaspar Chajul for their colonial outpost in the mid-sixteenth century. The town lies right beneath the Cerro San Andrés, with its prominent traditional altar on the summit, and just 8 kilometers (5 miles) south of the sacred Ixil ceremonial site at Juil.

According to oral history, zealous Dominican missionaries encountered one problem after another in their efforts to construct the church in Chajul in the late decades of the 16th century and to convert the resistant Ixil population. After the enormous wooden church beams had been hewn and hauled into town on the shoulders of hundreds of forced laborers, a squabble broke out over where to locate the church building. The western half of the town was populated by Ixil families forcibly resettled from nearby villages, whereas Ixil communities from northern Chajul around Ilom

---

THE TALE OF EL SEÑOR DE CHAJUL

The early Spanish missionaries' greatest challenge was converting the Ixil to Catholicism. As this history was recounted to me, Dominican missionaries devised a cunning plan to lure the local population away from the ancestral altars in the surrounding mountains into the new church at San Gaspar Chajul. A carved statue of Jesus of Golgotha was imported from the capital and secretly transported to the mountaintop at Juil, where Ixil ancestors believed that a "saint of miracles" resided among an ancient ceremonial site. In those days, as is still true today, an ancient altar at Juil drew sacred calendar priests from across the northern Cuchumatanes to attend the "dawning" ceremonies that marked the New Year in the sacred Maya calendar. Positioning their statue in Juil, the missionaries summoned the population of San Gaspar Chajul, telling them to go to Juil, singing and shouting, and that a deity would materialize. Lo and behold, this statue of Jesus appeared in the traditional sanctuary of the Maya gods. The Spanish had the statue transported to the church in San Gaspar Chajul.

Not to be outdone by this deception, however, Maya priests apparently stole the statue at night and returned it to Juil the next day. Oral history relates how this tug-of-war was definitively resolved when the Spanish posted guards at the altar to keep the "source of miracles" in the church. Eventually, two wooden sentries were substituted to protect *El Señor de Chajul,* as the figure of Jesus of Golgotha came to be known.

—AS RETOLD BY ANA LAYNEZ OF CHAJUL

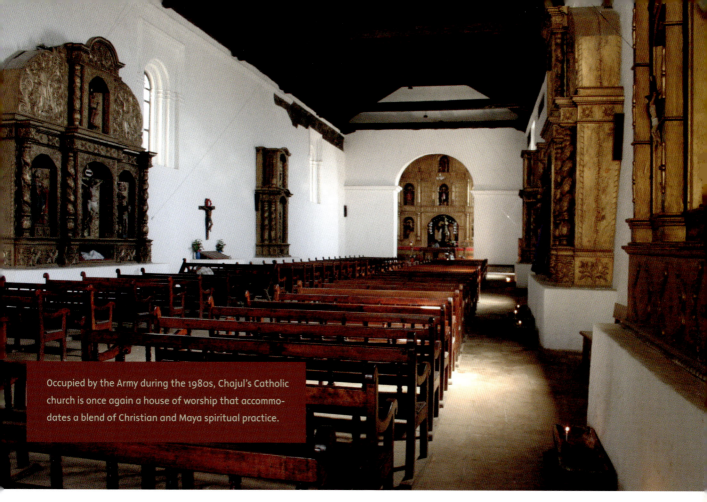

Occupied by the Army during the 1980s, Chajul's Catholic church is once again a house of worship that accommodates a blend of Christian and Maya spiritual practice.

occupied the eastern section. In order to placate both factions, the church building needed to straddle both communities. When completed, its double doors opened in the "Cantón of Chajul," while the altar was technically in the "Cantón of Ilom." According to mid-nineteenth-century parish records, the church measured 80 staves long (58 meters, or 190 feet) and 14.5 staves wide (10.5 meters or 34 feet).[80] Indigenous labor crews hauled the three bronze bells from the Spanish colonial capital of Santiago, present-day Antigua.

Entering the Catholic church, one's eyes slowly adjust to the solemn shadows of the cavernous interior. Soft daylight filters in from the half-dozen high windows near the rafters. Two rows of stark wooden pews flank a center aisle, drawing one's gaze forward, past a series of ornate wall entablatures enfolding weary saints to the gilded backdrop of the sacristy and the statue of Jesus of Golgotha. Near the front, at floor level in the central aisle, is an adapted Maya altar of flickering candles. A typical scene here on a quiet weekday morning offers a reminder that the Ixil found ways to accommodate many of their spiritual practices within the rituals of Catholicism. In addition to an Ixil gentleman sitting the front pew, head bent in prayer, a young couple kneels on the floor to light candles in the indigenous "candelabra," while a traditional spiritual guide begins a lengthy incantation in Ixil. The circle of candlelight picks up the color of rose petals reverently scattered around the altar and casts its glow on the kindly face of *El Señor de Chajul*.

Historic Houses

Elements of the oldest houses in Chajul's center date from the late sixteenth century, when Dominican

RIGHT: Many older adobe houses around Chajul's central plaza are several hundred years old. New construction often combines re-bar and corrugated tin with the traditional vernacular of wooden beams and columns and clay rooftiles.

monks assigned land around the plaza to the Ixil leaders "recruited" to carry out their agenda. In 2002, with funding through the European Union–financed "Proyecto Ixil," twenty of these historic houses received funding for minor renovations. These venerable dwellings reflect a hybrid Spanish-Ixil style that came to dominate the local vernacular. A deep front veranda is faced with hand-hewn arched beams, supported by heavy carved columns. Adobe brick walls, plastered white inside and out, support a tiled roof, keeping out the mountain chill at night and the sultry heat of the noonday sun. Thick front doors, sometimes with a tiny, hinged window at eye level, complete a once-closed façade to the street.

Behind the front wall, the design of these homes is consistent with domestic Ixil traditions. A principal front room, often with hard-packed dirt floor, serves for family meals and gatherings. It opens onto a small patio and kitchen garden. Two or more small rooms in back sleep the extended family on beds and straw mats (*petate*). Much of the private family activity occurs out back, often including a separate cooking shed, washing basin, sauna (*temascal*), and latrine. Perched on the clay ridge tiles of many of the older houses are numerous ceramic religious symbols and human and animal figurines, a traditional homage to the spirits and the natural world that sustain and protect the dwelling's inhabitants.

On the interior walls of several of the oldest houses are remnants of frescos believed to date back to the late sixteenth or early seventeenth century. Anthropologist Benjamin Colby mentioned seeing these frescos when he did his research here in the 1960s. Accompanied by a local guide from ADMI, I was able to see several of the surviving frescos. (I paid a requested donation and was asked to refrain from taking photographs.) The faded remnants of these wall paintings, which originally may have covered all four walls of the main room in the house, depict an elaborate ceremonial procession in earth tones of red, browns, and yellows. In one section, Maya nobles are depicted in feathered and woven costume; several figures brandish swords and lead what appear to be roped captives. A series of nine flowered symbols adorn the upper section of an adjacent wall; I was told that these represent the nine months of human gestation.

According to the grandmother of this household, these frescoes were painted by her many-times "great-grandfather," who worked as a master mason during construction of the Catholic church. Unfortunately, there are no surviving descriptions or drawings of the seventeenth-century church; it is impossible to know whether the colonial architects envisioned frescos. The semicircular niches on either side of the exterior front doors today, however, reveal interesting vestiges of wall paintings—in the domed section, two stylized monkey-like figures, and below, partial figures and a horse in procession. Ancient ceramic artifacts and remnants of painted plaster of temples and ceremonial structures in this region attest to the existence of highly skilled masons, wall painters, and other talented artists in the employ of the ancient Ixil rulers, long before the arrival of the Spanish.

The oldest adobe houses in town have now been patched, windows have been inserted, and additions have been built with rebar and cement block. Each year, more TV antennas sprout from the rooftops and more motorcycles crowd the front porch at night. Despite this inevitable advance of modern technologies, many aspects of Ixil domestic life have changed very little over the centuries. In the shelter of the front veranda, family members assiduously dry firewood for cooking and heating, and attic eaves are piled high with harvested maize. Every afternoon, the neatly swept veranda is populated with homemade wooden benches and stools; sweaty saddles and bridles hang from heavy roof beams; women bend over their colorful backstrap weaving, while children and elders work quietly shelling beans or de-graining maize cobs for the evening meal. With changes on the horizon, Ixil elders, like seventy-five-year-old Don Gaspar, speak forcefully about the duty of the younger generation to honor

ABOVE: Traditional adobe blocks made from clay, sand, and fibrous material such as straw or pine needles, insulate dwellings from the summer heat and winter chill.

ABOVE: Collector and curator of Museo Maya Ixil demonstrates the ancient Maya cerbatana.

and preserve the older homes and spirits of their ancestors:

> To guard and care for this house was the request of my great-grandparents. Both my father and my grandfather obeyed that mandate to preserve the home of our ancestors. The richness of our history and our culture are kept in the ancient paintings of the house; each painting is a mystery that encapsulates the history and life of our ancestors.

Museo Maya Ixil

Visitors to Chajul will want to seek out Felipe Rivera Caba, an avid collector of Ixil historical artifacts, for a chance to view his fascinating private museum. Felipe works a regular job at the BanRural, but dedicates his spare time to exploring for and preserving Chajul's cultural heritage. The tiny museum is housed in a traditional home along Chajul's main street into the plaza. What Felipe may lack in terms of organized display and lighting for his impressive collection, he makes up for with a personal tour of pre-Hispanic ceramics and jades, and an unusual assortment of musical instruments, the ancient *cerbatana* or blowpipe, and household furnishings rarely seen today.

ABOVE: Strikingly bold and endlessly colorful, the majority of women in Chajul continue to weave and wear traditional dress (traje) from head to ankle.

MARKET EXTRAVAGANZA IN CHAJUL

On Tuesday and Friday mornings, rain, or shine, the marketplace below the church bursts into a riotous bloom of color and activity. Vendors with baskets, scales, tables, and tarps walk, wheel, and trot into the marketplace early in the morning. Practiced hands unpack and arrange produce for sale. Hundreds of people from the nearby region converge here to buy or sell food products and other necessities. The scene is largely dominated by women of all ages carrying out this ageless routine. Market days are clearly an occasion for women to showcase their weaving, coin-silver earrings, and to crown their heads with the traditional

Bi-weekly market in Chajul's central square is an absolute feast for the eyes and kitchen hearth — a fascinating panorama of tradition and transition.

pom-pom-tasseled hair tie, twisted artfully around their glossy hair. The regality of traditional dress against the artful arrangements of local produce is an intricate tapestry of Chajul life and culture. Market day is an unforgettable experience for any visitor. It is also the best way to find out about the real cost of living in the Ixil region.

The bounty of this well-watered mountainous terrain is a wide variety of produce and, in warmer areas, two annual crops of maize. In the "warm lands" to the east, bananas, limes, oranges, avocados, sweet potatoes, tomatoes, spicy peppers, melons, palm fruit (*pacaya*), honey, and cardamom seeds are harvested. From the "cold lands" come wheat and oats, potatoes, broccoli, cabbage, carrots, collards and other greens, and peas. Wherever there is space around the compound, squashes—*güisquil* and *chilacayote*—climb the walls and roof. Every household seems to grow a few fresh flowers, peppers, and herbs.

Maize and beans provide the critical proteins in the Ixil diet. Beef, pork, or poultry is purchased mainly for holidays or special occasions. I am content to be a vegetarian in the Ixil, unless a neighbor offers to pluck a rooster for a sumptuous chicken soup (*caldo de gallo criollo*). Permanent kiosks that fringe the Chajul marketplace carry other staples: eggs, rice,

ABOVE LEFT: Organic arabica coffee grown and processed by the farmers' cooperative, Asociación Chajulense. **ABOVE RIGHT:** Smallholder coffee is depulped with a small hand-held machine, washed, and dried in the sun in household patios.

cooking oil, refined sugar, cakes of unrefined brown sugar, onions, garlic, black beans, maize, salt, and mineral lime used in cooking tortillas.

The "home goods" section of the market rounds out the picture of domestic life here. You can always find candles and incense used in traditional offerings and ceremonies, local clay pots and plastic pots for water, flat metal or clay *comal* for cooking and reheating tortillas, pots and pans, woven palm sleeping mats (*petate*), baskets, maguey string bags from Cotzal, wool blankets from Momostenango, umbrellas, shoes, sandals, and soap. For the menfolk, the market carries boots, rope, bridles, saddles, shoulder bags (*morral*), and, of course, the traditional palm-fiber hats. The hardware kiosks supply machetes, an essential tool in everyday life for both men and women; every young child learns to wield the machete, whacking weeds, chaff, and wood. Young boys and men are clients for the ubiquitous stall or tarp piled high with recycled Western hand-me-downs—jeans, T-shirts, and jackets—a hugely profitable business in Guatemala.

ASOCIACIÓN CHAJULENSE: AN ENGINE FOR ECONOMIC DEVELOPMENT

Like a phoenix rising from the flames, Chajul's coffee cooperative was built on the ashes of an earlier agricultural cooperative destroyed during the civil war. Many rural cooperatives in Guatemala received initial capital and training from the progressive Catholic missionaries in the mid-1900s. Unfortunately, they became easy targets of army campaigns to eliminate indigenous organizations and rural support for the insurgency. In 1988, following widespread devastation of Ixil villages and farmlands, a group of farmers in Chajul approached the Italian priest for assistance to relaunch the cooperative and provide seed stock to the starving population.

The new cooperative was named *Va'l Vaq Quilo* ("One Sole Voice"), commonly referred to as Asociación Chajulense. It has a major economic presence in Chajul and across the Ixil region, with over 2,000 members from fifty-seven communities. The cooperative's administration is housed in the renovated building of its prewar predecessor, *Unión Ixil*, adjacent to the Catholic church.

The real hub of activity from December through March is the coffee warehouse. In 2007, the Asociación Chajulense exported 1,000 tons of organic beans to Europe and American coffee roasters. One can visit the bustling coffee warehouse operations off the new road from Chajul to Cotzal. In one part of the warehouse, coffee beans that have been de-pulped, washed, and sun-dried in the front yards of co-op members are weighed, recorded, and stored in 100-pound bags (*quintal*). In another part of the building, the "green" beans are funneled through a labor-intensive sorting process. During two shifts per day, twenty women staff a conveyor belt, skillfully weeding out mottled or deformed beans. Quality beans are then re-dried to further reduce moisture content and re-bagged as "oro" (gold) for export. Arcadio Galindo, the director of the cooperative, was on hand the day we visited, and proudly announced that their organic coffee earned a premium price on the world market.

In addition to the coffee, the Asociación promotes honey production and a women's weaving and micro-credit project. It runs a local radio station in Chajul, Sola Voz (1500 AM Radio), and is expanding into cultural and ecotourism through the Posada Vetz K'aol. Cooperative products—including woven bags, placemats, traditional clothing, mountain honey, and freshly roasted coffee—are sold at cooperatives near the plaza and in the Posada.

Asociación Chajulense
14005 San Gaspar
Chajul—El Quiché
Telephone: (502) 7755-1261
Guatemala, C. A.
www.AsociacionChajulense.org

The Asociación leverages its coffee production and marketing connections to attract national and international support for a range of income-generation and community development efforts. One of its principal partners is the Fundación Ixil, launched in 2009 and spearheaded by an energetic board of businessmen and educators, including its President, Ricard Estrada, cofounder of Catelejo Corporation in Guatemala and Bill Fishbein, owner of Coffee Exchange and founder of the development-focused foundation called Coffee Kids (www.CoffeeKids.org).

CHAJUL TRADITIONAL DRESS: FUSION OF MYTH, ART, AND MANUAL DEXTERITY

For more than twenty years, I have been drawn to the epic display of man, beast, and nature woven boldly and brightly into *huipiles* from Chajul. From the sparse design of the ceremonial *huipil* to the lush tapestry of daily wear, the Chajul *huipil* is a visual invocation to the "Heart of the Sky and Earth," and a celebration of the Maya cosmovision. At the core of this vision is the belief that humans owe their existence to supernatural forces governing life and balance in the universe. Through prayer and mindfulness to the spiritual dimensions of the world around them, humans can merit divine protection

ABOVE: Chajul elder in regal traditional dress; the woven shawl (rebozo) draped over the head for sun protection.

ABOVE: Chajul weaver, wearing her own huipil inside out to reduce wear and tear, recreates elements of the Ixil Maya cosmovision on her back-strap loom.

and the life-sustaining gifts of nature. Chajul's *huipil* is unmistakable: iridescent eyes, jeweled wings, and torsos of pulsating color radiate their watchful presence and emboldening spirit in the lives of their mortal celebrants.

The Chajul *huipil* is woven in two rectangular pieces, forming a coherent, but not necessarily symmetrical, design. Like that of Nebaj, the warp and weft threads are doubled for greater warmth and durability. A circle is cut out of the finished pieces for the head, and the side seams are sewn up to leave tight-fitting openings for the arms. With great skill, the boxy *huipil* is tucked into an ankle-length wrap-skirt (*corte*) and secured with a wonderfully decorative belt (*faja*) that ties in back with multi-colored pom-poms.

Chajul distinctive regional dress, or *traje*, includes several colorful accessories. While young girls wear their hair loose or in a ponytail, women wind their hair on their heads with a hair ribbon (*cinta*) knotted off the center forehead with a flourish of pom-poms. Women enjoy multiple ear piercings, and dangle beads and coins threaded on tassels of fuchsia or tomato-red yarn (traditional necklaces and earrings called *chachal*). Women say that they never leave home without their shawl (*rebozo*). This essential and versatile piece of clothing is woven in two pieces, about a meter long, with a warp of thin colored stripes of blues, red, orange, white, and green, and a busy warp-faced design in the same set of colors. Customarily draped frontally—across the chest and back over the shoulders—the shawl is also commonly folded on top of the head to provide shade against the midday sun. In full regalia, this combination of bright colors, bold designs, pom-poms, and jewelry produce a truly unique and electrifying elegance.

I am interested in the evolution of Maya weaving styles and inquire about older *huipiles* to see how much has changed in the lifetime of the current elders. Chajul *huipiles* from the early 1900s were woven in simple white cotton and sparsely adorned with small, stylized birds, maize symbols, and geometric designs. Local ceremonial *huipiles* were similarly white, embellished at the collar with a thick sunburst of purple silk embroidery (from a mollusk dye) and commonly featured the image of the mythical double-headed raptor, called the *Kot*. By mid-century, when colored cotton threads became more common in the highlands, the everyday *huipil* turned bright red, with woven figures and symbols on the central chest, back, and shoulders in a variety of primary colors.

Today, while a version of the ceremonial white *huipil* is still woven for special occasions, a full range of colors and a more-prolific weft-faced design has eclipsed the austerity of the grandmothers' era. The Chajul marketplace is a veritable rainbow of colored canvases. Contemporary *huipiles* now come in every background color, and intricate icons and patterns have taken on greater depth and animation.

During the late afternoons in San Gaspar Chajul, many women dedicate an hour or two to their latest weaving project. They unroll their tidy bundle of rods and threads, securing one end of the backstrap loom to a post on the veranda, and the other to a belt around their hips. Perched on a weathered stool or seated on a *petate* mat in the softening light, the weaver's adroit fingers and shuttle create an artistic and cultural tapestry. There is no written pattern to follow, only examples of other designs and each weaver's dexterity and vision for her master plan.

ABOVE: Chajul weavers delight in a broad repertoire of color and design, artfully combining traditional and modern elements and color schemes.

WEAVING LESSONS WITH A MASTER

To develop a better appreciation of this ancient art, I commissioned a Chajul weaver to teach me the basics of backstrap loom weaving. I was paired with María by the Asociación de la Mujer Maya Ixil (ADMI), and spent many delightful hours under her patient tutelage. María's Spanish was excellent, but in fact, our lessons were conducted almost entirely through demonstration, repetition, and

RIGHT: For the novice weaver, learning the art and skill of the ancient backstrap loom is an experience in wonder, trust, and non-verbal communication.

many peals of laughter about my two left thumbs. I had never woven anything, so we started at ground zero. For my first attempt, María suggested that I start with a white table runner. In hindsight, maybe a narrow belt would have been more realistic for a novice like me. Every time I return to Chajul, I bring the masterpiece-in-progress to continue my weaving lessons and further our friendship. I highly recommend that interested visitors, especially textile enthusiasts and weavers, take a few lessons from an Ixil master.

I purchased my first set of wooden weaving pieces and leather backstrap on my way through the Chichicastenango market, where specialized vendors of backstrap loom "kits" and extra implements attract a lively throng of weavers. Every Ixil girl receives her first set of weaving implements at a young age and keeps them for life. As young as age four or five, girls are initiated into the ancient arts of Ixchel, the Maya goddess of backstrap loom weaving, by their mothers and grandmothers. They start by winding their own balls of thread and weaving narrow belts, progress to small decorative cloths, and by their teenage years, complete their first *huipil*.

María checked my bundle of beautifully sanded

pieces and leather backstrap to see if I had all the necessary equipment: two round end-rods, one double-pointed and laterally tapered batten rod, three or four weft dowels, a smooth shuttle, and a wooden pick. She accompanied me to a local thread vendor to purchase a pound of white cotton, plus red and orange accent threads.

Back on the porch of the ADMI offices on a typical sunny afternoon, María taught me the time-honed steps of weaving. We set up the revolving spindle to wind the skeins into balls of double-stranded thread. She demonstrated how to hold the threads in the fingers of one hand to allow the double thread to wind evenly on a ball in the other. I learned how to conduct my hands, hesitantly, then "musically," to feed the ancient warping board (*heradora*) with a rhythm of cotton thread. María's hands were so sure and swift, expertly honed over thirty years' worth of daily weaving. After winding the requisite number of double-stranded threads for the desired warp, María transferred the warp threads to the end-rods of the backstrap loom. With subtle tension on the warp, She "groomed," counted, and secured alternating double threads to the heddle rods.

The patient process of setting up the loom consumed an entire afternoon. I was simply awed by the "dancing" movements of María's practiced hands and fingers. "All of the fingers work (*Todos los dedos trabajan*)," she explained. My two left hands of all thumbs provided amusement to passersby, and María's daughter and a friend stopped by after school to add their encouragement and assistance as the sun set on my first day of weaving lessons.

On subsequent days, María and I continued my apprenticeship. I learned to alternate the sheds (the opening between the upper and lower strands of the warp), thread the shuttle evenly, and to tamp the weft threads down with the tapered batten. María's patient "Do as I do" helped me to internalize the rhythm, body movements, and arm muscles necessary to produce an even weave. At the end of each session, I rolled my precious loom into a neat and tidy bundle, just as María demonstrated. "The loom goes everywhere with us," María explained.

COOKING LESSONS: TORTILLAS AND B'OXB'OL

When in Chajul, do as the Ixil do. Ixil women have taught me to form perfect tortillas and prepare several culinary specialties. The preparation of special dishes is time-consuming and labor-intensive, involving a trip to the market, overnight readying of ingredients, stoking the fire, washing, grinding, chopping, folding, tying, boiling, roasting, toasting, steaming, taste-testing, more cooking, stacking, counting, covering, and arranging. Everyday cooking is often a multigenerational effort among the household women. When cooking for traditional celebrations, the quantity of food prepared doubles or triples, and the hands of other women in the extended family, as well as close friends, transform the work into a major social occasion.

To inquire about cooking lessons, visit the ADMI offices located two blocks downhill from the marketplace. Advance notice of at least a day is essential in order to obtain the freshest ingredients in the market. Plan on a half-day of preparation, cooking, laughing, and sharing. Such a culinary experience will tantalize the palate and instill a yearning for Ixil *tamalitos* and *tamales* for the rest of one's life.

Tortillas

Every meal includes tortillas; Ixil women calculate seven tortillas per person per meal. Here are the instructions for Preparing Ground Maize (Masa or che' in Ixil) for a Family Meal

- De-grain 5 pounds of maize kernels.
- Soak maize in enough cold water
- Add 2.5 ounces of powdered mineral lime (*cal*).
- Cook on low heat for 1.5 hours.
- Test by taking one cooked kernel and squeezing gently between two fingers; liquid spurts from

ABOVE: Maize-stuffed b'oxb'ol and tortillas, the staff of daily Ixil sustenance.

- the kernel when the maize is cooked.
- Remove from the fire and cool for two to three hours.
- Rinse maize lightly to remove the lime.
- Grind the soaked maize at the neighborhood maize mill (Q1/libra or pound).
- Shape and cook the tortillas.

B'oxb'ol (Maize-Stuffed Greens with Tomato Sauce)

This aromatic and nutrition-packed dish is an Ixil specialty, prepared whenever the succulent chard greens (*acelga*) or güisquil (small green squash) leaves are large and plentiful. There is an Ixil saying: "Anyone who tastes *b'oxb'ol* will live here forever." I have sampled traditional food all over the world, and I admit that *b'oxb'ol* is indeed a powerful lure. I look forward to this treat every time I return to the Ixil region.

On a chilly, rain-soaked market day—good for growing greens but not hiking—sisters-in-law María Pérez and Ana Laynez of ADMI invited me to learn how to make these delicious maize-stuffed greens with tomato sauce. We started with a mountain of freshly washed greens and a small tub of ground maize meal (*masa*). The maize had been soaked overnight in mineral lime and a pinch of wood ash. The magic of this recipe is in the freshness of the ingredients. As I learned, it also takes manual dexterity to split the greens neatly along the vein to create two halves, to spread four fingers of *masa* on the leaf, and to adroitly fold and crimp the leaf around this stuffing.

María and Ana worked patiently with me on technique, holding my hands in the right position, demonstrating how to add a few drops of water to smooth the *masa* onto the leaf, laughing as I finally mastered the gentle squeeze to seal the leaf. Too quickly, too much, too loosely results in green porridge! A large blackened pot, one-third full of water with a dash of salt, was set to boil on a wood-saving stove in the corner of the family living-kitchen-dining room of the old house. When the water reached a low boil, María gingerly layered the stuffed greens into the pot for a twelve- to fifteen-minute steam bath. Using the traditional basalt mortar and pestle (*piedra de moler*), steamed tomatoes, chili peppers, and a dash of salt were ground into a pungent sauce.

> **IXIL LEGEND OF SAN ANDRÉS**
>
> *Our ancestors hunted birds and small animals in the mountain forests with wooden blowpipes (cerbatanas) and darts. They returned with their bags full of game. One morning, the hunters departed early for the mountain, carrying leftovers from the evening meal and coals from the hearth to reheat their lunch. Just as they were about to eat, they saw a beautifully adorned white horse approaching, its rider formally dressed in hat, red jacket, and white pants. The rider addressed them, asking if they were about to eat. The hunters answered that they were, and inquired where the rider came from and where he was going. He answered,*
>
> *"I am only here to visit my animals and the birds that sing so sweetly. I see that you have killed many, and it makes me angry that you have taken things that are not yours. I will forgive you this time, because I imagine that you did not understand. However, the next time you seek to hunt birds in this domain, you must come and ask my permission. Do not hesitate to visit me. My house is on top of the mountain. If you need a place to rest or sleep, you may stay in my house. If you come without food, do not worry. All you need to do is ask me, and I will provide for you."*
>
> *Henceforth, the Ixil people understood that a great spirit protects the animals and birds of the mountains. Whoever needs to take living things from nature to survive must first ask permission, and then offer thanks to the provider and protector of this domain.*
>
> **—AS RETOLD BY ANA LAYNEZ OF CHAJUL**

HIKING TO CERRO SAN ANDRÉS

Rising 200 meters (600 feet) above the plaza and the Catholic church in San Gaspar Chajul is the tabletop summit of San Andrés. Since ancient times, the Ixil have gathered on this height for prayer ceremonies and to give thanks to the beneficent spirit of the mountain for the nourishing gifts of nature. Especially during important fiestas, wafts of smoke and sparks of fireworks rise into the starry night above the mountaintop (see Appendix 1: Calendar of Fiestas in the Ixil Region).

BELOW: Ixil farmers sow their own selected and preserved seed corn adapted to local growing conditions.

One beautifully clear and crisp January morning, I recruited several friends from the women's cooperative to hike with me to visit the legendary "saint on the mountain." We followed the road north out of town, in the direction of Juil. Within a short distance (half a kilometer), a large boulder on the right side of the road marks a footpath up the slope. The path climbs steadily around maize fields and up through the thinning tree cover below the summit. The sweeping view from the now-treeless mountaintop explains why this site was chosen for sacred ceremonies. Built into natural rock outcroppings are several traditional altars, blackened by countless seasons of prayer.

ABOVE: Every year Ixil farmers slash and burn forested areas to plant maize. Future economic sustainability depends on adaptation of soil enhancing techniques, such as alley cropping and cover crops.

HIKING CERRO PAXIL, "MOUNTAIN OF THE SACRED MAIZE"

Halfway between the town of Nebaj and Chajul is the *aldea* of *Xo'lk'uay* translated as *lugar de la troja,* or "place of the granaries"). The Cerro Paxil rises to the east above this tiny roadside community and harbors a small cave near its summit, where Ixil legend traces the discovery of maize by a mouse, a bird, and eventually, the thirteen mountain gods of the surrounding region.

Maize (*Zea mays*) is indigenous to Mesoamerica; carbon-dated maize cobs from a cave in Oaxaca, Mexico, suggest that the domestication of this critical staple crop began more than 6,000 years ago. Successive civilizations adapted maize cultivars to varying microclimates throughout the region, and eventually, the crop was introduced into other parts of the world.

The centrality of maize among the Maya is reflected in their Creation myths and legends, the sacred rhythms of the solar and agricultural calendars, and the celebration and sanctity of the sowing, harvesting, storing, and daily consumption of maize. The *Popol Vuh*, the sixteenth-century "transcription" of an ancient hieroglyphic "Council Book" of the K'iche' lords, is steeped in sacred imagery of maize: After defeating the evil Lords of the Underworld to avenge their fathers, one of the Hero Twins rises in the sky, as the Sun and symbolic Maize God; the twins'

THE DISCOVERY OF MAIZE ON CERRO PAXIL

Today, Ixil elders still gather their grandchildren around the hearth fires to recount this tale about the discovery of maize on Cerro Paxil.

In ancient times, a curious carpenter bird, named "Pantzuruk," spied a mouse crunching on a kernel of maize near a narrow rock crevice at the summit of Cerro Paxil, and asked him what he was eating and whether there was more.

"This is the dusk and the dawn," said the mouse. "And there is an eternal source deep inside this rock." After much cajoling, the clever Pantzuruk convinced the mouse to share five kernels of the hidden treasure. The gluttonous bird gulped down the hard grains and returned to beg for more. The lucky Pantzuruk, however, was unable to guard his secret: As he flew about the countryside, he dropped evidence of the undigested kernels. Eleven gods who were brothers ruled the surrounding mountains. The eldest spotted these kernels and witnessed the hearty maize plants that sprouted straight and strong from these seeds. The mountain gods summoned the birds of the kingdom to identify the source of these miraculous kernels, for they wanted to feed their future sons and daughters. In this way, they captured Pantzuruk, tied him up, and threatened to kill him if he did not bring them more kernels. Pantzuruk promised to lead them to the rock if they would release him.

Ignoring their youngest brother, Juil, who they disdained as a "pesky mosquito," the older mountain gods gathered around the rock to crack it open. Try as they might, they failed, and they argued among themselves. As a last resort, they called upon Juil, because they believed his cunning to be unparalleled. True to character, the youngest god laughed at the hubris of his brothers and their hands, bloodied with fruitless toil. He advised them to dig a huge hole and to hide themselves and cover their eyes and ears. A huge explosion ensued, cracking the rock wide open. By the time the older gods recovered, the clever young Juil, knowing that his brothers would cheat him of his fair share, had carried away a vast quantity of the maize on mules. The chastened gods, nevertheless, divided up the remaining fortune among their baskets: The maize that had burned was black, the part blasted by the explosion was golden, and the untouched maize was pure white. The gods gathered for prayer that their children would harvest two maize crops each year.

And such it is today, that the Ixil community shares the sacred maize and celebrates their good fortune and sustenance every year.

—AS RETOLD BY ANA LAYNEZ OF CHAJUL

---

grandmother and the original midwife, *Xmucane*, ultimately fashions the first successful men—the gods' Fourth act of creation—out of yellow and white maize meal.[81]

Maize continues to be the lifeblood of every Ixil family. In every home, a granary or crawl space under the roof is piled high with sun-dried maize; the next season's seed corn dangles from the rafters. The de-graining and soaking of kernels is a daily routine; grinding, patting, and flipping of toasting tortillas is the music of every mealtime. White, yellow, and occasionally blue maize is fashioned into tortillas, tamales, and the hearty maize drink, called *atol*. When Ixil elders talk about this staple crop, they speak about its cultural significance, and rarely its value as a cash crop.

> *Maize was never grown for commercial purposes, but to conserve our culture—a culture that is rooted in the earth and in the creator and former of the universe. To say that maize is not profitable is only to show the ignorance of those who undermine our culture and contribute to our children becoming alienated from their origins.*
>
> —Elder from Nebaj

During the time of La Violencia, the army used to burn our planted fields and harvests so that we would not be able to eat. But they did it also that we could not be able to cultivate the land or practice our rites and ceremonies. And this is how they tried to destroy our communication with our ancestors.[82]

—Woman from Chajul

In ancient times (and still in parts of the region today), Maya priests announced the day for sowing maize, which was celebrated by prayer ceremonies, special meals, and mobilization of the entire community. The maize cultivation cycle begins in late March or early April, before the onset of the rainy season. Farmers clear the maize field (*milpa*) and till the soil with the ancient hoe (*azadón*). Burning off of crop residues was common practice, but this is now increasingly discouraged in order to prevent forest fires. At sowing time, traditionally on a full moon in late April or early May, the men and boys in the family (plus neighbors in the tradition of mutual assistance, *u lotcho'm xula'*) depart early for the prepared fields. The head of the family distributes corn seed into the shoulder bag (*morral*) of each planter. He ceremonially initiates the sowing by poking a long-pointed stick into a hillock and depositing five kernels. Beans and squash are frequently intercropped with maize. The planting team works in unison along the contours of the field to ensure regular spacing and saturation of the entire plot. On this day, Ixil women prepare especially hearty tamales, called *tzi'ukal*, and carry these to the fields at lunchtime. These are protein- and salt-packed tamales of stewed tomatoes, peppers, meat, and ground maize designed to give strength and restore electrolytes to the hardworking field crew.

Despite the twin pressures of population growth and declining soil fertility, the Ixil continue to shun commercial, hybridized maize in favor of traditional cultivars adapted to local growing conditions and cultural preferences. The use of chemical fertilizers has proliferated among families that can afford the investment in higher yields. Ixil communities grow several types of maize, each with a distinct flavor and use in the culture. A tall, white maize variety yields two to three large ears of soft and sweet maize per stalk and is used in the rich traditional drink, *atol*. Another variety of white maize, with smaller ears and harder kernels, is abundantly grown for its adaptability to soil conditions, reliability, and good storing quality. A type of yellow maize is favored for its richer taste and higher vitamin content. Blue or black (*negro*) maize and a multicolored (*pinto*) maize are also grown in smaller quantities. Each maize color holds spiritual significance. The four colors are paired in Maya cosmology with the cardinal directions (white for north, yellow

for south, black for west, and red for east). Some among the Ixil say that the maize colors also symbolize different skin colors of the human races, as well as elements of the human body: white for bones, yellow for skin, red for blood, and black for hair.

Harvest begins in late October and continues through January in some areas. A small quantity of fresh, sweet maize is harvested early to roast over the fire or steam in the husk for the hot drink, called *k'oyum*. Most of the maize crop remains on the stalk to dry; it is shucked in the field and hauled home for storage in a granary (*troja*), or attic of the house.

Among the Maya and other Mesoamerican cultures, legends abound concerning the origin of the sacred maize. Many share some features—an insect or mouse that hoards a mysterious stash of kernels within a high mountain rock or cave, a covetous bird, wildcat, or fox that discovers the grain, and gods or early mortals who seek the sacred source and after much toil and trickery, ultimately crack open the repository in an explosion and burst of fire. According to anthropologist J. Eric S. Thompson, Mam, K'iche', and Kaqchikel legends refer to the mountain of *Paxil*, although this mountain appears in many different locales.[82]

The Ixil have their own Paxil Mountain, pierced by a deep cave at the top, where traditional Maya priests hold prayer ceremonies every year to give thanks for the sacred maize. I inquired about hiking to this cave and was encouraged to visit this cultural site by Ixil friends. Out of respect for local custom, however, it is important for travelers to avoid visiting on days of active ceremonies and to seek a local guide to accompany them on this forty-five-minute hike. This short hike offers a close-up look at the meticulously tended maize fields, the slash-and-burn deforestation that is creeping up the steep slopes because of population pressure, and beautiful views of the lush Chajul countryside. The final five-minute vertical scramble, which is slick in the rainy season, is slow going and calls for a stout walking stick.

SOAKING IN THE MAYA SAUNA

At the end of a long day hoeing or harvesting, chopping and hauling, walking and washing, tending and cooking, Ixil families bathe and relax in the traditional sauna, or *temascal* (*chuu* in Ixil). The beehive-shaped sweat lodge of adobe brick is an appendage to most traditional houses in this region. Most are not head-height: One enters the *temascal* on hands and knees through an opening draped closed by a towel or blanket. Inside are simple wooden benches or stools on a dirt floor, and an open hearth with several large stones. An hour or two prior to bathing, the wood fire is stoked and pots of water are set to boil and cloud the blackened interior with a cleansing steam. When embers glow and the rocks radiate, it's time for bathers to bask in the intense heat, occasionally pouring a cup of heated water over the hot rocks or themselves to wash away the day's grime and weariness. The *temascal* is used medicinally, for relief of colds, fatigue, aches, and pains. After a woman has given birth, her sisters and mother assist her to steam away labor pains in the temascal and bathe the newborn for the first time.

We were invited one chill January night to experience the pleasures of the sauna. With barely room for three of us, we perched on a plank bench around the glowing hearth. I draped a towel over my head to cut the intense heat as it worked its way into our bones. Within ten minutes, the dust of the day's hike trickled down our faces and backs, replaced by soothing warmth. We rinsed ourselves in several cupfuls of steaming water before braving the reentry into the chill night air outside, glowing and reinvigorated. I highly recommend visitors try a *temascal* bath, available for the asking at a small cost. Bring your own wrap, towel, and a bottle of water.

TRADITIONAL MUSIC IN CHAJUL

"Knowledge of traditional instruments and ancestral music is being buried with the elders in this region," explained Ana Laynez, president of ADMI, "and

ABOVE: Ixil musical instruments combine ancient drums, turtle shells, and gourds, as well as artisanal replications and adaptaions of string instruments and horns.

with this loss, important expressions and celebrations of Ixil culture."

During one of my visits to Chajul, Ana organized an unforgettable recital of uniquely Ixil music. We assembled after the workday was completed in the front room of a traditional adobe dwelling, and a dozen men from the community trooped in with their instruments in worn cases or wrapped in old cloths. The musicians were mostly older men and formed two traditional ensembles; several younger men looked like apprentices, taking their cues from the elders. These musicians perform locally, commissioned by families for special occasions (engagements, weddings, and funerals) and by the community for local elections and fiestas.

I recognized several instruments, including violin, guitar, and a modified trombone. The percussion section, however, was highly unusual. It included a turquoise-painted tortoise shell, a leather-covered wooden box (*tupa*), and a venerable slit-log drum (*tun-tun*). The drum was so heavy that it required two men to transport it; its hardwood shone with an aged patina. When I inquired about the age of the drum, two elders responded in unison: "It is 818 years old." I did the math: 2006 minus 818 = AD 1188, more than three hundred years before the arrival of the Spanish, perhaps even before this region was subjugated by the K'iche'. I asked them how they had managed to preserve the instrument through the ages, and throughout much turmoil. They explained that successive community elders had hidden the drum, "to safeguard and preserve the voice of their ancestors."

The two groups of musicians performed for an hour. The horn and violin led a "dialogue" of melodious tunes. The guitar joined in with a spirited voice. Three drums beat earnest and often-insistent rhythms in a wide range of tonalities—the softer *tock-tock* of the tortoise shell, the medium-range *tam-tam* of the cowhide drum, and the solemn *ton-ton* of the ancient split-log drum. The musicians played with great concentration and seriousness. A senior member, dressed in the Chajul traditional red-and-black jacket, explained that there were eight basic song variations, each related to one of "eight stages of the Ixil life cycle, from birth to death." The concert brought tears to the eyes of several of the gathered Ixil women. One declared that she had not heard some of the tunes for many years; another whispered that these melodies reminded her of relatives who were killed or "disappeared" during *La Violencia*. Fortunately, the musicians eventually struck up a lighter tune, perhaps one for courtship or marriage, and smiles returned to the faces of the performers and our tiny audience. A weathered Ixil elder stood up, unexpectedly bowed in front of me, and taking my hand, led me in tight dance circle in the flickering lamplight.

Abundant rainfall and forest cover feed the year-round Xak'b'al River as it flows north through Nebaj and Chajul.

The melodious rhythmns of this somber concert lingered with me for a long time... so different from the light-hearted marimba, another instrument with ancestral Maya roots. I continue to seek out traditional music when I travel in the region, and have heard from older musicians about their difficulty in finding younger apprentices to preserve the traditional lifesongs of Chajul.

EXPLORING NORTHERN CHAJUL

Most of Chajul's territory lies to the north of the municipal capital, in the high mountain cloud forests of unparalleled isolation and beauty. The ancient Ixil settled the fertile river valleys of Chajul's northern slopes around 500 BC, cultivating maize on sunlit hillsides and hunting prized jaguar pelts and quetzal plumage in the virgin forests. Pre-Hispanic traders and warriors probably navigated paths along the Xak'b'al River and mountain valleys between the Maya city-states of the Petén lowlands and their brethren, or rival, kingdoms in the western and central highlands. Ixil farmers and traders have traveled these same routes for centuries.

Farmers from the cool mountain slopes previously journeyed to the Ixcán to carve out additional maize fields in this unclaimed territory; since 1900, thousands of Ixil migrant laborers have traveled to coastal and Ixcán plantations of others. During the civil war, these northern Chajul forests sheltered Guatemalans fleeing to refugee camps in Mexico, Communities of Population in Resistance, and makeshift camps of the Guerrilla Army of the Poor.

Until 2000, only persons with local knowledge, pack animals, and rugged four-wheel-drive vehicles could access the remote *aldeas* of northern Chajul. During the rainy season, even the few rutted rural roads were largely impassable except by foot. Few outside goods reached these mountain villages; maize, coffee, and firewood had to be hauled out by foot or by mule-back.

Much is now set to change in northern Chajul.

BELOW: Juil is one of the most important pre-Hispanic settlements and sacred sites in the Ixil region, with a sweeping view in all directions.

[153]

ABOVE: Juil residents, several children and their father, accompanied us over streams and through woods and fields to the ancient sacred altar and temple ruins nearby.

In 1997, over the protest of Ixil communities, the government appropriated 450 square kilometers (175 square miles) of Chajul's tropical cloud forest to create the Visis Cabá Biosphere National Reserve. While this action affords "protected status" for some of the region's last remaining virgin forests and fauna, it is not certain that the government will steward these resources any better than local communities have done.

Beginning in 2002, foreign-financed engineers with dynamite and a fleet of earth-moving equipment began construction of a new road from Chajul's cabecera north to the Ixcán municipality. Multinational ventures have purchased extensive swaths of land along the Xak'b'al River, and the first of a series of hydroelectric dams commenced operation in 2011. These developments have prompted rising concern among indigenous communities. Although year-round roads will facilitate travel and commerce, many express fears that improved access will usher in a new wave of outsiders to buy up their land and expropriate control of the region's resources. Emboldened community organizations have recently stepped up their demands for a settlement of historic land disputes and an equal voice in the social and economic development of their ancient homeland.

The new road now stretches from the municipal capital to Amajchel, about 40 kilometers (25 miles) of winding, climbing, and plunging road leading into the heartland of northern Chajul municipality. By pickup truck in the dry season, a trip from the cabecera to Ilom takes three to four hours. Careful planning, including bringing along supplies for an unexpected overnight in a small village, is advisable.

Juil

The community of Juil (also spelled *Hu'il*, pronounced "Wheel") lies 8 kilometers north of Chajul cabecera, a fifteen-minute drive, or a half-day hike. According to Ixil legends, Juil was the youngest of eleven Ixil mountain deities, and the one who cracked the Paxil Mountain open to release the sacred maize. Juil is among the earliest Ixil settlements in the region. The ancient ceremonial site on the summit of Juil Mountain is regarded as the most important traditional altar in Chajul, if not the region, drawing Maya priests and traditional spiritual pilgrims from across Guatemala. According to anthropologist Benjamin Colby,

> *The sacred shrine of Hu'il . . . was central to the calendrical system. It was a place of pilgrimage for diviners, priests, curers, and ordinary folk, not only from all three dialect areas of Ixil country*

but from neighboring language areas as well. The Ixil say that "Aanhel [angel] Hu'il is what holds the world together."[83]

In recognition of the cultural importance of Juil, the European Union's "Project Ixil" organization (2002–04) financed the reconstruction of a traditional Maya altar (*casa oratoria*) on the mountainside, as well as a small guesthouse (*posada comunitaria*) to welcome visitors near the town center. The Guatemalan army razed Juil during the civil war and rounded up survivors into a barren encampment (another of the army's "development poles") straddling the road into northern Chajul. Present-day Juil retains the appearance of crudely designed wartime settlement, with one rutted main street flanked by a small church, schoolhouse, and cluster of tiny shops. One has to walk through the lush river valley at the bottom of the town and into the gently enfolding mountains to appreciate the allure of ancient Juil.

The pre-Hispanic ceremonial site, once populated with Maya temples and plazas, sits on a high ridge below the summit of Juil Mountain (2,745 meters, or 9,000 feet), surveying a vast panorama of the Ixil homeland. The historic site is a pleasant, hour-long hike from the village. My companions and I engaged a local farmer as our guide; as we walked through the village, numerous enthusiastic children joined us. We walked southeast from the town center into the valley below, crossing the village stream on a split-log footbridge. A worn footpath meandered through pastureland blooming with calla lilies, and over a series of cattle fences scaled by log "ladders," and up the foothills of Juil Mountain. As we approached the ceremonial site, our guide explained how the Guatemalan army had forced villagers to dig holes around the sacred site in search of Maya artifacts. Unfortunately, the looting of ancient sites in Guatemala is nothing new, but the Ixil people remember the systematic wartime plundering and desecration of ancient Juil as particularly offensive.

Today, the Maya New Year dawns on a symbolic reconstruction of an ancient altar and prayer center (*casa oratoria*). Twenty wooden pillars, carved with the glyphs of the twenty sacred daygods in the Maya calendar, support a rectangular enclosure atop a pyramidal, stone foundation. There is a raised altar with four wooden crosses against one wall of the inner sanctuary. There are ample signs that the altar is regularly used for traditional prayer ceremonies, including pools of melted candles and wilted flowers. The unmistakable aroma of *pom* incense blends with the fragrance of the pine needles that carpet the sanctuary floor.

To the north of the oration center, tucked just below the mountain's summit, the hand-hewn stones of the ancient Maya lie scattered and camouflaged in the midst of a maize field. With our guide, we searched through elephant-eye-high maize to locate a few telltale blocks of stepped temples that anchored this Classic Period (AD 200 to AD 900) site. Clearing the underbrush with a machete, our guide exposed the truncated stone torso of an ancient Ixil "warrior prince." According to a local account, the upper half of the stela was lopped off and carted away by helicopter during the civil war. Like many other pre-Hispanic ruins in the region, this site has never been scientifically documented and has suffered the ravages of "unofficial" plundering. To appreciate what remains of this prized sacred center, one would need to visit at the end of the maize harvest (January–March), when the rubble and contours of ancient Juil could be seen more clearly. (This is on my "to-do" list.)

The new "guesthouse" on the main road in Juil offers two dormitory-style bedrooms (Q25), for overnight visitors. Hostess Doña Juana also offers simple cooked meals and the guide services of family members and neighbors for those who wish to visit the ancient archaeological site. Guests should bring their own blankets or sleeping bags to spread on woven straw *petate* mats.

The Visis Cabá Biosphere National Reserve

The Visis Cabá Reserve begins just north of Juil, encompassing 450 square kilometers (174 square miles) of magnificent misty mountains, a critical watershed for northwestern Guatemala. The ecology of the tropical cloud forest varies with altitude and exposure to light. It nourishes an immense variety of flora and fauna: giant cedars and ceibas, mahogany, many species of pine, orchids and epiphytes, howler monkeys, and hundreds of birds, including the elusive national bird, the Resplendent Quetzal (*Pharomachrus mocinno*).

For thousands of years, Ixil communities have lived in and from these vast forests, valuing their natural resources as part of their ancient cultural patrimony and harvesting its abundant flora and fauna. From these dense forests came tropical nuts and fruits, fibers, resin, and wood, as well as prized jaguar pelts and exotic feathers. Prior to 1997, this cloud forest and its abundant resources were classified as communal, or *ejido,* land reserved, managed, and sustainably harvested for the common benefit of the Chajul communities.

Today, twenty-two Ixil communities ring the perimeter of the reserve, with a combined population of about 1,150 families, or roughly 10,000 inhabitants as of 2010. Despite the government's creation of the Reserve, Ixil from the surrounding communities continue to visit revered sacred springs and ancient prayer sites within the forest and to forage for traditonal forest products.

BELOW: Felipe Marcos Gallego is an environmental engineer (ingeniero ambiental) and the coordinator of the Universidad Rural center in Santa Cruz del Quiché. He is one of an increasing number of young Ixil professionals building a better future for this region, and has written extensively about the ecology of the Visis Cabá.

In the Voices

In the voices
Of the old trees
I recognize the words of my ancestors
Nightwatchers of the centuries,
their dreams are in the roots.

En las Voces

En las voces
De los arboles viejos
Reconozco las de mis abuelas
Veladores de siglos,
Su sueno esta en las raices.
—**Humerto Ak'abal**

(*Our Culture is Our Resistance: Repression, Refuge, and Healing in Guatemala,* by Jonathan Moller and Ricardo Falla, et al.)

The Maya vision of the cosmos describes the intricate and interdependent relationship between man and nature. Ancient Ixil legends, traditional prayers, the lyrics and poems of modern artists mirror this mystical relationship, as so simply and eloquently in the following poem by K'iche' poet, Humberto Ak'abal.

Ixil community leaders have petitioned the Ministry of the Environment to return protection of the Visis Cabá Reserve to Chajul. They contest government intentions and believe that their ancestral lands are more vulnerable to illegal logging and resource exploitation without the active surveillance of local communities who have a vested interest in their preservation. To date, their renewed petitions have been denied.

To explore the ecology of the Visis Cabá, visitors should hire a local guide from one of the villages bordering the reserve. Inquiries can be made in Juil or Vichox (just beyond Juil) for access to the southern section of the reserve, or in Jua' or Chel, for access to the northern section.

Beyond Juil, the road traverses misty west-facing slopes that are 3,000 meters high (9,850 feet high) to the tiny hamlet of Visiquichum, and then plunges via hairpin turns into the Xak'b'al River valley. On a sunny day, the unfolding panoramas of northwestern Guatemala are simply magical. Rising into the distant clouds are the highest peaks in Ixil country, Paramos Grande (3,350 meters) and Cerro Sumal (3,320 meters) in Nebaj, and beyond, the mountains of Todos Santos Cuchumatán in the Department of Huehuetenango.

In the foreground, dotting the high slopes, are a half-dozen Ixil villages, the sparkle of a few corrugated tin roofs and patches of maize fields revealing their locations among the thick forests. The road cuts are daring, dramatic, and certainly dangerous during the rainy season. Landslides are common, washing out tree cover and burying ravines below in mud and rock; a gigantic road grader is on perpetual duty. Even in the dry season, several waterfalls along this route refresh dusty travelers. The road crosses the Xak'b'al River at the bottom of a narrow ravine, where the river is less than 50 feet across, climbs steeply up the opposite bank, and snakes cautiously northward several kilometers along heavily eroded valley contours.

Around a bend in the road, the river valley opens into a fertile cauldron. On the left, a secondary road climbs northwest to substantial settlements in Finca La Perla, Sotz'il, and Ilom. Straddling the river near the town of Jua' is the new Xak'b'al hydroelectric dam. Families living in the valley bottom have benefited from the dam construction, providing labor and selling land along the river for a price that is ten times the normal rate. Beyond Jua', on the east side of the Xak'b'al, passable roads lead north to Chel and east to Amajchel and Cabá, former Communities of Popular Resistance during the civil war.

Sotz'il and Ilom

Oral history and shreds of archaeological evidence locate the earliest settlement of the Ixil Maya in the vicinity of Ilom by 500 BC. The providence of the early, Preclassic Ixil remains unresolved. Linguists point to the west, since Ixil dialects are distantly related to Mam. Local historians, however, believe that the ancient Ixil also had strong connections to Preclassic Maya city-states of the Petén lowlands. The name *Ilom* is derived from *Illomb'al,* meaning "lookout" and "place of rest." For millennia, the Ixil used Ilom as a waypoint, coming from the high mountains to the tropical lowlands, to extend the maize season and to trade with communities to the north. Renewed interest in the early archaeology of this region may eventually shed more light on the early Ixil colonies.

The distance from Jua' in the Xak'b'al River valley to Ilom is only about 10 kilometers, but beware that seemingly short distances on these secondary roads may require much more time than expected. Until recently, the road appeared too challenging for my rented vehicle. In the spring of 2010, however, at the

ABOVE: Mountaintop Sotz'il residents continue to petition Government to settle questionable transfers of their ancient community lands to outsiders in the late 19th and early 20th centuries.

end of the dry season, a fresh road grade opened up new vistas for me. I drove though Sotz'il (3 kilometers up the road) and to Ilom in under an hour, getting my first look at these northern *aldeas*. Torrential rains, like those that pummeled Guatemala in mid-2010, regularly wipe out rural roads; travelers need to verify passable road conditions before setting out for remote destinations.

Sotz'il and Ilom enjoy a milder geography and climate than their high mountain neighbors to the south. Altitudes across the northern foothills of the Cuchumatanes range from 1,300 to 1,000 meters (4,300 to 3,300 feet). When nights are frigid in San Gaspar Chajul, the air can feel almost balmy in Sotz'il. Airy, wood-plank construction (*tablones*) replaces insulating adobe brick in local house construction; citrus, banana, plantains, and tree ferns shade family compounds. The gentler topography and temperatures support two maize crops a year and attracted outsiders here in the late 1800s to acquire land for coffee plantations.

SOTZ'IL

Reflecting the postwar population boom, the population of Sotz'il has sprawled beyond its original ridgetop niche, with sweeping views southward into the Xak'b'al valley and north to the Ixcán. The road winds up through a crowded amphitheater of dwellings that terrace the sun-drenched hillside and town center. I drove slowly through the town at noontime. Family life spilled into the roadway; neighbors shared blaring music from a boom box; elders in traditional dress mixed with young schoolchildren in sports caps and backpacks. An overnight stay here would certainly involve laying out one's sleeping bag in the home of a local family.

ILOM

Ilom is located strategically in the foothills of the northern Cuchumatanes, its southern back to the misty high mountains and its northern gaze into the lush tropical lowlands of the Ixcán municipality. Alluring traces of ancient Ilom mark the landscape of this *aldea*. Remnants of temples, tombs, ballcourts, and plazas with sacred altars have been documented nearby in Maravilla (Chajul) and Sajsivan (Nebaj). Downstream from the new hydroelectric installation, where the Rio Xamala' joins the Xak'b'al River, an ancient site, termed Xak'b'al, is being rescued and preserved with contributions from the dam's foreign investors. The rich archaeology and artifacts recovered from these sites confirm strong cultural and trading links between ancient Ixil kingdoms and the dominant lowland city-states from the Early Classic Period through the Late Classic Period (AD 100–900). Available evidence also lends more credence to the tales of an eccentric antiquarian priest encountered by John Lloyd Stephens in the 1840s, who relayed indigenous accounts of a large city, "with turrets white and glittering in the sun," visible from a mountaintop near Ilom.[84] Lincoln pursued this intriguing tale in 1940 and scanned the horizon from Ilom, writing "it was impossible to see anything but heat mist over the jungle."[85] From the road above the present-day town of Ilom, steep valley walls rising from the Rio Xamala' limit the view out to the Ixcán, where dense jungle growth most certainly consumed or camouflaged any remnants of ancient Maya settlements.

Ilom's population has recovered from the beatings of the civil war and the confines of the army encampment and "development pole" established here. Today,

BELOW: The earliest migrants of Ixil-speaking Maya to the present-day region settled in Ilom's temperate valley climate between the steamy Ixcán lowlands to the north and the foggy Cuchumatán Moutains to the south.

the town looks and feels like a booming frontier outpost, complete with the sombrero'd horseback rider that galloped past as my pickup truck inched down the rutted incline to the town center. Judging from the numerous shiny tin roofs and roadside *tiendas*, residents of Ilom continue to thrive, like their predecessors, on trade and traffic across the nearby Mexican border at Barillas.

Finca La Perla

From a ridge above Sotz'il, Finca La Perla comes into view to the south, its telltale and daredevil airstrip bisecting a cluster of farm buildings. The headquarters of this extensive coffee plantation occupy an elevated, east-facing promontory, looking over an enormous swath of prime land that the elders of Ilom and Sotz'il still claim as their rightful ancestral territory. For more than a century, Finca La Perla (along with Finca Santa Delfina and related land claims) has been at the epicenter of repeated clashes and court cases between various outside owners of the Finca and Ixil communities of northern Chajul. The tale of this convoluted land dispute is not unique to the Ixil region or to Guatemala; however, I write about the details of this particular case because it is one of the better-documented tales of numerous historic land disputes in the region.

For this reconstruction of facts, I am indebted to historian Elaine D. Elliott and her linguist husband, Stephen Elliott, who grew up in Nebaj from 1952 to 1969, the eldest son of American linguists Raymond and Helen Elliott.[86] This story also gives readers an appreciation of just how complicated and intractable many such land disputes in Guatemala have become, fostering misunderstandings, resentment, and animosity as they fester unresolved.

The history of Finca La Perla dates back to the late 1800s. While the practice of the state commandeering of indigenous land began in the colonial era, it accelerated rapidly under President Barrios's national land-reform agenda. Indigenous lands not previously surveyed and titled were essentially up for national appropriation and reallocation. The subsequent race to register municipal claims throughout Guatemala was fraught with problems. Sparring between municipalities over ancestral borders and marshaling legal expertise to document claims with the National Land Registry proved perilous and costly to most indigenous communities. In some cases, land courts settled competing claims by awarding disputed parcels to third parties. In other cases, bribes and political influence enabled savvy outsiders to carve out land titles ahead of municipal authorities. Local and national politics, occasionally involving corruptible indigenous officials, played a big role as the national "land grab" escalated.

Prior to receiving an initial municipal title in 1900, Chajul municipal authorities lost ancestral land to outsiders' claims, as well as to the government's establishment of a new Ixcán municipality entity. Chajul also lost the opportunity to secure additional acreage in the northern *aldeas* of Ilom and Sotz'il, when President Estrada Cabrera deeded several large land parcels to himself and to loyal government soldiers from Momostenango. Initial confusion about the legality and location of the soldiers' grants languished and was compounded over the next twenty years by the acquisition of these and other land parcels by a Mexican-born Ladino, Lisandro Gordillo, who had served as municipal secretary in Chajul. Gordillo proceeded to clear land for a coffee plantation, but allowed Ilom and Sotz'il villagers to grow maize on unused land.

Chajul municipal officials eventually sued Gordillo in 1928 for the return of the soldiers' lands, providing evidence that the disputed titles actually referred to territory in Momostenango to the west. Although two lower courts decided in favor of Chajul, Gordillo's claim (and suspected bribery)

Afternoon rays illuminate the farm buildings of Finca La Perla and the gravesite of its former patron, Luis Arenas, shot by members of the Guerrilla Army of the Poor in 1975.

prevailed in Guatemala's highest court. In a temporary reversal of fortune, Gordillo offered to sell the disputed land back to the communities of Ilom and Sotz'il when he was faced with bankruptcy. Chajul authorities, however, balked at the proposition that they should pay Gordillo for what was essentially "stolen" property. When the landowner soon appeared with a land surveyor, local villagers suspected Gordillo was planning to sell their land to someone else and threw him in jail. Seeking revenge, Gordillo trumped up a communiqué to Nebaj that "Ilom had been invaded by Lacandon tribes," implying that he, himself, had been murdered by his captors. Government soldiers were dispatched to rescue Gordillo; three men from Chajul were publicly whipped and three others executed for their rebellion. Thus, Ilom and Sotz'il lost an opportunity to regain their rightful lands, and Gordillo sold several parcels, including Finca La Perla, to a Swiss national, Francisco Fernando Egger Foster.

When Jackson Steward Lincoln visited the plantation in 1939, he was extravagantly wined and dined by the Finca's Swiss owner. Lincoln makes mention of an ancient Maya ceremonial site, including an impressive "stone temple with steps about 30 x 60 meters" located amid the coffee trees on Finca land.[87] By 1934, bankers had repossessed the insolvent Finca La Perla.

For five years, as the coffee plantation floundered, local farmers from Sotz'il and Ilom families cultivated the maize fields, paying minimal rent to the bank.

In 1941, Luis Arenas added Finca La Perla and Santa Delfina to his already-extensive plantations in the Ixcán to the north. He built an airstrip to fly coffee production down to Nebaj and fenced off finca land, estimated at over 86 *caballerías* (about 3,900 hectares). Breaking with former landowner practice, Arenas permitted only full-time finca workers, a majority of whom were Ladinos and K'anjob'al Maya from Santa Eulalia, to farm idle plantation acreage. Land-poor villagers from Ilom and Sotz'il, who supplied the majority of seasonal labor for the coffee harvest, lost all access to their former *milpas* on the Finca.

The land prospects of Ilom and Sotz'il families seemed brighter for a few years during the reformist "Decade of Spring." As the governments of Arévalo (1945–51) and Árbenz (1950–54) advanced their ambitious land-reform agenda, the owner of Finca La Perla faced expropriation of significant "vacant" acreage for redistribution to landless local petitioners. In a conciliatory gesture, Luis Arenas voluntarily transferred 4 *caballerías* (about 180 hectares) to Ilom in 1946, the area on which the present-day town of Ilom is located. Between the various acts of Congress and the national land redistribution program known as Decree 900, Arenas was slated to lose 90 percent of his finca holdings in northern Chajul. Apparently, Arenas was so enraged that he offered his personal services to the counterrevolutionary Guatemalans and Americans plotting to overthrow Árbenz.[88] When the National Liberation Movement and CIA operatives deposed Árbenz in 1954, all acts of land redistribution were nullified. Finca La Perla remained intact, and the communities of Ilom and Sotz'il lost another chance to own a piece of their ancestral lands.

In 1975, the Guerrilla Army of the Poor launched its first salvo against those it viewed as the entrenched oligarchy by targeting the aging owner of Finca La Perla. In hopes of rallying indigenous communities to their cause, the EGP shot Luis Arenas on June 7, 1975, which was payday at the Finca.[89] In this bloody aftermath, local reaction was confused and muted. Many indigenous laborers on the Finca feared for their jobs. Ixil villagers from Ilom and the Sotz'il area feared they would be held accountable for the landowner's murder. Indeed, these villagers suffered the full brunt of government retaliation. When the Guatemalan army launched its "scorched earth" campaign in the early 1980s, army soldiers, together with members of the Finca's civil patrol, carried out the grisly torture and execution of scores of "suspected" guerrillas and sympathizers in Sotz'il and Ilom. As coffee production on the Finca took a beating from the escalating violence, the Arenas family deftly maneuvered to consolidate worker loyalty and buoy production. In 1984, they reorganized the legal entity of *Finca la Perla y Anexos, S.A.* and sold 40 percent of the new stock to permanent plantation staff on multiyear loans bearing 0 percent interest. Few plantation workers from Ilom or Sotz'il were beneficiaries in this ownership transfer.

The latest chapter in the narrative of Finca La Perla has, once again, heightened tension in northern

RIGHT: Scenes from Chel: Catholic church with Ixil symbols stuccoed into the façade, caldron of drying cardomom, rural evangelical mission.

Chajul. The 1996 Peace Accords created the legal groundwork for institutional remediation of disputed land claims, as well as for the rights of indigenous communities to organize and advocate for their rights and interests. The Accords cautiously emboldened communities in northern Chajul, encouraged by indigenous rights organizations, to renew their long-standing claims against the Finca. This political hot-potato issue was tossed back and forth between official organizations charged with land remediation, but without resolution.

In 2004, under mounting political pressure and declining coffee prices, the Arenas Méndes family sold a key piece of disputed land along the Xak'b'al River to a Honduran-owned industrial conglomerate. The land was sited for a 50-meter hydroelectric dam, to be constructed with multinational financing. In 2007, as access roads and dam construction commenced, the Mesa Regional Ixil, representing thirty-six indigenous Ixil organizations, protested the land sale and the proposed hydroelectric project. They argued that they were not opposed to dam construction, but to the fact that the electricity and profits generated would not benefit local communities. The Mesa group also renewed its demands for government to resolve long-standing land disputes between the communities of Ilom and Sotz'il and the owners of Finca La Perla.

As of this writing, I know of no further progress or resolution of Ixil community petitions. The Xak'b'al Dam is complete and has begun operating; plans for

Chel serves as a reststop for transport of migrant labor and produce to and from farms and ranches of the tropical Ixcán territory north of Chajul municipality.

further dams are on the drawing table, and it remains to be seen how these will affect villages above and below the dams. Electric transmission towers and lines march in regular cadence across the mountain ridges and valleys of northern Chajul, but most Ixil families still cannot afford to install electric lights. Ixil families that sold land along the river or for electric towers are expanding their homes and replacing ceramic roof tiles with shiny corrugated tin, but their windfall represents but an ephemeral reprieve from grinding poverty. Meanwhile, the foreign energy conglomerate has magnanimously financed the archaeological preservation of ancient Xak'b'al, a bittersweet reminder that once, not so long ago, Ixil kingdoms ruled these vital waterways and vast forest resources.

Chel and Beyond

From the new bridge above the Xak'b'al Dam, an improved road continues northeast to Chel, about 3 kilometers beyond Jua'. After Ilom, Chel is the largest *aldea* in northern Chajul (estimated population as of 2012: 700 families). The altitude is about 1,200 meters (4,000 feet), but the ecology on the north side of the Visis Cabá heights feels tropical. The houses in the town of Chel, a mixture of Ixil and Ladino families, are all wood-plank construction, some with thatched roofs. A shallow river rumbles through the town on its way west to join the Xak'b'al.

I visited Chel on market day and was able to walk around town, talk with vendors, and join other townsfolk for a bit of shopping and swapping. Chel functions as a collecting and trading-hub point for produce from the northernmost *aldeas* of Chajul: smallholder cardamom and coffee, bananas and plantains, orchids from forests around Amajchel and Caba to the east, citrus, pineapples, and bamboo. The gentle topography north from Chel makes this town a transit point for hundreds of migrant workers from Chajul and Nebaj, who make their way through here for seasonal work on Ixcán farms and ranches beyond Finca Estrella Polar and Amajchel.

LIMITLESS HORIZONS FOR THE IXIL: EXPANDING EDUCATIONAL OPPORTUNITIES

Returning to Chajul's municipal capital from remote mountain villages, I sense this town's magnetic attraction for young students who yearn to study beyond the limited horizons of a one-room, rural primary school. It has been only twenty years since primary education became available in every district in the Ixil region. Now, with 65 percent of Guatemala's population under the age of sixteen, there is an exploding demand for formal education. The 1996 Peace Accords recognized the rights of the indigenous population to be educated in their native language, although truly bilingual education remains limited due to a shortage of certified Ixil teachers and bilingual pedagogic materials.

There was only one primary school in the *cabecera*, when I first visited the area in 2005. Enrollment topped 600 children, divided into morning and afternoon sessions, but an equal number of the town's children could not attend. Either their parents could not afford the inscription fees and school uniforms, or there was simply no room to accommodate them. Class size exceeded forty students, and a starting teacher earned Q1,500 per month. At that time, a few successful students went on to Chajul's new middle school (*básico*), for grades seven through nine, but there were still no local options for high school and preprofessional training (*diversificado*). Only a handful of local families could afford the costs of further education, which meant sending their children to private high schools in Nebaj or Santa Cruz del Quiché.

In 2004, a new nongovernmental organization, Limitless Horizons Ixil (*Horizontes sin Límites Ixil, Il'eb'al y'el y y'ae'b'al Ixil*), opened its doors in Chajul to do just what its name implied—help students and their families see beyond the limiting horizons of their mountain valleys. Katie Morrow, a young American social worker, and Pedro Caba, an Ixil university

ABOVE: The new library of Limitless Horizons Ixil's ((Horizontes sin Límites Ixil, Il'eb'al y'el y y'ae'b'al Ixil) is a raving success, heralding a great leap in educational ambition and opportunity for families and youth in Chajul.

graduate from Chajul, started the organization with a vision to address rural poverty by educating the next generation. Run by a tiny staff of Ixil and Americans personnel, Limitless Horizons has grown in five short years to provide annual scholarships for about seventy-five students to attend middle and high school. The organization runs an after-school program for intensive homework help, mastery of basic computer skills, and a variety of community-enterprise development workshops. In 2009, Limitless Horizons opened the first community library in Chajul municipality, which was so popular that it moved into expanded space in 2011!

I sponsor four Ixil students through Limitless Horizons. The first in their families to attend middle (*básico*) and high school (*diversificado*), they are full of enthusiasm and dreams for the future. I receive a handwritten letter from them every year, and enjoy a chance to catch up in person when I am in Chajul. Visitors should be sure to visit Limitless Horizons' offices and library, which are located a three-minute walk downhill from the municipal plaza, next door to the *Comedor las Gemelas*. Find out how to sponsor Chajul students or to volunteer at www.LimitlessHorizonsIxil.org.

When President Alvaro Colom rode to victory with strong indigenous support in 2008, he announced a goal of universal education and started by abolishing inscription fees at public schools. In Chajul's cabecera there are several new schools, including a Methodist-supported primary and secondary school, a private nondenominational middle school, and a new public middle school. The majority of students enrolled in middle and high school live in or nearby this town, but a growing number hike in each week, one to two hours from their villages, lodging with local families during the week to pursue their education.

Nevertheless, rural indigenous children must still overcome daunting obstacles in order to complete their formal education. According to Chajul municipal statistics, less than 25 percent of all children complete primary school; 5 percent, middle school; and only 1 percent ever finishes high school. There are many reasons for this dismal picture, and one of the main ones is still cost: public schools are nominally free, but parents have to buy uniforms, shoes, notebooks—not to mention the additional living expenses if a student needs to board away from home. Foregone income and help at home is also a major cost factor. A punishing national curriculum, lack of bilingual and culturally relevant materials, and inadequately trained teachers contribute to high failure and dropout rates.

Despite these challenges, my "street thermometer" shows change and vibrancy in Chajul. As I meander through the market or enjoy the afternoon light in the central plaza, young students stop to talk or solicit help with their English lessons. Often our conversation leads to "What's next after *básico* or *diversificado*?" I am impressed with the passion in their voices as they talk about their ambitions—among them, to become bilingual secretaries, teachers, agronomists, doctors, and entrepreneurs. I hope their dreams come true. The future of the Ixil region depends on it.

BELOW: Sponsoring a smart and deserving teenager to pursue her education and dreams is a mutually rewarding commitment.

CHAPTER 6
Cotzal

OPPOSITE: Photo by Beth Lentz. At lower altitudes than Nebaj and Chajul, the municipality of Cotzal enjoys gushing, year-round waterfalls, like this one at Santa Avelina. **ABOVE LEFT:** Spiney maguey is cultivated in Cotzal's arid zones for its milky sap used in indigenous medicinal remedies and liquor, and leathery spines that yield fiber for rope and twine. **ABOVE RIGHT:** Young girl in distinctive Cotzal woven blouse.

Overview - Cotzal is the smallest of the three Ixil municipalities, encompassing only 182 square kilometers (about 70 square miles) in the southeastern section of the region. Ixil linguists offer several interpretations about the origin of the name, "Cotzal": *Tz'a'la Vitz,* meaning "land between the mountains," and *Ko'tutz'a'lavitz,* derived from the expression, "Let's go to the warmer lands." Indeed, Cotzal is sandwiched between mountain ridges rising to 2,000 meters (6,560 feet) along its northern boundary with Chajul and peaks of 2,500 meters (8,200 feet) along its southern border with the Quiché municipalities of Uspantán and Cunén. Within these borders, spectacular waterfalls, lush palms and tree ferns, and wafts of sultry heat dramatize Cotzal's undulating topography, which slopes gradually in some sections and precipitously in others to about 1,000 meters (3,300 feet) at the eastern end of the Cotzal River valley. On days when it can be drizzling and damp in Chajul or Nebaj, a short jaunt downhill into Cotzal's balmier landscape offers a welcome change of climate. In Cotzal's sheltered valleys, tropical palms, pines, and hardwoods shade smallholder plots and plantation expanses of Arabica coffee, and trees laden with avocados, bananas, plums, and citrus moderate the sultry heat of the rainy season in hamlets of modest adobe and wood-plank houses.

Ixil ancestors are thought to have migrated into the area of Cotzal's hospitable climate during the Early Classic Period (AD 250 to AD 550). Archaeological evidence points to continuous occupation of a number of ancient sites through to the era of K'iche' domination across the western and central highland areas of Guatemala (AD 1250 to AD 1450). Pre-Hispanic temples and ceremonial centers were clustered along the fertile Cotzal River and perched high on mountain plateaus and ridges. After being initially ambushed by the combined forces of Cotzal and Uspantán in 1529, a second Spanish regiment eventually overpowered and defeated these Maya communities in 1530. The conquerors built a church and administrative base on the site of an exisiting Ixil village and baptized it "San Juan Cotzal." Today, most people refer to this municipality simply as "Cotzal."

DIRECTIONS TO COTZAL

Cotzal's capital (*cabecera*), and the largest town in the municipality, is only a short drive of twenty minutes from the capitals of Nebaj and Chajul. From Nebaj center, follow the main road north from Nebaj's El Triángulo gas station to a major juncture marked by the Ixil headquarters of the Academy of Mayan Languages and signs pointing right to Cotzal and left to Chajul. The road to Cotzal leads in northeasterly direction, about 17 kilometers of beautiful rolling hills and valleys to Cotzal's *cabecera*. Minivans and passenger pickups depart Nebaj for Cotzal from a stop in front of Hotel Nebaj. Two daily buses leave from Nebaj's bus terminal in the back of the market for the towns of Cotzal, Santa Avelina, and the Finca San Francisco; inquire for schedule of out and return trips. From Chajul center, Cotzal is just 9 kilometers; minivans for Cotzal depart from the town plaza in Chajul and pick up passengers at the southern entrance to town, where the roads to Nebaj and Cotzal intersect.

BETH LENTZ, U.S. PEACE CORPS
When this guidebook was just a glimmer of an idea, I received a cheerful email from a U.S. Peace Corps volunteer, Beth Lentz, in Cotzal. She was completing two years of teaching environmental sciences in Cotzal's municipal capital. Fluent in Spanish and conversant in Ixil, Beth was embraced by children, parents, and teachers in Cotzal, and was an enthusiastic explorer of the region's ecological and cultural landscapes. She easily enticed me into visiting her with this invitation:

Cotzal is one of the most beautiful and picturesque municipalities in the Department of Quiché. It has a mild climate, forests everywhere, and plenty of rain so that it is green year-round. There are places to enjoy oneself, whether outdoors or with the people in their homes. You will have to accustom yourself to people staring at you and kids yelling "gringo"; people everywhere want to know where you are from, why you are here, and how to say their own names or favorite expressions in English. The pace of daily life is slow, and no one is really in a hurry for anything. So, relax, take your time, and enjoy your visit to Cotzal.

Beth eventually spent four months helping me research and document Cotzal traditions and transitions. The next Peace Corps volunteer to be posted to Cotzal, Josh Kyller, focused his efforts on village food security and soil fertility. Josh hitched a ride with me on several occasions to distant *aldeas*, and this guidebook benefited from his knowledge of local agriculture and the perpetual struggle of indigenous families to feed their families and send their children to school.

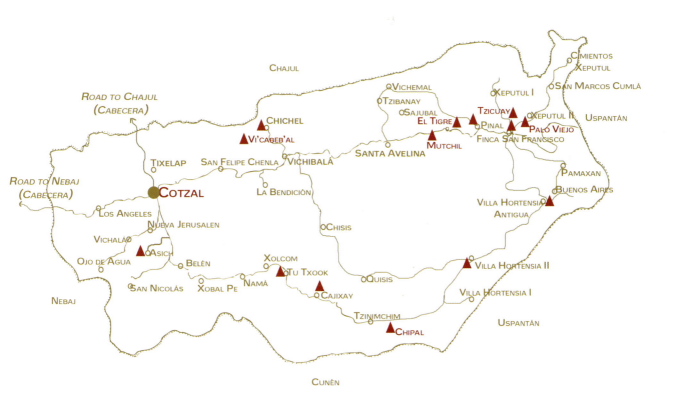

ABOVE: Photo by Michel de la Sabelier. Wood-slat houses are better adapted to the tropical climates of lower altitudes in Cotzal's eastern region.

Lower altitudes and warmer temperatures also explain why outsiders started to prospect for land in Cotzal in the late 19th century. In 1885, the munipality was granted title to 401 *caballerías* (18,200 hectares) of its ancestral land claims. The Italian-descendant Pedro Brol and Spanish Heberra Ibárgüen families rapidly acquired some of the most fertile land in the municipality for coffee, sugar, and maguey plantations, and cattle production. The land-holding census of 1964 indicated that 119 "non-indigenous" owners controlled over one-third of all registered farm acreage in the municipality; of these, several large properties controlled several thousand hectares of prime land.[90]

Local antagonisms over political infighting and land ownership erupted into early civil war violence in Cotzal, when the sons and heirs of Pedro Brol were both murdered. Since the war's end, however, falling world coffee prices, coupled with continued land conflicts, have resulted in the sale of significant plantation acreage in Cotzal to former workers and to Ixil families within nearby communities. Finca San Francisco is still the largest landholder and employer in Cotzal today, and is run as a semiautonomous entity within municipal boundaries.

The population of Cotzal is estimated at 28,000 (as of 2012). Ixil-speaking inhabitants represent about three-quarters of the population, with K'iche'-speaking Maya and Ladinos accounting for about 15 percent each. Steady population growth and declining soil fertility is straining Cotzal's land and forestry resources. The average population density has risen to 1.4 per hectare, but this crude measure does not account for non-arable land, nor the highly skewed distribution of registered land holdings. According to a 2003 survey, 55 percent of the registered land area at that time was held in parcels of less than 1 hectare; 34 percent of land area was in plantations and "multifamily" holdings (including plantations that lodge permanent workers) larger than 45 hectares, including several substantially larger holdings.[91] Struggling to recover from the dislocation and losses of the civil war, the majority of Cotzal families are coping with unprecedented levels of food insecurity and economic marginalization.

Poverty is not a new phenomenon in Cotzal, nor is seasonal labor migration to supplement subsistence farming. What seems new since the end of the civil war, however, is the growing trend in multiyear out-migration and the consequent erosion of family and community cohesion. According to the last official census in 2002, more than 50 percent of the region's population is under seventeen years old. For Cotzal's youth, TV, cell phones, the Internet, and hawked CDs portray an external world that is beyond their families' means. Among the Ixil municipalities, Cotzal has experienced the greatest tension and difficulty in curbing incipient youth unrest. In my visits to schools here, I have sensed an acute hunger for learning, coupled with worry and frustration about about future employment prospects, whether in the fields or towns.

A member of Cotzal's health commission offered the following blunt prescription: "Our youth need a more positive outlook for the future; this means better education, gainful employment, healthy activity, and the knowledge that their initiative and hard work will make a difference in their lives and community." This can be said of all youth in Guatemala today, but the rural isolation of Ixil communities and limited resources compounds the anxiety felt by youth, parents, and community leaders about the future.

Although such challenges appear especially daunting in Cotzal, I have also witnessed the other side of the equation: incredible resilience, industriousness, creativity, and community commitment at work to build a brighter future for Cotzal. Visitors to Cotzal will see this spirit in the bustling biweekly market in the municipal capital, spilling out of the indoor marketplace with a boundless display of traditional products. Cotzal weavers keep their shuttles busy, building on their reputation for fine textiles to market their crafts to tourists at home and abroad. Public and NGO-run schools enrollment is at full capacity.

Traditional farmers and villagers are gradually embracing new technologies for the home and fields. Every year, more families install wood-saving stoves, water-filtration buckets, and other healthy and energy-saving practices introduced by nongovernmental organizations and staffed by Ixil entrepreneurs. The organic coffee cooperative in Santa Avelina provides sustainable returns for its membership. Three hundred and fifty of Cotzal's formerly landless families are applying new methods of intensive agricultural production and securing land ownership within cohesive communities assisted by Agros International. Increasingly, civil society in Cotzal is exercising a louder voice and a more concerted role in the economic and political life of the municipality.

Visitor Services in Cotzal

The historic town center of Cotzal is cradled on the slopes of a low mountain ridge, at 1,800 meters (5,900 feet), facing the rising sun across a broad river valley. Compacted into a tight grid since colonial times, the town's streets and footpaths radiate outward in a more organic sprawl from the nucleus of the Catholic church, principal plaza, and municipal offices. The narrow and treacherously steep streets demand skillful navigation and more than an ounce of temerity; all vehicle traffic to and from points within the municipality transits through this bottleneck. During the rainy season, the precipitous streets become gushing spillways. Needless to say, the easiest way to explore the *cabecera* is by foot. The town is much smaller than Nebaj or Chajul, but shares the modernizing bustle of downtown Nebaj, complete with a growing fleet of brazen three-wheel *tuk-tuks*. Commercial development, half Ladino and half indigenous-owned, has crowded out the traditional adobe and tile structures in the town center. Concrete-block and laminated tin roofing are in the ascendancy, and the local hardware stores conduct a

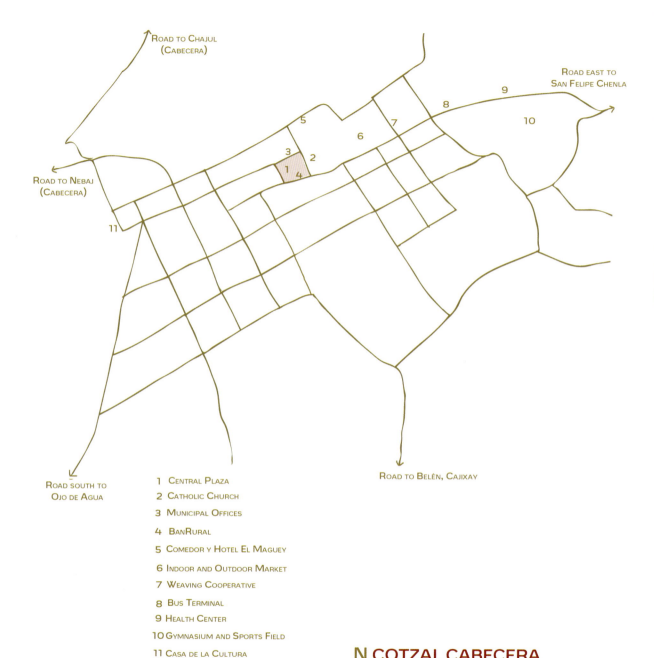

booming business. Recent growth has expanded onto a plateau above the town center and into the valley below. The municipal health center, town soccer field, and a covered recreational center sit on flat valley land at the east end of town, on the road to the second-largest town in Cotzal, Santa Avelina.

The distinctive characteristics of the Cotzal's tropical climate and historic culture remain clearly visible throughout town. Banana trees and brilliant bougainvillea luxuriate in family compounds. Pineapple, citrus, avocados, and tomatoes are piled high in market stalls. On the side streets, women stretch, spin, and wind the tough maguey fibers for the rope and net bags sold all over Guatemala. And, the indigenous women of Cotzal continue to weave and wear a stunning version of the traditional *huipil* in the regal blues and greens of the once-prized Quetzal feathers.

LODGING

The choices for visitor accommodations, particularly for groups, are limited here. During a recent visit, several new small hotels were under construction. I advise visitors to ask at the municipal offices for the current status of guesthouses and families that offer "home stays" (bed-and-breakfast with a family) for a few Q per night.

Hotel y Comedor Maguey is an older, established small guesthouse, offering a half-dozen simple bedrooms above the restaurant, several with a window, all with shared bathroom: Q100/night/double room or Q60/single. Telephone: (502) 4087-7129 or 4030-9311.

FOOD

- *Hotel y Comedor Maguey:* A reliable favorite; the kitchen is open beyond the small dining area, and one can inquire, "What's for dinner?" For lunch or dinner, they offer savory chicken, steak, and pork plates for Q20–25. A heaping plate of eggs and beans, with tortillas and coffee or tea, costs just Q12.
- *Comedor Los Cobanerita* attracts a regular clientele, serving hot traditional fare for Q10–20.

On major market days, Saturday and Wednesday, mini-eateries on the upper floor of the market cater to vendors, shoppers, and intrepid tourists who want to take break from the fray and enjoy a hearty soup, tamales, beans and eggs, coffee, the traditional hot maize drink, *atol,* and, of course, fresh tortillas—a quick meal on the go for Q5 to Q10. My rule of thumb: If it's piping hot, it's safe to eat. Best to bring your own bowl, cup, and spoon!

Basic food supplies and quick bites can be purchased any day of the week from a number of mini-stores, as well as from a number of semi-permanent market stalls in back of the market building. Street vendors sell fried chicken, chips, and fresh tortillas at noon and suppertime. Storefront kiosks on almost every block are open from morning to night with a limited inventory of nonperishable snacks, cooking oil, drinks, and canned foods.

BANKING AND HEALTH-RELATED SERVICES

The BanRural office is located on the central plaza; as of June 2012, there was no ATM facility in Cotzal. A large general store across from the Central Park sells a range of durable goods, and half a dozen small pharmacies offer a limited supply of over-the-counter medicines and herbal alternatives. The health clinic (*Puesto de Salud*) is staffed by a full-time doctor, several nurses, and supplemented by two Cuban doctors.

GUIDE SERVICES

I recommend that visitors seek out local guides to explore Cotzal and provide translation (Ixil to Spanish and vice versa), as most places of interest are not well marked or lie on private or communal property.

- The *Cooperativa Tejidos Cotzal* offers visitors a two-day package of eco- and cultural tourism, including a visit to Cotzal's beautiful waterfalls, outdoor picnics, culinary and weaving demonstrations, and discussion of Ixil history and culture; Q75–100 per person for groups of four or more (www.tejidoscotzal.org). A week's notice is recommended. Contact: (502) 4621-9725 or 4605-5967; TejidosCotzal@gmail.com. Cooperative manager, Pedro Marroquín Chamay: (502) 5877-2821; marroquin393@hotmail.com.
- Consult *Guias Ixiles* at El Descanso in Nebaj center for tour guides familiar with Cotzal; Telephone: (502) 5847-4747 or 5749-7450. Website: www.nebaj.info/home.html; Email: miguelbrito@SolucionesComunitarias.com. For English-only speakers, contact turismonebaj@gmail.com.

Explorations in Cotzal

TRANSFORMING COTZAL'S COLONIAL PLAZA

A decade after the signing of the Peace Accords, municipal authorities in Cotzal redesigned and renovated the central core of the town to soften its colonial austerity and realign its functions with service to the community. The new intimate arrangement of bougainvillea-shaded pergolas and benches now invites townsfolk to enjoy a few minutes on a park bench while waiting for an appointment at the bank or municipal offices, or to rendezvous near the new fountain with friends and family. The municipal offices also experienced a facelift with fresh coats of paint, and are teeming with young professionals scurrying about, pleased to answer questions or give directions.

The central plaza and Catholic church stand on the only level spot in the entire town. Rising just a few steps above the plaza, the Catholic church remains solemn and imposing. Just inside the entrance, hundreds of tiny wooden crosses encircle a wall-mounted statue of the crucified Christ. Each cross bears the name and date of someone from Cotzal who was killed or "disappeared" during the civil war. There is also a small memorial to Father Guillermo (Bill) Woods, a beloved Maryknoll missionary shot down in his plane by the army in 1976. Father Bill Woods championed the cause of landless poor and helped to develop cooperative farming villages in the jungles of

RIGHT: Renovation of the central plaza in Cotzal has made it a welcoming meeting place and bustling venue for spillover of the market.

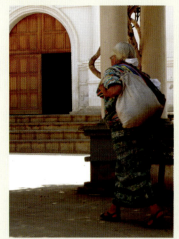

the Ixcán, beginning in the late 1960s. Up to the time he was assassinated, Father Bill ferried produce and medical supplies in and out of the remote settlements.

Historically, the biweekly market unfolded on the central plaza, every square foot right up to the front door of the church covered with a mosaic of tarps, baskets, and produce piled high. In step with the 2005 renovation of the plaza, a three-story indoor market building was constructed just behind the church complex. The new structure provides shelter for vendors and buyers from the blazing sun and drenching downpours, but unfortunately lacks the beauty, flexibility, and energetic ebb and flow of a traditional outdoor market. On Saturdays, the biggest market day of the week, people pour into Cotzal from all across the region, spilling beyond the confines of the indoor market, back onto the central plaza. All streets surrounding the plaza are crammed with colorful produce, chirping poultry, squirming piglets, and bleating kid goats. Market day gets off to a feverish pitch by 7:00 a.m., cresendos in the noonday sun, and tapers off with a mass exodus by midafternoon.

PRESERVING IXIL LANGUAGE AND IDENTITY

Language functions as a mirror of culture. For 500 years, the Spanish and their descendants sought to darken this glass, to supplant indigenous languages with Spanish, and to homogenize ethnic identity under Ladino norms and values. However, the 1996 Peace

Photo by Juan Clemente Raymundo Velasquez. A Chajul grandmother relates the sorrows and changes she has witnessed over her 80 years.

Accords reaffirmed the cultural rights of indigenous communities. Today, most road signs and billboards in the Ixil region are written in both Spanish and Ixil, and preschools and primary grades offer at least some bilingual instruction. Indigenous community radio stations reinforce this progress, broadcasting a major portion of their programming in Ixil.

The Peace Accords also provided for an official commission, the Academy of Mayan Languages, to advise and implement the new mandated commitment to indigenous languages. The Academy has twenty-two offices in Guatemala, one for each of the Maya languages still spoken today. Tomás de la Paz Pérez, the coordinator of the Academy's Ixil branch office, described the Academy's noble, and often daunting, mission:

> The objective of the Academy is to assure that the indigenous languages are not lost. There are some languages that only have about forty speakers, and the majority are elderly people. It will be hard to rescue those languages, but with the help of the Academy in those areas, the language will not be lost completely.

The Academy researches the grammar and linguistic origins of local idiom, provides linguistic workshops to teachers and municipal officials, and recommends rules on the spelling and grammar of written Ixil. There are two facilitators in each of the three Ixil municipal capitals to coordinate the reinforcement of Ixil language studies and to prepare bilingual materials for schools.

Despite these efforts, the fight to preserve indigenous culture and language is an uphill battle. National and global messages bombard these communities in direct and subtle ways every day, through the medium of information technology, increased labor mobility, urbanization, and even T-shirts and tourists. Ixil teens enthusiastically embrace change; few understand the implications of losing their mother tongue.

Ixil elders shake their heads and lament the assault on traditional Ixil culture. For them, it is not just about the loss of respect for one's elders, or about changes in dress and lifestyle. Conversations with this older generation have helped me understand just how deeply their personal identities and roles within the community are tied to the teachings and spiritual beliefs of their ancestors.

"Grandchildren no longer use their given Ixil names."

In the naming of a newborn, the legacy of the grandparents and a traditional spiritual blessing was formally passed to the newest generations. If the newborn was a first son, he took the name of his paternal grandfather; if a first girl, the name of her paternal grandmother. A second son or daughter inherited the name of his or her maternal grandparents. Later children were often named after other elder family members. The Catholic Church recognized only Christianized first names in the baptismal records, but Ixil names were used within the family and local community. Today, with the continued erosion of traditional Maya spirituality, many families have dropped the Ixil naming custom altogether. In an ironic commentary on the times, I recently heard that some Ixil youth use an interactive Maya calendar "horoscope" via the Internet to research the Maya deities and traits associated with their birth dates (www.mayacalendar.org/mayan-horoscope.php). There is now a Maya Calendar "widget" for one's computer desktop as well as an "app" for iPhones!

"We must remind our children that the elders have much value; they hold our history in their heads, not in books. The elders are the books of life."

The vast majority of Ixil elders never learned to read or write, but they are the repositories of oral legends, ancestral spiritual custom (*costumbre*), and family history. Just as grandmothers teach their granddaughters the arts of weaving, grandfathers plant the first seeds and

ABOVE: Photo by Chris Percival. Maximilliano Poma Sambrano, a dedicated teacher and community advocate.

bestow the traditional blessings on the *milpa*. In this way, young people learn to show respect for their elders; according to an older tradition, children were not supposed to walk in the shadow of an elder—in other words, they were to follow the leader from a honorable distance. Respected adults in Ixil communities are elected as "adjunct mayors" (*alcaldes auxiliares*) and form a council of traditional authorities (*principales*) who represent the community in municipal affairs and resolve local conflicts and petty crimes. Traditional rights and laws of the community have been passed down orally from one generation to the next.

"Who will bury me as I buried my parents, in the sacred traditions of our ancestors?"

Burial rites of the Ixil are a mixture of ancient Maya and Christian traditions. They believe that a prompt and proper burial is necessary to release the spirit of the deceased. Failure to pay such respect may result in a restless and angry spirit that lingers in a form of purgatory to haunt the living. When someone dies, there is an urgency to clean and dress the body in traditional clothing and personal affects, and to bury the coffin in a ceremony with candles, incense, and flowers that remember the deceased, but also his or her relatives who have passed before.

Fortunately, a few important voices in the Ixil community today are trying to bridge the emerging cultural divide between generations. These are typically the parents of today's youth. They experienced firsthand the desecration of Ixil culture during the civil war and are often the first in their extended family to have received a formal education. They know what is at stake for their cultural patrimony, but also understand that conscientious change and modernization can serve to strengthen and safeguard Ixil identity.

A Teacher of Ixil Language and Culture

Maximilliano Poma Sambrano, whose given Ixil name is Tzima, is a strong advocate and teacher of Ixil culture. He studied in Cotzal through middle school and seized the rare opportunity to finish high school in Antigua, then attend the University Mariano Gálvez in Guatemala City. Maximilliano has published five books on the Ixil language, including a dictionary, grammar book, and several translations of books for children into Ixil. Passionate about the preservation of Ixil culture, he teaches Ixil language studies in several regional secondary schools.

Q: *How did you become so involved in the study of Ixil linguistics?*
A: Growing up, people thought that it was wrong and unproductive to study our culture and language. What was seen as important was learning Spanish. After completing *básico* [middle school] in 1988, I went to Antigua and began studying the Ixil language and culture. I realized that we are too often looking

Ixil elders proudly safeguard their ancestral heritage.

ahead, and [thus often] fail to look back at the past, to see what we can learn from it, to understand what our ancestors taught us and how they lived. This worried me, because for me, the past is very important. So, little by little I started learning more and more about my own indigenous culture. When I studied at the university, I met more people who were interested in the same things.

Q: *What happened when you returned to Cotzal with this enthusiasm?*
A: When I returned to Cotzal, no one was really interested in the Ixil language and teaching it. Luckily, the Catholic Church needed translations of the Bible, so I took that opportunity to help. With this work, we wrote the first Ixil translation. However, slowly I came to realize that the Church was not promoting Ixil beliefs, language, or culture, but trying to change what people thought, 100 percent. They were imposing their beliefs on others instead of building on present beliefs. . . . In Ixil, *Kub'aal* means "our owner," and someone who cares for us. I realized that I didn't have to be part of the Church for someone to look after me because God is everywhere, like it says in the Bible. Today, there are many divisions within Cotzal . . . Rather than unite people, religion has divided them . . . I am very spiritual and I practice what my parents taught me, and I have seen benefits as a result of my spirituality.

Q: *With new technology and social norms, do you see Ixil people respecting their traditional culture and practices?*

A: There have been many changes over the past few years. Here in Cotzal we now have electricity, paved roads, phones, cable television, and Internet access. These changes have improved our quality of life and made it easier for us. Despite these changes, we still need to respect and practice the culture so that we do not lose all of our history. We should continue to respect Ixil names. One of my friends told me that he tried to register his newborn son under a particular Ixil name and they told him that he could not do it because it was not a "registered" name. These are incidents that should not occur. All of my children have Ixil names, and I was proud to go register them in the municipality with those names. We should be able to accept technology but preserve the past at the same time.

Q: *As a bilingual teacher, what changes have you seen in education over the years?*

A: The kids in primary school, especially kindergarten through third grade, don't have a very big vocabulary. It is hard to explain assignments to kids only in Spanish at this level, because they don't understand completely. Before and during the war, the idea was to learn Spanish, because [although] everyone knew Ixil and spoke it at home, to get ahead and find work, you had to learn Spanish too. So, teachers were told that they shouldn't speak Ixil to their students because they wouldn't learn that way. The problem is that the message is more direct in Ixil, and the kids do better work because they fully understand the assignment. After the Peace Accords, people realized that it was okay to speak a little Ixil in class and to teach how to read and write the language, not just to speak it. Today, teachers explain in both languages when needed, and the kids continue to learn Spanish. Some think that there should be no Ixil spoken in schools, but I disagree; insisting on Spanish only is simply a form of taking away our identity.

ABOVE: Photo by Beth Lentz. Traditonal Ixil brides wear a long ceremonial huipil woven specially for the grand occasion.

IXIL MARRIAGE CUSTOMS

There are two steps to an Ixil marriage: the formal asking for the woman's hand in marriage (*la pedida*), and the wedding ceremony and celebration. The traditional Ixil community recognizes a couple as married after satisfactory conclusion of the formal *pedida;* however, a church wedding ceremony or civil ceremony in the municipal office confers the legal title of marriage.

The *pedida* is held in the home of the young woman. Seeking advice of the elders within the family and among close friends is an integral part of the discussions. The invitees, along with the hopeful couple and the young man's parents, gather first at the young man's home and walk together to the young woman's home in a large group. The neighbors and community turn out in the street to watch the small parade of people and view the couple soon to be joined together.

At the young woman's house, a table has been set up where the parents of the intended couple discuss their children's decision to marry, talk about the roles of each one, and give advice on how young people should treat each other and the roles and obligations of each. The couple is seated at the head of the table. Typically, the man's family comments on the role of a wife: to care for the children, provide food for the family, to obey and respect her husband. The woman's family speaks about the role of a good husband: to provide for his wife, respect her, and treat her well. Others make comments and suggestions. When all has been said and a verbal agreement is reached, the couple is granted permission to marry. The two families share a celebratory meal.

BELOW: Photo by Michel de la Sabelier. Ixil elders play an important role in caring for and educating their grandchildren.

A church wedding usually follows several months later, with sufficient time for elaborate preparations and expenses on the part of both families. On the appointed day, the marriage ceremony commences at the man's family home, where the couple and family wait inside for the assembly of friends and the presiding priest, pastor, justice of the peace, or lawyer to arrive. Everyone walks together, surrounding the couple, to the site of the ceremony. The Ixil bride wears a *huipil* woven especially for the event, often draped by a woven white veil. The groom dons white pants, the traditional woven red jacket, and a palm-fiber hat. Wedding bands are not exchanged in a traditional Ixil marriage.

When the wedding ceremony is completed, the newlyweds are literally showered with blessings for a prosperous life, as papier-mâché bells filled with maize, beans, and rice rain down on the happy couple. The wedding party walks through the town or village to the groom's home, where a wedding feast is waiting. Huge pots of rice, meat, tamales, and hundreds of tortillas feed the multitudes. Gifts are presented to the newlyweds, small things they will need to start their life together in their new home, including a new shawl from the sisters or mother of the bride, which will be used to wrap and carry the firstborn child.

BIRTH TRADITIONS IN AN IXIL FAMILY

Traditional preparations to welcome a new child begin as the woman approaches her time to deliver. The husband and parents of the pregnant couple, the *abuelos* ("grandparents," also interpreted as "forbearers"), attend to the small needs of the expectant mother. Community "godparents" (*padrinos*) for the newborn are chosen. A local midwife is consulted and contracted to help with the delivery. A segment of traditional believers engage a Maya priest to conduct prayers for the health of the mother and infant. Pregnant women are peppered with precautionary old wives' tales.

The majority of Ixil women still give birth at home, unless a complication is anticipated or one arises during labor, in which case every effort is made to transport the ailing woman to the nearest community health post, or *Puesto de Salud*. On the day of delivery, the pregnant woman's mother (*abuela* to the newborn), and sometimes either the mother-in-law and/or a midwife, take charge of the birth preparations and delivery. A reed mat (*petate*) covered with a clean cloth is placed near the hearth and a pot of water set to boil. When labor has advanced, the birth assistants support the woman to a squatting position, and the newborn's grandmother (or attending midwife) receives the infant. The umbilical cord is cut with a sterilized knife or scissors and tied with cotton thread.

Immediately following the birth, the assistants wait for the placenta to be expelled; to expedite this process, hot chili peppers may be burned on the fire to precipitate sneezing and final contractions to release the afterbirth, which is customarily burned on the hearth. The new mother rests with a drink of sweet maize *atol* and is refreshed with a cleansing of natural soap, *jaboncillo*, made from the sap of a local tree called *Tzoo*, or *Tzojon*. The newborn is swaddled in wraps woven by a family member. On the next day, mother and child are treated to an herbal bath in the traditional sauna (*temascal*), while the *abuela* administers a special massage to her daughter and new grandson or granddaughter. Finally, a joyous announcement of the birth goes out to the extended family and neighbors, who gather at the house for the celebration with small gifts and celebratory *tamales* or *b'oxb'ol*.

Not so long ago, the Ixil mother and newborn baby received the extended family's attentive nurturing for forty days after the birth. The husband's job was to keep the hearth stoked and provide for extra resources in an emergency. Sisters and *abuelas* prepared hearty meals and kept the home safe from "lurking" dangers; for example, traditional superstition holds that evil spirits can be transmitted through the medium of domestic animals and common metal objects, such as forks and machetes. Today, the recovery period has shrunk to only a few days, and not many women pay attention to such old wives' tales. Ixil women tell me that they return to regular routines soon after delivery, but that many traditional birth practices and precautions do help save lives.

I interviewed an Ixil midwife to understand how the teachings of this ancient profession are reinforced by modern practices today to reduce maternal and infant mortality. Now in her fifties, this Cotzal community midwife related how she was "called" to join the profession through a recurrent dream: "Someone was handing me a book on how to be a midwife.

ABOVE: Ixil Maya children are treasured by their parents and the extended community.

When the same dream came to me again, I realized that it was a sign." At the age of eighteen, she entered into an apprenticeship with her mother-in-law. Traditional midwives observe and assist community elders for several years before they are ready to work on their own.

Several years ago, this midwife attended a Ministry of Health course for midwives and obtained her official certification. The cost for her services is Q25 for an assisted delivery, including prenatal and postnatal care. Generally, she is contacted three months into a pregnancy, and visits the pregnant woman every other month to palpate the belly, offer advice on personal hygiene and nutrition, and suggest activities the pregnant woman should avoid. When the time approaches for delivery, the midwife determines if the baby is in the correct position; if not, she will attempt to reposition the baby through gentle manipulation or recommend that the pregnant woman go to the hospital in Nebaj for delivery. Her advice to pregnant women: "Go to the *Puesto de Salud* to get vitamins, eat lots of vegetables and greens, and never buy medicines without a doctor's prescription. Go to the clinic or hospital if the baby is in a breech position or after twelve hours of labor. Following delivery, drink lots of water to cleanse the body, and rest for ten days."

CONTINUITY AND CHANGE IN COTZAL WEAVING

The common Cotzal *huipil* is created in three rectangular panels, densely adorned with miniature figures and symbols in horizontal ranges. A love of color harmony shines through the dominant tones of either blues and greens or reds and pinks in the common *huipil*. Elegantly pleated and tucked into a dark-colored wraparound skirt (*corte*), the boxy blouse is tidily secured with a woven belt (*cinta*). In the past, the two-meter-long belt was adorned with huge multicolored pom-poms knotted at the waist in front, but these extra flourishes have largely disappeared from common use. Similarly, few women in Cotzal today tie their hair up with the traditional red hair ribbon (also called *cinta*) that formerly ringed their head like a regal halo. A bold striped shawl, in reds, greens, and black, with heavily brocaded weaving on both ends, completes the *traje* of Cotzal.

Men in Cotzal, like those in Nebaj and Chajul, have all but abandoned the costume of their grandfathers for Western-style clothing. On formal occasions, however, Cotzal men still don a traditional outfit, consisting of a woven red jacket (*saco*) with black embroidery on the sleeves, white pants, and woven belt, plus the ubiquitous palm-fiber hat.

As in Nebaj and Chajul, Cotzal backstrap loom weaving has seen significant evolution in use of color and style of design within recent generations. The expanding market in cotton and acrylic threads, Ladino and Western influence, increased interregional travel and trade, and greater freedom of artistic expression contribute to a growing diversity of Cotzal weaving today. Although the cost in time and materials for the traditional *huipil* edges up every year, a majority of Cotzal women still continue to weave their own *huipiles* and *rebozos* as a matter of strong cultural pride and identity. For many, an hour or two of daily weaving may lead to a bit of much-needed cash if they can manage to sell a new or used piece of their handicraft.

Formerly white, the solid background color of the Cotzal *huipil* today spans the whole color spectrum. Weft-faced designs now cover the entire blouse, including the side sleeve panels, in an intricate and integrated tapestry. Venerable older women of Cotzal recall weaving their first *huipiles* from natural cotton that they spun and dyed themselves. They describe picking the seeds and twigs from the raw, harvested cotton, hand-carding the fibers, and then rolling the fibers in hands lightly coated with honey to bind the fibers. After twisting and spinning the cotton fibers with a weighted whorl, the threads were hung in the sun to dry. They produced their own natural dyes: red hues from flowers or seeds of the *achiote* plant (*Bixa orellana*), greens from leaves and vegetables, oranges from carrots, onions, and oranges, and blues from the native indigo plant. The

SO, I STARTED WEAVING . . .

This humble tale of learning to weave, shared by Teresa, an accomplished weaver in Cotzal, offers comfort and encouragement for all beginning weavers:

I started weaving because I didn't like the huipiles *that my mother gave me to wear. They were very simple and didn't have animal figures, only figures representing the wind and the four cardinal points embroidered on the collar. I wanted a beautiful* huipil, *and [I knew] that I would have to weave it myself. So, I started weaving, watching my mother. The first* huipil *I wove embarrassed me. The birds didn't have tails or beaks, and the designs on one side of the* huipil *were upside-down. The sleeves were a bit better [than the center panel], because I did those after I had learned my mistakes. But the sleeves never really fit with the body of the* huipil. *My mother was critical of my work, but she had invested money in the thread, so I had to wear my first* huipil. *I was so embarrassed, but then I learned to weave better quickly!*

quantity of raw cotton needed to weave a *huipil* cost about Q5 sixty years ago.

Cotzal weavers today enjoy access to a dizzying array of colors and manufactured threads, but the prices of these (mostly imported) threads have skyrocketed. The raw material cost of a *huipil* today ranges from Q100 to Q200, depending upon the quality of cotton and intricacy of design. A new Cotzal *huipil* in the market or from an expert weaver sells for Q500 to Q2,500; however, weavers barely recoup the cost of the thread in the discounted sale of a used blouse or shawl.

Despite recent evolution in colors and style, the Cotzal *huipil* perpetuates an ancient Ixil celebration of the life-giving forces and rhythms of the sacred universe. The collar opening and design represent the Creator, at once the sun and the Maize God, *El Corazón de Cielo* ("Heart of the Sky"). Four emblems embroidered around the collar carry a host of sacred meanings according to Cotzal weavers: the four cardinal and sacred dimensions of the universe, the four phases of the moon, and supernatural spirits associated with sunrise, sunset, wind, and rain. A veritable necklace of sacred emblems is bound together with a thickly embroidered band of multicolored leaf motifs, described by some as the new growth of "pine blossoms." One weaver interpreted this motif to represent the pine resin incense (*pom*), which is burned at sacred Maya ceremonies and the fragrant pine boughs and needles that commonly carpet the area surrounding the traditional altar.

The body of the Cotzal *huipil* is intricately populated with symbolic imagery of the sacred calendar and mythologies. Translation of weaving vocabulary varies among weavers, and knowledge of older sacred traditions may be fading with the younger generations. Several older Cotzal women offered the following consistent interpretations of common weaving patterns and icons: The chevron pattern represents the wind and air associated with the sacred calendar daygod, *Iq'*. Bird figures symbolize nature, wealth, and the daygod, *Tz'ikin*. Symbols for maize, sugarcane, and the color green are associated with authority and the daygod, *Hunaapu*. The zigzag pattern represents both the sacred mountains and lightning. The triangle symbolizes the Creation of the universe and the three sacred hearthstones placed in the night sky by the primordial gods.

Colors also have their significance: red, the color the rising sun, east, blood of sacrifice, and red maize; white, the color of the light of day, north, white maize, and purity; black, the color of the earth, darkness, west, and black or blue maize; yellow, the color of yellow maize, fire, south, and human skin. I find it fascinating to "read" a *huipil* with its weaver, and I encourage textile-loving visitors to do the same.

Reviving the Double-Headed Eagle Design

While I was talking with Cotzal weavers about tradition and change, I learned about an older *huipil* design featuring an elaborate double-headed eagle pattern that had completely disappeared from local weaving vernacular. A respected older weaver, Doña Catarina, spoke passionately about learning to weave

Cotzal master weaver, Doña Catarina, shares design and technique with the next generation.

ABOVE: Lovingly preserved fragments of a 100-year old huipil from Cotzal provide the template for an ambitious revival of the "double-headed eagle" (Kot) design.

as a child, and about the loss of many old and sacred weaving traditions of the culture. She expressed a passionate desire to revive several older *huipil* designs she had learned as a child from her grandmother.

The mythical double-headed eagle, referred to as *Kot,* figures prominently in Ixil oral tradition. Iconic symbols of the eagle appear in several forms of Ixil material culture today, most notably in the *huipiles* and on carved wooden doors and shutters of Chajul. Maya myths and ancient artifacts are populated with powerful bird imagery. In the Creation myth, the primordial gods dispatch the raptor, *Xecotcovac,* to pluck out the eyes of a failed attempt to forge humans out of wood, because the beings lacked heart and humility. The ancient Maya "tree of life," a symbol of the universe, frequently depicted a bird in the upper branches. The Ixil legend of the *Kot* represents a local fusion of Maya symbolism. Recounted and embellished by generations of Ixil grandparents, it was told to me like this:

When the gods created humans, they sent a huge double-headed raptor to protect them from danger and predators. However, once the raptor had devoured all the jaguars and other enemies of Man, the giant bird turned to devouring humans. To disguise and protect themselves, humans started carrying large baskets or heavy sticks on their heads as they went to and from their fields. The ravages of the raptor did not stop until one day it plucked up a man carrying an especially heavy load on his head. By the time the giant bird reached its nest on the top of a distant bald rock, it was so weak from exhaustion that the man was able to kill it. From the blood of the Kot sprang an eagle and a snake, both good and evil.

Upon hearing this gruesome tale, I wondered out loud why Ixil women would want the *Kot* emblazoned on their blouses. I was told that the double-headed eagle has come to symbolize the protective power of the gods, and the victory of good over evil.

I joined in the enthusiasm of Cotzal weavers to revive the *Kot* design and agreed to underwrite the minimal costs of an apprenticeship for twelve young weavers with Doña Catarina. The details were finalized effortlessly by email: high-quality thread matching the ancient colors was purchased, and the weavers met together once a week for the better part of a year to learn the design and associated weaving techniques. When the Kot *huipiles* were nearing completion, I returned to celebrate their accomplishments. Many of the women expressed gratitude for the opportunity to study with Doña Catarina.

"For years now," Doña Catarina recounted, "I have been searching, even in the *aldeas*, for evidence of the *Kot* design woven by my grandmother, but I have not found a single one." She took her thick long hair braid in her hands, and pointing to the gray hair creeping in, explained that she was getting old now and did not want her grandmother's designs to die with her. Doña Catarina gingerly unwrapped a threadbare scrap of an old *huipil* woven from homespun cotton with natural dyes. She spread the delicate piece next to one of the newly woven replicas. We crowded around this ancient remnant, grateful for its existence and the initiative of Doña Catarina to resurrect this piece of Cotzal's cultural heritage. When the fascinating and heartwarming morning of sharing came to a close, we cemented our bonds of friendship over a delicious lunch of spicy Cotzal *caldo de rez* (beef soup). We identified our next project together: to revive another older ceremonial *huipil* design in the lush blues and greens of the surrounding mountains and *milpas*.

Cotzal Women's Weaving Cooperative

Cooperativa Tejidos Cotzal was organized in March of 1997 to assist war widows in generating income. The cooperative is now open to any weaver who wants to participate. It works to develop and sell new products at Guatemalan tourist fairs and artisanal exhibitions for export. Pedro Marroquín Chamay, an artistic and entrepreneurial young man who grew up in Cotzal, manages the cooperative. The cooperative sells its products through several outlets in the United States, Antigua, and Quetzaltenango, and is always eager for more contacts to sell abroad. The cooperative store is located on the street behind the main market in downtown Cotzal.

Cotzal weavers are now offering an appealing two-day package of eco-cultural tourism for groups of four to six persons for Q75–100 per person. For information about this brief immersion in Cotzal's local culture and scenic beauty, contact:

www.TejidosCotzal.org
Telephone: (502) 4621-9725
Email: TejidosCotzal@gmail.com
Co-op Manager: Pedro Marroquín Chamay
Telephone: (502) 5877-2821
or Email: Marroquin393@hotmail.com

BELOW: Photo by Beth Lentz. Cotzal woman in ceremonial dress (traje) with rods and battens of the back-strap loom acquired as a young girl and assiduously maintained for a lifetime of weaving.

The Ixil region is blessed with the year-round abundance of water.

COOLING OFF IN COTZAL'S WATERFALLS AND SWIMMING HOLES

The mountainous geography and plentiful rainfall in this region translate into glorious waterfalls, swimming holes, and year-round rivers that nourish the villages and the crops. In the lower, steamier altitudes of Cotzal, several of these cooling-off spots are a destination for the local population and eco-adventurers alike.

Chamul River Swimming Hole is a ten-minute walk from the town center of Cotzal, along the road to Nebaj. This bathing spot is said to be an important part of a Cotzal childhood, although accumulating trash along the banks would make me hesitate to take a dip. A walk along the river's edge is nevertheless delightful, and a year-round stream constantly refreshes the water of the natural swimming hole. If one is seeking a more private dip, follow the trail along the river 500 meters upstream to the *Pool of the Priest*, fed by a small waterfall.

Santa Avelina Waterfall lies about 1 kilometer, or a twenty-minute walk, from the center of Santa Avelina (a thirty-minute drive from the town of Cotzal). These falls are the largest in the municipality, about 150 meters, and the most frequently visited. The charge to visit is Q5. It is refreshing to wade or swim in the cold water, or to simply enjoy the mist from the cascade. These falls are particularly

ABOVE: From December to March, the Ixil coffee crop is hand-picked, hand-processed, and sun dried to reduce moisture content to about 10% before sold to the Maya Ixil cooperative or other traders

popular during Easter week (*Semana Santa*), when Cotzal families flock here with picnics, and local vendors offer snacks, ice cream, and drinks.

Chichel Waterfall is stunning and more remote, about 10 kilometers from the town of Cotzal. At Vichibala, the road to Chichel branches north. The waterfall is a forty-five-minute walk from Vichibala, or twenty minutes from the village center in Chichel. Follow the road to the soccer field in Chichel and ask any villager for directions. Springs in Chajul feed the Chichel waterfall, which careens over the rocks from a height of 100 meters. A series of sunlit pools below the falls beckon intrepid bathers. The area around the waterfall is tranquil and shaded by trees that play host to a variety of birdlife and colorful bromeliades (a variety of epiphyte or "air plant" that lives on another tree or plant and derives water and nutrients from the air, rain, and soil or surrounding organic matter). The local landowner charges an enjoyment fee of Q5 per person, and has provided several picnic tables and cookout pits.

IXIL GOLD: CERTIFIED FAIR TRADE ORGANIC COFFEE IN SANTA AVELINA

From the onset of Guatemala's "coffee boom" in the late 1870s through the mid-twentieth century, the bulk of the country's largest export crop was produced on large foreign or Ladino-owned plantations. National land reform and labor mandates passed during the term of President Barrios (1873–85) effectively opened huge tracts of indigenous lands and delivered the cheap indigenous labor that was required to establish Guatemala as a major world producer of *Arabica* coffee. The warmer and lower altitudes of Ixil country were invaded by adventuring coffee barons at this time. Many Ixil smallholders also planted small plots of coffee trees and sold their harvest to nearby plantation owners or other middlemen.

Prices for Guatemalan coffee beans rose with robust world demand, reaching US $168 per 100 pounds for *Arabica* in 1986. The following year, however, world prices plummeted to US $85, reacting to oversupply coupled with an economic downturn among coffee-consuming countries. The crisis translated into the ruin of many Guatemalan coffee plantation owners and economic panic for smallholder coffee farmers. At the end of the civil war, many communities of indigenous farmers reestablished agricultural cooperatives to eliminate middlemen. World coffee prices, however, remained depressed into the 1990s, forcing coffee cooperatives to reassess their options. The two largest Ixil coffee cooperatives, the *Asociación Chajulense* and the *Cooperativa Integral de Comercialización Maya Ixil*, decided to focus on organic coffee. This turned out to be a smart strategic decision. Today the two cooperatives are members of the Federation of Organic Coffee Producers of Guatemala and are proud to boast that their members' shade-grown, organic coffee receives top price on the world market.

I met with Andrés Cruz Martínez, manager of the Ixil Maya Cooperative. The cooperative is headquartered in Santa Avelina, 10 kilometers (a half-hour drive) from Cotzal's municipal capital. A delicious steaming cup of freshly roasted coffee greeted me upon arrival. The cooperative's warehouse hummed with activity, as the early harvest (December through May) was weighed, processed, and bagged for export. Andrés recounted the story of the cooperative's humble beginnings, with twenty-eight members and exports of only 560 *quintales* (56,000 pounds). Today the cooperative has grown to 135 certified organic coffee growers and processes 2,500 *quintales* (250,000 pounds) for export. In 2007, Ixil Maya sold for US $180/100 pounds—a premium of 65 percent over the average world price for nonorganic coffee! The cooperative contracts most of its produce with a roaster from San Diego, California, but is constantly scouting for discriminating coffee importers who recognize both quality and the cooperative's commitment to

BELOW: 100 pounds of ripe red coffee berries yield about 20 pounds of "green" beans.

improving the lives of Ixil coffee farmers.

Sixty percent of Cotzal's small farmers grow some coffee, but only a portion qualifies as high quality and certifiably organic. To produce the best quality requires a minimum three-year investment in planting, natural fertilizing, pruning, and shading the young coffee trees before they begin to produce. The trees produce for up to eight years before they must to be uprooted and replaced with new seedlings. Farmers must pick the coffee cherries at the peak of their ripening, remove the fruit pulp from the seed or bean, and wash and then dry them slowly in the sun. Since it rains periodically even in the "dry season" (November to May), the coffee harvest must be assiduously tended on patios, tarps, or any convenient flat area, to reduce the moisture content to 12–15 percent. Too little drying results in mildew and too much leads to cracking. The harvest of ripening coffee cherries and their processing at home continues over several months. Smallholders hand-sort the dried beans for uniformity and then deliver their beans to the cooperative for quality control and weighing. The success of the cooperative depends on all of the members doing their utmost to uphold quality standards. In order to sustain the highest quality, the cooperative provides regular workshops to its members and those who want to join.

Each year, organizations that certify organic coffee production visit Santa Avelina to inspect the growers and the processing operation. They test a minimum of 30 percent of terrain where cooperative coffee is produced, conducting inspections on randomly selected stands of coffee. Organic certification costs a whopping US $3,000 a year! If one member does not have proper paperwork or has used chemicals, the entire cooperative suffers. In 2004, the Ixil Maya Cooperative received its Fair Trade certification, granted to democratically organized farmer organizations who agree to uphold a number of guiding fair trade principles. These principles include a guaranteed minimum floor price and premiums for certified organic produce, commitment to social justice and community development, and promotion of environmentally sustainable practices.

Producing for the cooperative requires investment, knowledge, and vigilance, and is not easy for its members. But, according to Andrés Cruz Martínez, it means better living standards for Ixil farmers:

> *There are many benefits to being a member in the cooperative. I have already seen the changes in the lives of some of our members. Before, they could not buy clothes for their children or shoes to go to school. Some kids didn't go to school due to the costs. When their kids were sick, they couldn't buy medicine, but today, they are doing all of these things.*

Strong demand and premium prices for their coffee have enabled the Ixil Maya Cooperative to expand membership and services. The cooperative launched a bakery project for women, computer training for members and their families, and promotion of wood-saving stoves.

Visitors interested in learning more about organic coffee production and the Ixil Maya Cooperative are encouraged to contact the manager in advance of a visit.

Cooperativa Integral de Comercialización Maya Ixil
Telephone : (502) 7861-2846 or 7861-2847
Email for Cooperative Manager, Andrés Cruz Martínez: andrespmayaixil@yahoo.com

MAGUEY: THE FIBER OF COMMERCE

Towering, tough, and thriving for up to a hundred years, the native maguey plant (also known as the Century Plant and agave) has long been a mainstay of Cotzal's economy for the production of rope, bags, nets, and hammocks. The thorny succulent is particularly suited to arid conditions and thrives even on marginal soils across Central America. The Aztecs and Maya milked sweet agave sap for a variety of medical uses, including a fermented libation called *pulque*. Even though synthetic bags have made inroads into the market for maguey, many Cotzal families still grow a few plants as a cash

BELOW: An ancient utilitarian crop, maguey fiber extraction and weaving of loose net produce bags has been a mainstay of the Cotzal economy – a better alternative than plastic.

crop. The stretchy net maguey bags (*red*) secure baskets of produce all over Guatemala and are still essential to indigenous commerce. Cotzal's equivalent of "Miss America," elected during the municipality's annual fiesta, is crowned the *Flor de Maguey*.

This traditional craft is painstaking and time-consuming. When the barbed, cactus-like maguey leaves reach 1 to 2 meters in length, they are hacked off by machete. Farmers then burn the leathery leaf to remove the exterior skin, setting the pulpy interior to dry out in the sun. The dried, fibrous structure is beaten with a wooden mallet and hand-separated into individual strands, and then washed and dried once more. The rough sinews are then coaxed into great lengths of rugged brown twine by feeding the fibers into two spinning wheels set apart by 20 to 30 meters. The finished twine is sold in bulk or worked locally into rope and every shape and size of utilitarian bag. Recently, textile designers have rediscovered maguey, elevating the utilitarian fiber into fashion accessories and breathing new life into artisanal maguey production in Cotzal. Fiber artist and textile historian Kathryn Rousso offers a fascinating, in-depth examination of the history and culture of maguey in Mexico and Guatemala in her recent book, *Maguey Journey: Discovering Textiles in Guatemala* (2010).

DEVELOPMENT IN THE COTZAL RIVER VALLEY: THE CASE OF FINCA SAN FRANCISCO

Directions from San Juan Cotzal to Finca San Francisco.
From Cotzal center, a good road leads through San Felipe Chenla, Vichibalá, Santa Avelina, and Finca San Francisco. This is the most heavily populated area of Cotzal, among the rolling hills and fertile Chamal and Cotzal river valleys that wend an easterly route. Traditional Ixil agriculture of maize, beans, squash, and the spiky maguey mix with smallholder coffee, tomatoes, avocados, and snow peas bound for export. With a steady drop in altitude, sultry heat and humidity rise; insulating adobe-brick homes give way to light and airy wood-slat (*tablones*) construction; banana, mango, avocado, and citrus trees shade family compounds. Beyond Santa Avelina (17 km from the *cabecera*), the road

winds downhill another 8 kilometers, onto the extensive property of Finca San Francisco, straddling the Cotzal River. Several ancient Ixil centers were located on the banks of this river; to my knowledge, however, none have been preserved, and the sites are inaccessible to casual visitors. The river swirls past the working headquarters of Finca San Francisco and swerves northward. At that juncture, the road forks left to the far northeastern aldeas of Cotzal and right, to the mountaintop villages of Buenos Aires and Pamaxan and the southeastern mountain communities that border on Uspantán and Cunén.

Finca San Francisco: History and Recent Developments

Italian descendant and former labor recruiter, Pedro Brol, laid eyes upon the fertile lands of the Cotzal River valley in the last decade of the nineteenth century. Brol moved quickly to obtain a large jigsaw-puzzle piece of land in eastern Cotzal from the National Land Registry in 1903. With friends and growing influence, Brol accumulated additional acreage in Cotzal and neighboring Uspantán, transforming the lush tropical forest into one of the largest and most productive coffee plantations in all of Guatemala. At its height, Finca San Francisco commanded 6,800 hectares, employing several thousand seasonal workers for the annual coffee harvest, and exporting upwards of 100,000 *quintales* of green coffee. Since the civil war and the weakening of world coffee prices, Finca owners have reportedly sold a number of parcels to their workers, while other pieces are the subject of ongoing land disputes. The current extent of their land ownership is unclear, but Finca San Francisco continues to command a strategic section of the Cotzal River valley and to harvest a fertile cauldron of coffee plantation in the valley bottom and surrounding hillsides.

For the last century, Finca San Francisco marked the end of the road in eastern Cotzal. Daily bus service from the *cabecera* unloaded and reloaded passengers at the Finca gates. Unlike many other commercial coffee farms in Guatemala, Finca San Francisco did not encourage visitors; transiting through Finca property by foot or vehicle, was controlled by armed guards until mid-2011.

In 2008, with coffee revenues declining, Finca San Francisco partnered with the Italian energy conglomerate, ENEL, to build a hydroelectric dam on the Cotzal River and sections of Finca property. This development opened a new chapter in the historically tense relationship between Ixil communities, the Finca, the Cotzal mayor (*alcalde*), and government officials. Ixil leaders were aware of the graft that had quietly greased the wheels of land and resource concessions in northern Chajul. They had witnessed the contentious development of the Xak'b'al hydroelectric dam on Finca La Perla lands long disputed by the communities of Ilom and Sotz'il.

In January 2011, when the mayor of Cotzal had repeatedly ignored community petitions for information about the future Cotzal dam, Ixil representatives blockaded the main road between the municipal capital and the Finca at San Felipe Chenla and refused to allow the construction equipment of ENEL or the Finca San Francisco to pass. Citing the constitutional rights of indigenous communities to be consulted and to approve development projects within their districts, Ixil representatives demanded full disclosure of the hydroelectric project from the government and the mayor of Cotzal; the permanent opening of a public road through the Finca San Francisco; and direct negotiations with ENEL for reparations, as well as social and economic investments in the affected Cotzal communities. For several months, tensions escalated as Ixil communities held firm in the face of pressure from as high up as the president of Guatemala, who threatened to brand them as "terrorists" and to dispatch the army to open the road.

At the time of my most recent visit to Cotzal in mid-2011, a potentially confrontational situation had fortunately been defused. The blockade had been

Coffee plantation of Finca San Francisco blankets all but the steepest slopes and hilltops of the ancient Cotzal cloud forest.

lifted. Direct negotiations were under way between Ixil community representatives, ENEL, the Finca, and the government to address community questions and demands. The evolution of these discussions is worth watching, and not only for the future of Ixil community relations and economic development in the Cotzal River valley. A new model of consensual dialogue between the government, national and multinational investors, and indigenous communities throughout Guatemala is needed in order to meet the pressing challenges of social and economic development in a progressive and equitable manner.

The road through Finca San Francisco has been opened for through traffic, but Finca guards do not encourage visitors to linger on plantation property. For those of us who depend on a cup of Guatemalan coffee to get us going in the morning, even a glimpse of this coffee operation in full swing is a reminder of the labor- and land-intensive costs of this prized commodity. Finca coffee cannot compete in price with certified organic production of Ixil coffee cooperatives, but its sheer volume and a well-oiled infrastructure make it a formidable player among Guatemalan exporters. The nucleus of Finca operations consists of a cluster of administrative buildings, coffee-depulping stations, drying platforms, and storage warehouses on the southern bank of the Cotzal River. A whitewashed church and a half-dozen canteens and small stores cater to permanent staff and the seasonal influx of laborers who lodge in rustic bunkhouses or commute daily from nearby towns and villages during coffee harvest season.

Do not miss an opportunity to drive or hike up the road from Finca San Francisco to Buenos Aires on the mountaintop above. The impressive centennial plantation envelops the surrounding valley slopes in an undulating canopy of shade trees and dark-leafed Arabica coffee that thrive in the dappled sunlight. Here and there, a venerable Ceiba, tufted bamboo, graceful tree ferns, and tropical hardwoods grace a most majestic landscape. When the coffee is in bloom, the heady fragrance is intoxicating. As the berries ripen, the thickly planted slopes hum with harvesters for several months, each day selecting the reddest fruit and hauling bulging sacks of produce to collecting points. Coffee pickers earn about Q80 (US $10) per 100 pounds of berries, representing one to two days' labor. Compare this to the price of two cappuccinos in Paris or New York!

BELOW: Hydroelectric dam construction has proven extremely contentious in Guatemala, often planned without local participation or approval and lacking mitigation of long-term economic and social impact on affected communities.

NAVIGATING THE SKYLINE FRONTIER IN SOUTHEASTERN COTZAL

Beyond the upper slopes of the Finca, the road deteriorates and zigzags up the last 2 to 3 kilometers to the mountain's crest. Daily life at the top of this arduous climb is for the truly hearty and valiant pioneers who have staked out farmland on some of the steepest and most marginal land in Cotzal. Pickup trucks and mules provision these remote communities. As its name suggests, the climate of the picturesque Buenos Aires is refreshingly cool and dry compared to the sultry valley below. The veranda of the new schoolhouse in town commands a spectacular view of the surrounding mountaintops. A local schoolteacher informed me that the villagers could arrange overnight accommodations for visitors at the schoolhouse or in village homes. From Buenos Aires, the return trip through Finca San Francisco to municipal capital of Cotzal is easily two hours by car, longer by bus, and best completed during daylight hours. A decision to continue in a southerly loop back to Cotzal requires a commitment of three to four hours by four-wheel-drive vehicle.

Rudimentary roads connect Buenos Aires to Villa Hortensia Antigua, Villa Hortensia II, and Villa Hortensia I, named by former plantation owners for the blue hydrangea flower. The terrain varies from rugged to ragged, from crest to gully. Even though the roads have improved somewhat in recent years, it is best not to attempt this particular stretch without a horse or a four-wheel-drive vehicle. Hearty hikers and accustomed Ixil villagers, no doubt, can take best advantage of the magnificent scenery. Between the thinly forested ridges at 2,000 meters (6,500 feet) and rocky streambeds 300 meters below, indigenous families carve out a meager living in the gentler folds and plateaus of this arduous landscape. Views from the skyline drive reveal the alarming extent to which the tropical forests have disappeared, exacerbating soil depletion and erosion. In March and April, before the onset of the rainy season, the hillsides are on fire, with farmers burning off weeds and crop residues before sowing maize. Chain saws and axes gradually gnaw into the remaining tree cover to clear new fields. There is little evidence that farmers practice anti-erosion measures; with every rainy season, more soil washes down the slopes and crop yields decline on these fragile lands. Within a few years, farmers are forced to apply fertilizers or to clear new land. It is a vicious cycle, all too common in Central America.

Villa Hortensia II and Cueva del Rey (Cave of the King)

Unless one is planning an all-day loop drive through Finca San Francisco, the shorter route to Villa Hortensia II is directly south from the municipal capital through La Esperanza and then east along the southwestern corridor through Belén, Nama, Cajixay, and Tzinimchim. A two-day, round-trip hike from Santa Avelina to Villa Hortensia II (consult the *Guía De Senderismo* or a local guide) leads past waterfalls alongside the rutted road to Chisis, by shortcuts and rugged climbing to the mountaintop village of Quisis, then down into Villa Hortensia II. Either way, the scenery is breathtaking, as one travels through intensely cropped hills and valleys and over high mountain ridges to finally drop precipitously down onto the plateau of Villa Hortensia II, and into the verdant river valley of the Rio Chipal.

I made this trip with friends in our trusty pickup truck, accompanied by U.S. Peace Corps volunteer Josh Kyller, who took advantage of the ride to stop in villages along the way and meet with local colleagues in their new initiative to promote market vegetable gardens. Having an open-bed truck always means having lots of passengers, local knowledge, and a chance to communicate to them how much we are enjoying our visit to their part of the world.

It is not hard to imagine why the Ixil Maya ancestors chose the location of Villa Hortensia II as a ceremonial and civic center. The geography offers clear

ABOVE: Villa Hortensia II sits atop the rubble of a pre-Hispanic Ixil settlement.

strategic advantages: a sweeping view to the rising sun, a protective ridge and a lookout to the west, freshwater spouting forth from the mountainside above, and the proximity of underground caverns. From the road cut above the town, recently widened by bulldozers, the natural setting of this ancient site is awe-inspiring; the only detraction is the unnatural grid of tiny streets imposed on this impressive promontory. Descending onto this elevated plateau, the road zigzags across mountain slopes recently cleared of trees for new maize fields.

Villa Hortensia II is literally built over the rubble of ancient temples and ritual ballcourts. Not surprisingly, the tidy village church sits squarely atop an ancient raised platform. All along the main street, the modest community has incorporated pre-Hispanic stones and walls into their dwellings. Town services include several tiny stores, a primary school, soccer field, and a cinder-block community center available for overnight lodging of visitors. At the east end of town, the road descends into the Rio Chipal valley, where a new bridge enables transport between this town and Villa Hortensia Antigua, Buenos Aires, and Finca San Francisco.

CUEVA DEL REY (CAVE OF THE KING)

For the ancient Maya, caves represented sacred gates to the Underworld, Xib'alb'a ("Place of Fear"), where primordial battles between life and death were waged and won to bring light into a new universe, and portals for communication with godly spirits. Caves and underground streams riddle the geography of Mesoamerica, characterized by a porous limestone base that dissolves to form underground caves and sinkholes (*cenotes*). The ancient Maya had no shortage of caves, where their divine leaders and priests erected altars to their gods and to their earliest ancestors from a great city in the east, referred to in the *Popul Vuh* as "Tulán Zuyua, Seven Caves, Seven Canyons."[92]

The Cueva del Rey is located on communal land in Villa Hortensia II. My companions and I intercepted the assistant mayor on his way home for lunch and asked permission to visit the sacred cave. He was pleased to give us an update on local developments in town, and indicated the route to the cave on the other side of the town soccer field. The ten-minute hike to the cave traces a well-worn foot and mule path over the southern lip of the plateau. The rocky path descends into the ravine alongside a cascading stream that splashes into sparkling pools below. A thunderous waterfall 200 meters above drowns out conversation.

Although unmarked and obscured by dense vegetation, it is not too difficult to find the cave entrance, about 10 meters above the streambed and quite near the path. Ixil legend says that the spirit of the great K'iche' leader, Tecún Umán, traveled through this cave into the Yucatán. The rough mouth of the cave is about 1 meter wide and a half-meter high. Visitors are obliged to enter this sacred realm on their hands and knees. Thin rays of daylight illuminate the features of a large chamber inside, roughly 20 meters long and 10 meters wide, with a height of 10 meters in the center section. It is clear at once that this cave was used for prayer ceremonies; seven curving steps (perhaps a reference to the mystical number seven that reoccurs in so many instances in the *Popol Vuh*) descending to the cave floor are hewn into the cave wall. The cave glistens with stalactites, and a small stream trickles through large rocks on the cave floor. Melted candle wax from previous prayer ceremonies coats a natural altar on these rocks. A flashlight reveals several natural tunnels leading off the main chamber; a cursory investigation did not reveal other interior rooms.

Caves were once guarded community secrets and used regularly by Maya priests for traditional prayer ceremonies. Today, the ancient customs are definitely on the wane; nevertheless, visitors are encouraged to treat these sacred sites with great respect and to ask local landowners or someone "official" in advance of exploring these caves and other sacred sites. Other well-known sacred caves in Cotzal include: Cueva Cajixay in Cajixay, Cueva Xolko in Nama, and Cueva Vi'sivanko' (3 kilometers north by walking trail from Cotzal center).

ABOVE: Photo by Chris Percival. Cueva del Rey: entrance steps were carved out of limestone by Ixil ancestors.

BREAKING THE CYCLE OF POVERTY: AGROS INTERNATIONAL'S DEVELOPMENT MODEL

Along Cotzal's southwestern corridor, Villa Hortensia I, Cajixay, Belén, and San Nicolás are referred to as *Agroaldeas.* They have all benefited from the assistance of Seattle-based nonprofit organization, Agros International, to obtain loans and legal title to their land. Agros launched its activities in Guatemala in the early 1980s, focusing its support in the northern sections of Quiché and Huehuetenango. Today, Agros has integrated thirteen communities in the Ixil region into its development model, including seven in Cotzal, where the problem of landlessness is particularly acute. Their model is based on breaking the cycle of poverty, but they aptly define *poverty* as "broken relationships," getting at the heart of community disintegration, widespread distrust, and despair that characterized most Ixil villages following the civil war.

Agros assistance begins with a group of needy families committing to work together for the benefit of the entire community. An integrated program of community development, education and health care, and agricultural technical assistance continues for a period of seven to ten years, during which formerly landless families pay down their loans and achieve a degree of economic and social sustainability. A visit to one of the Agros villages illustrates how the consistent implementation of their model can significantly brighten the prospects of Ixil families within these communities.

Centro Tecnologico / Fundación Agros
Agroaldea El Paraíso
Nebaj
Telephone: (502) 5319-0849
Email: info@agrosixil.com
www.agros.org

BELOW: Reforestation and fruit tree cultivation are part of the Ixil school science curriculum.

Agro International's land redistribution and development model has given landless farmers a new lease on life and reduced economic migration to the cities and the U.S.

Agroaldea Villa Hortensia I

This is one of the former plantation properties of the Herrera Ibárgüen family. Due to poor soils and irregular terrain, it proved marginal for coffee production; plantation owners allocated land parcels to local Ixil families in exchange for four to five months' labor on the family's coastal sugar plantations. After being held by the Guerrilla Army of the Poor (EGP) for six months in 1977–78, Roberto Herrera Ibárgüen gave up his properties in Cotzal, a total of 2,633 hectares (approximately 6,500 acres) to the Guatemalan government in 1982.[93] The Guatemalan army burned Ixil houses and fields in and around Villa Hortensia I, forcing villagers to flee the area. Twelve years after the signing of the 1996 Peace Accords, landless families in Villa Hortensia I have finally received a loan for 688 acres from the government land trust agency, Fontierras, with the backing of Agros.

When I visited Villa Hortensia I in 2008, it appeared little more than a refugee camp in the middle of a rocky, thirsty, and barren landscape. Cotzal families that had resettled here after the war had nowhere else to go. Most existed on a bare survival diet, still dependent on annual migrations to plantations elsewhere to make ends meet. As of early 2011, this community is a changed and hopeful place. The community of 120 families is now three years into a fully participatory process to build basic infrastructure, preserve and enrich the soils, educate adults and children, and undertake productive and sustainable economic activities. According to the benchmarks of village progress, 83 percent of families now have access to water within 10 meters of their houses; 56 percent of school-age children are attending school; 44 percent of leadership positions in town are held by women; and families are now growing three nontraditional cash crops (snow peas, string beans, and potatoes) as well as raising some livestock. When I returned to the town, I scouted around for the children of Mario and María, who, according to Agros's annual village report, sell ice cream with a loan from the community credit program. The stalwart progress from three years ago to today lends new meaning to the village name *Hortensia,* as the hydrangea flower symbolizes "survival" among the Maya.

Agroaldea Belén

This beautiful, ridgetop village is another success story of the teamwork between Cotzal families and Agros. The community is easily accessible via a twenty-minute drive due south from the municipal capital or an uphill hike. I have passed through this verdant hamlet many times in the last few years, witnessing the backbreaking work of men and women clearing stones and stumps from the fields, replanting trees, and tending

BELOW: Families with tiny land holdings learn to semi-stall small ruminants, using manure and compost for natural fertilizer.

meticulously to a ripening crop of snow peas.

The Agros collaboration with twenty-five landless families began in 1998 with the acquisition of two small farms totaling 80 acres. After thirteen years of hard work and weekly Agros technical assistance, Belén celebrated its graduation from direct Agros support in mid-2011. The community has attained an impressive level of self-sufficiency and sustainability: 100 percent of villagers have access to water; 93 percent of school-age children attend school; women fill about half of the community leadership positions; five crops are grown for commercialization; and 83 percent of families own some form of livestock. Almost all of the villagers have repaid their land loans and finally have title to a piece of land that also supports their families.

Agros International builds partnerships between philanthropic communities (churches, schools, businesses, and families) and rural communities through their program called "Journey with a Village." It offers a mutual, long-term commitment of funders and farmers to secure a self-sustaining and self-governing community. It is a journey well worth taking!

BELOW: Cotzal school children join the fiesta parade.

RIGHT: Cotzal's annual Fiesta Titular engulfs the entire town and visitors from across the Ixil region in a week of merriment and relaxation.

CELEBRATING COTZAL'S ANNUAL FIESTA

When June 21 rolls around every year, the community of Cotzal turns out in carnival spirit to celebrate the birthday of their municipal patron, Saint John the Baptist. In fact, elaborate preparations for the weeklong fiesta begin months before the celebrations formally commence. Schools, businesses, and municipal services plan and construct elaborate floats for the town parade, selecting and pampering their candidate for the *Flor de Maguey* pageant ("Miss Maguey Flower"). Costumes and masks are rented and readied for street performances and traditional Maya dances. Storeowners and street vendors stock up with food and fireworks for the eager crowds, and families in and around the municipal capital prepare for the swarm of out-of-town guests and visitors who will crowd the town for the better part of a week. A local commission is appointed to ensure that the week's events roll out with more marimba, fanfare, and extravagance than the year before.

Cotzal's fiesta, like that of Nebaj (August 15) and Chajul (January 2) is a glorious, and sometimes riotous, display of traditional and modern culture and society in the region today. The *Flor de Maguey* procession launches the official festivities. Pickup trucks and wagons are transformed into a living tableau of some activity or theme that is central to San Juan Cotzal. Among the candidates for the *Flor* of Cotzal: a young woman spins maguey fibers into rope, another makes tortillas, someone weaves, and another sways to the

Photo by Beth Lentz. Cotzal's annual fiesta culminates in the fun-loving costumed *Convite*.

marimba. At the end of the day, the budding "Flowers" of the community reappear on stage in the community hall to showcase information about their host organization before a panel of judges. One lucky lady is chosen as the *Flor de Maguey*. The festivities offer many young Cotzal women a rare day in the sun.

People from miles around join the happy throngs that fill the streets of downtown Cotzal. Everyone has something to sell—steaming *tamales,* special breads, sticky cotton candy, sodas, sugarcane, and homemade popsicles. And most arrive with a few bills or coins. *Centavo* arcades siphon the spare change of parents so young boys can battle with the science-fiction monsters of the universe. Ixil elders hold tight to the hands of their youngest grandchildren, while the rest of the family takes off in different directions. The crowds can be intense; a side street or doorway of a shop presents a good perch to take a breather or get one's bearings.

A particular highlight of the fiesta is the *Convite,* an elaborate and costumed procession of dance, music, and performance in the best of Maya traditions. Historically, the actors in this allegorical drama were young men disguised as women. Today, however, children and young women often join the noisy throng, and their stunning masks and costumes represent both female and male characters—mythical, historical, and Disneyesque! The *Convite* engulfs the entire town of Cotzal in a day of drama, mystery, pranks, and good humor. With utmost secrecy, two partners have rented costumes weeks in advance and diligently practiced their dance steps. From dawn to dusk, they join other masked participants, parading from street to street, dancing to a mobile marimba and other musicians hired for the special event. At every designated stop around town, the colorful throng performs for about twenty minutes. In between sets of dancing, members of the *Convite* enter the homes of families who have invited them in for *tamales* and the traditional maize drink, *atol* (or other stronger drinks). No one knows who is behind the costume of the cartoon character, ancient Maya king, Spanish conquistador, pirate, politician, or devil. After the dancers complete a circuit of the town, they converge at the community hall for a final dance. Townspeople crowd in to watch. The suspense is finally lifted as the tired dancers take off their masks to reveal their identities.

Each day of the fiesta resounds with noise and lively activity. The crackle and boom of firecrackers send sparks and rockets into the midnight sky. Overhead, in the pitch-black Ixil night, brilliant constellations named for the Maya deities and the hearthstones of the Creation, cast a beneficent glow as Ixil children and parents surrender to weary sleep. The cock will crow before too many hours have passed, announcing that the Maize God has risen once again on a new Ixil day.

CHAPTER 7
Next Steps in the Ixil Journey

OPPOSITE: Ixil b'oxb'ol: steaming maize-stuffed mountain greens straight from the hearth.

I never imagined that an invitation from Ixil Maya weavers to visit their ancestral homeland would result in such an extraordinary journey. What began as a burgeoning interest in traditional textiles evolved into a veritable adventure

of discovery, through the mountains and villages, ancient caves and temple ruins, and crowded markets and bustling coffee cooperatives of the Ixil region. The journey soon extended into the homes of Ixil families, where I enjoyed lively conversations and rich storytelling traditions, deeply rooted in an ancient and enduring Maya culture. Little did I realize that having savored the luscious *b'oxb'ol*, freshly steamed from *milpa* maize and succulent greens, I would be smitten, as the village elders predicted, with the Ixil "homing instinct," and an unquenchable hunger for more. I have included the recipe for this uniquely Ixil dish (see Cooking Lessons in Chajul), complete with a pinch of ash from the Ixil hearth, so that other visitors may be infected with the same awe and affection that I feel for the Ixil Maya and their sacred mountains.

After five years of return visits to Nebaj, Chajul, and Cotzal, one phase of my own formative journey, like a cosmic cycle in the Maya calendar, has come full circle. And, like the clockwork of our lives, a new phase has already begun. Together with Ixil friends and enthusiasts, we have already mapped out some suggested next steps to help preserve the rich legacy of Ixil culture and to contribute to self-sustaining, locally planned development for the benefit of Ixil communities. In the Maya village tradition of mutual support, much can be accomplished with many heads and hands working toward common goals.

My own commitment is twofold: to encourage Guatemalan and international travelers to visit the Ixil region, and to help promote the organization of local information and resources ready to welcome and accommodate cultural, ecological, and volunteer tourists. As part of the research for this guidebook, my Ixil colleagues and I interviewed a number of Ixil individuals about their lives and professions, their experiences during the civil war, and their thoughts about recent trends and hopes for the future. One question we routinely asked was whether the interviewee thought that tourism could be a positive development for the region, and if so, what they believed the region had to offer visitors. I was struck by several common themes in the responses. On the one hand, they universally expressed pride in the cultural and natural *requezas* ("riches") of the Ixil homeland and traditions. On the other hand, many raised concerns, noting that visitors needed to be prepared for—and respectful of—what they would see and experience on their journey here.

I took these suggestions and concerns to heart, determined to write a different kind of guidebook. In addition to making a remote region more accessible to cultural, ecological, and volunteer tourists, it is my hope that this guidebook will offer visitors the opportunity to experience Ixil culture in a profoundly educational and personal way—to explore the natural beauty and diversity of the region, and to learn more about the local organizations that are working so hard to build a bright future for Ixil communities.

As this guidebook goes to press, I am already planning future journeys to Nebaj, Chajul, and Cotzal. With each passing year, I have observed new developments that are transforming the Ixil region. Change is arriving in the form of improved roads, cell phones, and television, through education, globalization, and necessity. In another decade, the face of the region will inevitably look different, raising important political, economic, and social questions for the Ixil communities and their leaders. One of the looming issues on the minds of many is what will happen to Ixil identity—language, religion, dress, family customs, and community rituals—the hearty fabric of Ixil culture that has enabled the Ixil Maya to survive the tests of time.

Conversations with Ixil friends and colleagues about this central question have generated a host of practical ideas to preserve the bountiful and ancient *requezas* of the Ixil region and culture. Some of these suggestions include:

- mapping the region with GPS and GIS tools in order to locate, mark, and relabel ancient sites and modern resources with their traditional Ixil names;
- developing multilingual signage, information, and guides to important Ixil cultural and historical sites;
- introducing a self-maintaining digital human-resource listing of organizations, professionals, and contacts in Nebaj, Chajul, and Cotzal;
- creating a physical, digital, and virtual repository of existing written resources pertaining to the region and its cultural artifacts (including photos of pieces in museums and other private collections), as well as recordings of traditional

ABOVE: Photo by Chris Percival. This guidebook offers visitors an opportunity to understand and experience the Ixil Maya culture and homeland in a deeply personal and respectful way.

- music and oral accounts of history, legends, and local lore;
- developing a reference to the ecological resources within the region, including an inventory of native flora and fauna within the myriad microclimates, along with a catalog of medicinal plants and other natural products that can be sustainably grown and harvested; and
- identifying voluntary, community-based mechanisms to solicit participation in these efforts and venues, encouraging visitors to share in the use and benefits of these cultural resources.

As a follow-on to this guidebook, I cannot imagine anything more rewarding than helping to promote this agenda.

This guidebook will be available in Spanish and e-book versions in 2013. For more information, please see the website for this guide and future Ixil explorations: www.GuatemalaIxilJourney.org.

APPENDIX 1: CALENDAR OF FIESTAS IN THE IXIL REGION

DECEMBER 31–JANUARY 1

Entrega de Varas Edilicias (Election of Communal Authorities). On December 31, newly elected communal authorities in the *aldeas* of Nebaj, Chajul, and Cotzal adorn their homes with palm and pine branches and invite neighbors and family members to a traditional prayer ceremony, asking for blessings on the responsibilities being invested in them and their office. At 6:00 a.m. on the morning of January 1, the leaders convene at the local municipal offices for a swearing-in ceremony with the elected mayor (*alcalde*) during the morning; firecrackers and celebrations follow this event.

JANUARY 2–6

Feria Titular de Chajul (Patron Saint's Festival of San Gaspar Chajul). The *cofradía* of Saint Gaspar Rey (one of the three "Kings of the Magi") parades King Gaspar's statue through the streets of Chajul, accompanied by traditional music and dances. Town festivities continue all week, with parades, traditional music, games, family gatherings, copious supplies of *tamales*, and firecrackers.

BELOW: Preparations of hearty tamales accompany every Ixil fiesta; this fortified tamale is carried to the family maize field (milpa) on the Day of Maize Sowing (Día de la Siembra).

JANUARY 15

Fiesta de Esquipulas (Feast of Esquipulas). This feast day marks a national celebration for Catholics in Guatemala, when they make their annual pilgrimage to the shrine of the 400-year-old "black" Jesus figure in Esquipulas, Department of Chiquimula. In the Ixil region, on the night of January 14, Catholics hold a silent vigil in church, followed by a celebration with traditional music and firecrackers.

FEBRUARY 1–3

*Día de la Candelaria (*Day of Candlemas*).* The patron saint day festival of Acul (Nebaj), the Day of the Virgin of Candelaria, is celebrated at the midpoint between the winter solstice and spring equinox, a time of anticipation for the Maya New Year. The image of the Virgin of Candelaria is paraded through the streets of Acul. Celebrants come from Nebaj and surrounding municipalities. This is a time of local baptisms and marriages and festivities include traditional music, dances, and fireworks.

FEBRUARY 22, 23, OR 24 (varies by year, as determined by the Maya Calendar)

Año Nuevo Maya (Maya New Year). Ceremonies begin the night before the New Year and continue through to the dawn, with traditional prayers, incense, candles, and flower offerings. In Nebaj, Chajul, and Cotzal, traditional community leaders, the *alcaldes auxiliares* of each village (*aldea*), convene in their respective municipal capital to await the dawn of the New Year and to observe traditional Maya prayers. On the following day, these leaders conduct prayer ceremonies in all the sacred corners of the town, accompanied by marimba music and firecrackers.

SECOND FRIDAY OF LENT (varies by year, between late February and mid-March)

Romería al Señor de Chajul (Pilgrimage to the Señor of Chajul). Catholic and traditional Maya believers converge on Chajul from all across the Ixil region (and beyond) to venerate the figure of Jesus of Golgotha in the Catholic church. All day, a steady procession of visitors wait patiently in the aisles for their opportunity to lay offerings of candles, flowers, and traditionally woven palm baskets at the feet of this colonial-era statue, known as "protector of the people," and believed to bestow curative powers. This is also a day throughout the Ixil region when people visit traditional Maya altars to conduct prayer ceremonies, including the altars on top of Cerro San Andrés above the town.

SEMANA SANTA OR EASTER WEEK (varies by year, between March 22 and April 25)

Semana Santa is the most important religious holiday in Guatemala; the entire country is on vacation. Festivities in Nebaj, Chajul, and Cotzal begin on the Sunday preceding Easter Sunday, with the blessings of branches (*la bendición de ramos*) and the procession of saints from the town cemetery to the Catholic church. On the following Thursday, the religious brotherhoods (*cofradías*) in each town lead the "sharing of bread and honey" for Catholics and non-Catholics in the early morning (3:00 a.m.), followed by a feast of traditional meals shared among friends and neighbors. From 10:00 a.m. to noon on Thursday, traditional Maya priests participate in the ceremonial "washing of the feet" of the members of the *cofradía*, followed by a reenactment of the Passion of Christ and a solemn procession accompanied by traditional trumpets. In some places, young people create scarecrow-like figures of Judas and hang these from different places around town; in joking spirit, they often put faces of political figures or famous people on these stuffed figures. On Good Friday, a solemn procession of the crucified Christ figure makes its way through the town, accompanied by traditional musicians. On Saturday, townspeople gather for walks outside, picnics, games, and music. Saturday evening, processions of the saints through town terminate with feasts among the *cofradía* and friends. On Easter Sunday, the resurrection of Christ is celebrated, with a final parade of the risen Christ figure through the streets.

APRIL 21 (approximately)

Día de la Siembra (The Day for Maize Sowing). The annual planting of maize lasts from three days to a week, and is traditionally accompanied by Maya prayer ceremonies, blessing selected seed corn from the previous harvest. The head of household ceremonially plants the first seed. On this day, women prepare a special recipe of hearty tamales and carry this to the fields to eat with the planting crew. In the warmer sub-climates of the region, some farmers are able to plant two crops a year; traditional prayers and rituals are associated with the first planting.

MAY 3

Día de la Cruz (Day of the Cross). Observed in Nebaj at the sites of eleven sacred crosses (Maya altars), placed by the founding ancestors around the town. Maya priests gather to petition their neighbors for funds to support the annual Maya rituals associated with local sacred altars. (Expenses include incense, flowers, candles, and the engagement of traditional musicians for important dates in the Maya calendar.) The vicinity of the sacred sites is cleaned, and traditional crosses may be repaired and painted. Family members gather to prepare coffee and lunch for the spiritual leaders. At 7:00 p.m., the Maya priests and neighbors gather at the particular sacred site to intitiate prayer ceremonies.

MAY 22 (approximately)

El Baile del Quetzal (Dance of the Quetzal). Organized by the traditional *cofradías*, twenty days (one "month" in the Maya calendar) after the Day of the Cross; each *cofradía* engages in activities and rituals related to their particular saint.

JUNE 19–24

Feria Titular de Cotzal (Patron Saint's Day Festival of San Juan Cotzal). Several days of intense festivities follow the birthday of Cotzal's patron, Saint John the Apostle (June 21), through the downtown streets. Festivities include the Miss Maguey Flower (*Flor de Maguey*) contest, horse races, costumed dancing, feasts, and firecrackers.

AUGUST 12–15

Feria Titular de Nebaj (Patron Saint Festival of Santa María Nebaj). The statue of Santa María de La Asunción is paraded through the downtown streets of Nebaj on August 15, preceded by several days of celebrations, a town parade representing organizations and businesses, marimba music, dancing, games, and fireworks.

SEPTEMBER 15

Día de la Independencia (Guatemala Independence Day). In Nebaj, Chajul, and Cotzal, this national holiday is celebrated with organized activities and contests, including parades and traditional dances.

NOVEMBER 2

Día de los Santos / Día de los Muertos (All Saints Day/Day of the Dead). On the evening of November 1, *Remoshno* ("Preparation for the Day of the Dead"), teenagers in Ixil towns organize into two groups—one to carry a cross, and the other, a bell. They run through the streets, visiting different houses where they are offered snacks, such as *elotes* ("roasted corn on the cob"), güisquil, or fruits. The idea is to scare the wandering spirits of the deceased back to the cemetery, where they will be remembered and honored the following day. On November 2, families gather in the local cemetary in a fusion of traditional and Catholic rituals, bringing palm leaves and flowers to decorate the graves, along with candles they will burn all day. Children and adults prepare for this day by making kites that they fly from the cemetery on November 2, to communicate with the departed family members and ancestors.

DECEMBER 24–25

La Navidad (Christmas). On Christmas Eve, Ixil friends and family come together to eat, attend church services, and engage musicians to fill the home and neighborhood with traditional accompaniment. Twelve midnight marks a deafening explosion of fireworks. On Christmas Day, families relax and visit friends and neighbors.

DECEMBER 26

Corrida del Niño (Day of the Christ Child). At daybreak, the bells of the Catholic church summon the assembly of the twelve cofradía groups to prepare a stable and manger at the altar of the church for the statue of the newborn Jesus. Families who observe this day create carpets of pine needles and flowers in the streets in front of their homes and proceed to the church, carrying small offerings for the Holy Child. Later, in the evening, the image of the newborn Christ in a manger is carried on a float through the town and along the beautifully carpeted streets. Candles, firecrackers, and special meals are prepared and shared among family and friends.

BELOW: Nebaj women ready to fill their market basket.

Young women from Chajul stop to chat in the market.

APPENDIX 2: GLOSSARY OF COMMONLY USED WORDS

IXIL			ENGLISH	SPANISH
NEBAJ	**COTZAL**	**CHAJUL**		
Cha'laxh. Tiixen.	Chajlentzik'axh.	Tchaqlaxh. Xeni. Xeni.	Good morning. Good afternoon. Good night.	Buenos días. Buenas tardes. Buenas noches.
¿Ma' b'a'nkuxh axh?	¿Kam ni tale'?	¿Kam tal axh?	What's going on?	¿Qué tal?
B'a'nkuxh in.	B'a'n ko'xh in.	B'a'n kuxh in.	I'm fine.	Estoy bien.
Nun ch'o'ne'.	In ya'v.	Oyb'al in.	I'm sick.	Estoy enfermo/a.
Koolinaj in.	Koolinaj in.	Koolina'qxh in.	I'm tired.	Estoy cansado/a.
¿Jatva'x ayaab'?	¿Jatva'l aya'b?	¿Jatva'x ayaab'?	How old are you?	¿Cuántos años tienes?
Ma'tve't in.	Ma't tek in.	Ma't vet in.	I'm leaving now.	Ya me voy.
La qilqib'.	La qil qib'.	Eel eeb'.	Take care of yourself.	Cuídate.
Cheel in.	Cheel in.	Tchel in.	I'll be right back.	Ya vengo.
Ko'on.	Ko'.	Ko'n.	Let's go.	Vámonos.
Oraaxh.	Mat'inb'a.	Ma'teb' in.	Good-bye. (the first part)	Adios.
Tii.	Ora'xh.	Na'xhb'a.	Good-bye. (the response)	Adios.
¿Kam ab'ii?	¿Kam ab'ii?	¿Kam ab'ij?	What is your name?	¿Cómo te llamas?
¿Ma' nasa'?	¿Ni tzik asa'a?	¿Na sa'e?	Do you like it?	¿Te gusta?
Nunsa'.	Nunsa'a.	Nik insa'e'.	I like it.	Me gusta.
Ye' unsa'.	Yu'nsa'a.	Ye' nik insa'.	I don't like it.	No me gusta.
Nunsa'.	Nunsa'a.	Nik insa'e'.	I want it.	Lo quiero.
Ye' unsa'.	Yunsa'a.	Ye' insa'.	I don't want it.	No lo quiero.
Ye' vootzaj.	Ye' vootzaj.	Ye' vootzaqle.	I don't know.	No sé.
Loq'chit jab'al.	Kaana jab'al.	Oqxh jab'ale.	There's a lot of rain.	Hay mucha lluvia.
Mam xo'q'ol.	Kaana xoq'ol.	Oqxh xooq'ole.	It's muddy.	Hay mucho lodo.
Maas che'v.	Kaana che'v.	Oqxh itche'v.	It's cold.	Hace mucho frío.
A'chit tz'a'e'.	Kaana tz'a'.	Oqxh tz'a'lale.	It's hot.	Hace mucho calor.
¿Kani'ch?	¿Kani'ch ija'mel?	¿Ke'ch ija'mil?	How much is it?	¿Cuánto cuesta?
B'an b'a'nil.	B'an b'a'nil.	B'an b'a'nil.	Please.	Por favor.
Ta'ntiixh.	Ta'ntioxh see.	Tantiuxh.	Thank you.	Gracias.
Paloj in.	Sa paal in.	Pal b'eeq in.	Excuse me. (to pass by)	Con permiso.
¿Kam oora cheel?	¿Kam oora cheel?	¿Kam oora tcheel?	What time is it?	¿Qué hora es?

IXIL			ENGLISH	SPANISH
NEBAJ	**COTZAL**	**CHAJUL**		
¿Kam asa'?	¿Kam asa'?	¿Kam asa'?	What would you like?	¿Qué quieres?
Ni vitz'aj.	Ni vitz'a.	Nik vitz'a.	I am thinking.	Estoy pensando.
Ni tzaj untzi'.	Nitzaj untzi'.	Kamyxh in tzaqa tzi'il.	I'm thirsty.	Tengo sed.
Nun va'ye'.	Nunva'ye'.	Kamyxh in t-va'y.	I'm hungry.	Tengo hambre.
Nonaj in	Noonaj in	Noonaqxh in.	I'm full.	Estoy lleno/a.
¿Ma' k'axk'oj ich?	¿Atil tzik ich?	¿Oqxh ik'axale?	Is it spicy?	¿Pica mucho?
Maas vata'm.	Nunkam tu vata'm.	Kamyxh in vata'm.	I'm tired.	Tengo sueño.
Loch in.	Loch in.	Lotch in.	Help me.	¡Ayúdame!
Ku'en.	Ku'en.	Ku'en.	Sit down.	¡Siéntate!
Si'u.	Ni'axh.	Avule'.	Come here.	¡Ven acá!
Chaa atzi'.	Chaatzi'.	Xhakalil.	Be quiet.	¡Cállate!
La kaa in tzitza'.	Toj kaay in tza'.	Ma't ku' in.	I'm getting off here.	Voy a bajar aquí.
Acha'vchitu'.	Tx'anel chitu'.	Josq'ilxhtu'.	It's beautiful.	¡Que bonito!
Acha'vchit u kutename'.	Tx'anel chit u kutenam.	Josq'ilxh u qutenam.	Our town is pretty.	Nuestro pueblo es bonito.
Naab'a	K'usal	Tx'aul	NebajCotzalChajul	NebajCotzalChajul
tenam	tenam	tenam	town	pueblo
kanoj	ee'	ee'	yes	sí
ye'le	ye'ka	ye'le	no	no
vi'xh	vi'xh	vi'xh	cat	gato
uk'a'	a'	a'	drink	bebida
kapee	kapeel	kapeel	coffee	café
ixi'm	ixi'm	ixi'm	dried corn	maíz
lee	lee	lee	tortilla	tortilla
pa'ich	pa'ich	pa'itch	tomato	tomate
paq' ich	Ta'l pa'ich	joxim ich	sauce	salsa
is	b'aq'b'och	is	potato	papa
chib'	chi'o	tchib'	meat	carne
ak'atx	t'el	katxhan	chicken	pollo / gallina
ta'l ak'atx	ta'l t'el	ta'l kaxhan	chicken soup	caldo de pollo / gallina
txikon	txikon	txikon	beans	frijoles
ta'l txikon	ta'l txikon	ta'l txikon	bean soup	caldo de frijol

IXIL			ENGLISH	SPANISH
NEBAJ	**COTZAL**	**CHAJUL**		
Xuum	Xum	Xuum	Flower	Flor
nimla ch'ich'	kamioneeta	kamioneta	bus	camioneta
xamal	xamal	xamal	fire / light / candle	fuego
k'ayib'al	k'ayib'al	k'ayib'al	market	mercado
b'ey	b'ey	b'ey	road / street	camino / calle
vatb'al	vatb'al	vatb'al	hostel	hospedaje
txutx	nan	txutx	mother	mamá
b'aal	tat	b'aal	father	papá
tz'akab'a'l	tz'ak	tz'akab'al	medicine	medicina
xu'm	xu'm	xu'm	flower	flor
nimlaq'ii	nimla q'ii	nimla q'ij	party / festival	fiesta
otzotz	otzotz	otzotz	house	casa
tzi'an	tzian	naatch	far away	lejos
najli	naja'	naqli	close	cerca

NUMBERS

ye'xhkam	ye'xkam	ye'xkam	zero	0 cero
ma'l	ma'l	va'l	one	1 uno
ka'va'l	ka'va'l	kaava'l	two	2 dos
oxva'l	oxva'l	oxva'l	three	3 tres
kajva'l	kaava'l	kajva'l	four	4 cuatro
o'va'l	o'va'l	o'va'l	five	5 cinco
vaajil	vaajil	vaaqil	six	6 seis
vujva'l	jujva'l	juqva'l	seven	7 siete
vaaxiil	vaaxajil	vajxajil	eight	8 ocho
b'eluval	b'eluval	b'elval	nine	9 nueve
laval	laval	laval	ten	10 diez
b'axaj	b'axa	b'axa	1st first	1° primero
ka'v	ka'v	ka'v	2nd second	2° segundo
toxvu	toxva	toxv	3rd third	3° tercero
kajvu	kaava	kajv	4th fourth	4° cuarto
motxtel	ya'eb'al	ya'teb'al	last	último

La Antigua, face of San Francisco church, completed in 1702.

BIBLIOGRAPHY

Adams, Richard N. "Ethnic Images and Strategies in 1944," in *Guatemalan Indians and The State: 1540–1988*, edited by Carol A. Smith, 144–162. Austin: University of Texas Press, 1990.

Ak'abal, Humberto. *Ajkem Tzij, Tejedor de Palabras*. Guatemala City: Cholsamaj, 2001.

Anderson, Marilyn, and Jonathan Garlock. *Granddaughters of Corn: Portraits of Guatemalan Women*. Willimantic, CT: Curbstone Press, 1988.

Asociación de la Mujer Maya Ixil (ADMI), and M. Brinton Lykes, with Proyecto FotoVoz. *Voces e Imágenes: Mujeres Maya Ixil de Chajul/Voices and Images: Mayan Ixil Women of Chajul*. Guatemala: Victor Herrera de Magna Terra, with the support of The Soros Foundation, 2000.

Asturias, Miguel Angel. *Men of Maize*. New York: Delacorte Press/Seymour Lawrence, 1975. Originally published in 1949 by Editorial Losada, S. A., Buenos Aires, Argentina, as *Hombres de Maíz*.

Asturias de Barrios, Linda (ed.). *Cuyuscate: Brown Cotton in the Textile Tradition of Guatemala*. Translated by Nancie L. González. Guatemala: Museo Ixchel del Traje Indígena, 2002.

Ayres, Glenn. *La Gramática Ixil (An Ixil Grammar)*. La Antigua, Guatemala: Centro de Investigacíones Regionales de Mésoamérica (CIRMA), 1991.

Becquelin, Pierre, Alain Breton, and Véronique Gervais. *Arqueología de la Región de Nebaj, Guatemala (Archaeology of the Region of Nebaj, Guatemala)*. Guatemala City: Centro Francés de Estudios Mexicanos y Centroaméricanos, Escuela de Historia, Universidad de San Carlos de Guatemala, Ministerio de Asuntos Exteriores de Francia, 2001.

Benz, Stephen Connely. *Guatemalan Journey*. Austin: University of Texas Press, 1996.

Brady, James E. "In My Hill, In My Valley: The Importance of Place in Ancient Maya Ritual," in *Mesas & Cosmologies in Mesoamerica*, Vol. 2, edited by Douglas Sharon, 83–91. San Diego: San Diego Museum of Man, 2003.

Breton, Alain, Anne Cazalès, and Miquel Dewever-Plana (photographs). *Mayas*. Chambray-lès-Tours, France: CLD Editions, 2002.

Carlsen, Robert S. *The War for the Heart and Soul of a Highland Maya Town*. Austin: University of Texas Press, 1997.

Carmack, Robert M. *The Quiché Mayas of Utatlán: The Evolution of a Highland Guatemala Kingdom*. Norman: University of Oklahoma Press, 1981.

Carmack, Robert M. *Toltec Influence on the Postclassic Culture History of Highland Guatemala*. New Orleans: Middle American Research Institute, Tulane University, 1968.

Carmack, Robert M., John D. Early, and Christopher Lutz (eds.). *The Historical Demography of Highland Guatemala*. Albany: Institute of Mesoamerican Studies, State University of New York at Albany, 1982.

Casa de la Cultura Nebajense. *Estudio de prefactibilidad para un Proyecto de Desarollo Turistico en el Area Ixil (Prefeasibility Study for a Tourism Development Program in the Ixil Region)*. Nebaj, El Quiché, Guatemala: Programa de Las Naciones Unidas Para el Desarrollo (PNUD/UNDP) and Programa De Desarrollo par Desplazados, Refugiados y Repartriados (PRODERE), 1992.

Christie, Jessica Joyce (ed.). *Landscapes of Origin in the Americas: Creation Narratives Linking Ancient Places and Present Communities*. Tuscaloosa: The University of Alabama Press. 2009.

Coe, Michael D. *Breaking the Maya Code*. New York: Thames & Hudson, 1992.

Coe, Michael D., and Justin Kerr. *The Art of the Maya Scribe*. New York: Thames & Hudson, 1997.

Coe, Michael D. *Final Report: An Archaeologist Excavates His Past*. New York: Thames & Hudson, 2006.

Coe, Michael D., and Mark Van Stone. *Reading the Maya Glyphys*. New York: Thames & Hudson, 2005.

Colby, Benjamin N. "The Anomalous Ixil—Bypassed by the Postclassic?" *American Antiquity* 41 (1976).

Colby, Benjamin N., and Lore M. Colby. *The Daykeeper: The Life and Discourse of an Ixil Diviner*. Cambridge, MA: Harvard University Press, 1981.

Colby, Benjamin N., and Pierre L. van den Berghe. *Ixil Country: A Plural Society in Highland Guatemala*. Berkeley: University of California Press, 1969.

Commission for Historical Clarification (CEH), *Guatemala: Memory of Silence* (Conclusions and Recommendations), 1999. http://shr.aaas.org/guatemala/ceh/report/english/toc.html; in Spanish, *Guatemala: Memoria Del Silencio* at http://shr.aaas.org/guatemala/ceh/mds/spanish/cap1/cap1.html.

De Arathoon, Barbara Knoke. *Símbolos que Se Siembran*. Guatemala: Museo Ixchel del Traje Indígena, 2005.

De La Cruz, Tabita Juana, Diego Santiago Ceto, and Lucas Mendoza Asicona. *Tilon Tatin Tenam Maya' Ixil, Monografía Maya Ixil* (*Monography on the Ixil Maya*). Guatemala: Academia de Lenguas Mayas de Guatemala, Direccíon de Planificacion Lingüística y Cultural (Academy of Mayan Languages, Office of Linguistic and Cultural Planning), 2008.

Deuss, Krystyna. *Shamans, Witches and Maya Priests: Native Religion and Ritual in Highland Guatemala*. London: Guatemalan Maya Center, 2007.

Diehl, Richard A. *Tula: The Toltec Capital of Ancient Mexico*. London: Thames & Hudson, 1983.

Elliott, Elaine D. "Feeding the Men of Corn: Ixil Land History of Ilom," unpublished paper, 1990.

Elliott, Elaine D. "Gaspar Ilom: Maya Resistance to the Western Ideology of Nature," master's thesis, University of San Diego, 1998.

Elliott, Elaine D. "A History of Land Tenure in the Ixil Triangle," unpublished paper, Centro de Investigacíones Regionales de Mésoamérica (CIRMA), 1989.

Elliott, Raymond, and Helen Elliott. "Ixil," in *Languages of Guatemala*, edited by Marvin K. Mayers, Summer Institute of Linguistics, 125–139. The Hague: Mouton & Co., 1965.

Esquivel, Julia. *The Certainty of Spring: Poems by a Guatemalan in Exile*, translated by Anne Woehrle. Washington, D.C.: Ecumenical Program on Central America and the Caribbean, 1993. Originally published in 1989 as *Florecerás Guatemala* by Ediciones CUPSA, 1989.

Falla, Ricardo. *Massacres in the Jungle, Ixcán, Guatemala, 1975–1982*. Translated by Julia Howland. Boulder, CO: Westview Press, 1994.

Fischer, Edward F., and R. McKenna Brown (eds.). *Maya Cultural Activism in Guatemala*. Austin: University of Texas, Institute of Latin American Studies, 1996.

Fischer, Edward F., and Carol Hendrickson. *Tecpán Guatemala: A Modern Maya Town in Global and Local Context.* Boulder, CO: Westview Press, 2003.

Foundation for the Advancement of Mesoamerican Studies, Inc, Crystal River, Florida. (http://www.famsi.org/mayawriting/codices/dresden.html)

Gall, Francis. *Diccionario geográfico de Guatemala.* Guatemala: Instituto Geográfico Nacional, 4 volumes, 1976.

Gleijeses, Piero. *Shattered Hope: The Guatemalan Revolution and the United States, 1944–1954.* Princeton, NJ: Princeton University Press, 1991.

Goldman, Francisco. *The Art of Political Murder: Who Killed the Bishop?* New York: Grove Press, 2007.

Gonzáles, Gaspar Pedro. *A Mayan Life.* Rancho Palos Verdes, CA: Yax Te' Press, 1995.

Gonzáles, Gaspar Pedro. *Return of the Maya.* Rancho Palos Verdes, CA: Yax Te' Press, 1998.

Gonzáles, Magda Leticia. "Más Allá de la Montaña: La Región Ixil," in *Guatemala: La Infinita Historia de Las Resistencias,* Manolo E. Vela Casteñeda, coordinator, pp 163-227. Guatemala: Secretaría de la Paz de la Presidencia de la República de Guatemala, 2011.

Gradin, Greg. *The Blood of Guatemala: A History of Race and Nation.* Durham, NC: Duke University Press, 2000.

Gragnolati, Michele, and Alessandra Marini. *Health and Poverty in Guatemala,* World Bank Policy Research Working Paper (Washington, DC: The World Bank, 2003).

Grube, Nikolai (ed.). *Maya: Divine Kings of the Rain Forest.* Cologne: Könemann Verlagsgesellschaft mbH, 2001.

Guatemala Peace Accords: Key Texts and Agreements (English version). Conciliation Resources (www.c-r.org/accord/guatemala).

Gugliotta, Guy, and Kenneth Garrett (photographs). "The Maya: Glory and Ruin," *National Geographic,* 212.2 (August 2007): 68–109.

Guzaro, Tomás, and Terri Jacob McComb. *Escaping the Fire: How An Ixil Mayan Pastor Led His People Out of a Holocaust during the Guatemalan Civil War.* Austin: University of Texas Press, 2010.

Handy, Jim. "The Corporate Community, Campesino Organizations, and Agrarian Reform: 1950-1954," *Guatemalan Indians and the State: 1540 to 1988,* edited by Carol A. Smith, 163–182. Austin: University of Texas Press, 1990.

Handy, Jim. *Revolution in the Countryside: Rural Conflict and Agrarian Reform in Guatemala, 1944-1954.* Chapel Hill: The University of North Carolina Press, 1994.

Harbury, Jennifer. *Searching for Everardo: A Story of Love, War, and the CIA in Guatemala.* New York: Warner, 1997.

Harbury, Jennifer. *Truth, Torture, and the American Way: The History and Consequences of U.S. Involvement in Torture.* Boston: Beacon Press, 2005.

Harrison, Peter D. *The Lords of Tikal: Rulers of an Ancient Maya City.* New York: Thames & Hudson, 1999.

Human Rights Office of the Archdiocese of Guatemala. *Guatemala: Never Again!* Recovery of Historical Memory Project (REMHI). Maryknoll, NY: Orbis Books, 1999. Originally published in 1998 in Spanish as *Guatemala: Nunca Más* by the Oficina de Derechos Humanos del Arzobispado de Guatemala.

Instituto Nacional de Estadística Guatemala (National Institute of Statistics of Guatemala). *Censos Agropecuarios* (*Agricultural and Livestock Census*) 1979, 2003; Investigacíon de Campo Grupo EPS, 2008 (www.ine.gob.gt/np/).

Instituto Nacional de Estadística Guatemala (National Institute of Statistics of Guatemala). ¿Como estamos viviendo? Encuesta Nacional de Condiciones de Vida, Principales Resultados (How Are We Living? National Survey on Living Conditions, Principal Results), 2006 (www.ine.gob.gt/np/).

International Center for Human Rights Research (CIIDH) and Mutual Support Group (GAM). *Draining the Sea: An Analysis of Terror in Three Communities in Rural Guatemala, 1980–84.* Washington, DC: American Association for the Advancement of Science, 1996 (http://shr.aaas.org/guatemala/ciidh/dts/nebaj.html).

Jenkins, John Major. "Introduction to the Mayan Calendar," *Tzolkin: Visionary Perspectives and Calendar Studies,* 1992, 1994 (http://alignment2012.com/fap4.html).

Chichicastenango market mask vendor juxtaposes the royal Maya jaguar with comic caricatures of Spanish conquistadors.

LaFarge, Oliver. *Santa Eulalia: The Religion of a Cuchumatán Indian Town*. Chicago: University of Chicago Press, 1947.

Land, Hugh C., and H. Wayne Trimm. *Birds of Guatemala*. Wynnewood, PA: Livingston Publishing Company, 1970.

Lebrun, David. *Breaking the Maya Code: The 200-Year Quest to Decipher the Hieroglyphics of the Ancient Maya* (feature documentary). Produced by Night Fire Films in Association with Arte France, 2008.

Lincoln, Jackson Steward. *An Ethnological Study of the Ixil Indians of the Guatemala Highlands* (typewritten text with manuscript notes and photos), 1940. Edited version published posthumously by Carnegie Institution of Washington, D.C., 1942.

Los Artisticos del Pueblo Ixil. *Songs of Resistance* (musical CD, recorded by Mark Arrneson, with accompanying English and Spanish translation), 2005.

Lovell, W. George. *A Beauty that Hurts: Life and Death in Guatemala*. Toronto: Between the Lines, 1995.

Lovell, W. George. *Conquest and Survival in Colonial Guatemala: A Historical Geography of the Cuchumatán Highlands, 1500–1821*. Montreal: McGill-Queen's University Press, 2005.

Mann, Charles C. *1491: New Revelations of the Americas before Columbus*. New York: Vintage Books, 2005.

Manz, Beatrice. *Paradise in Ashes: A Guatemalan Journey of Courage, Terror, and Hope*. Berkeley: University of California Press, 2004.

Manz, Beatrice. *Refugees of a Hidden War: The Aftermath of Counterinsurgency in Guatemala*. Albany: State University of New York Press, 1988.

Martin, Simon, and Nikolai Grube. *Chronicle of the Maya Kings and Queens: Deciphering the Dynasties of the Ancient Maya*. London: Thames & Hudson, 2000.

Maturin, Anthony. *Pilgrimage to Chajul: Tales from Guatemala*. Christchurch, New Zealand: Quoin Press, 1996.

Mayers, Marvin K. (ed.). *Languages of Guatemala*. The Hague: Mouton & Co., 1966.

Menchú, Rigoberta, and Elisabeth Burgos-Debray. *I, Rigoberta Menchú: An Indian Woman in Guatemala*. Translated by Ann Wright. London, UK: Verso, 1984. Originally published as *Me Lllamo Rigoberta Menchú y Así Me Nació la Conciencia*. Barcelona, Spain: Editorial Argos Vergara, S. A., 1983.

Miller, Mary Ellen, and Karl Taube. *An Illustrated Dictionary of the Gods and Symbols of Ancient Mexico and the Maya*. London: Thames & Hudson, 1993

Moller, Jonathan, and Ricardo Falla, et al. *Our Culture Is Our Resistance: Repression, Refuge, and Healing in Guatemala*. New York: PowerHouse, 2004.

Montejo, Víctor. *The Bird Who Cleans the World and Other Mayan Fables*. Willimantic, CT: Curbstone Press, 1991.

Montejo, Víctor. *Testimony: Death of a Guatemalan Village*. Translated by Victor Perera. Willimantic, CT: Curbstone Press, 1987.

Montejo, Víctor. *Voices from Exile: Violence and Survival in Modern Maya History*. Norman: University of Oklahoma Press, 1999.

Montejo, Víctor, and Luis Garay (illus.). *Popol Vuj: Libro Sagrado de Los Mayas* (*The Popol Vuj: Sacred Book of the Maya*). Toronto: Un Libro Tigrillo, Groundwood Books/House of Anansi Press, 1999.

Montenegro, Gustavo Adolfo. "El Lugar de Jaguar," *Prensa Libre,* July 25, 2005

Ortiz, Dianna, and Patricia Davis. *The Blindfold's Eyes: My Journey from Torture to Truth*. Maryknoll, NY: Orbis, 2002.

Payeras, Mario. *Days in the Jungle: The Testimony of a Guatemalan Guerrillero, 1972–1976.* New York: Monthly Review Press, 1983. Originally published in 1981, Havana, Cuba, as *Los Días de la Selva.*

Perera, Victor. *Unfinished Conquest: The Guatemalan Tragedy.* Berkeley: University of California Press, 1993.

Recinos, Adrián. *Popol Vuh: Las Antiguas Historias del Quiché, Traducidas del Texto Original, con Una Introducción y Notas.* Mexico: Fondo de Cultura Económica, 1947.

Recinos, Adrián, and Delia Goetz (trans.). *The Annals of the Cakchiquels,* Chonay, Dionisio José, and Delia Goetz, trans. *Title of the Lords of Totonicapán.* Norman: University of Oklahoma, 1953.

Región Ixil, Quiché-Guatemala: Guía De Senderismo. Madrid: Solidaridad Internacional, 2005.

Rousso, Kathryn. *Maguey Journey: Discovering Textiles in Guatemala.* Tucson: University of Arizona Press, 2010.

Schele, Linda, and Peter Mathews. *The Code of Kings: The Language of Seven Sacred Maya Temples and Tombs.* New York: Simon & Schuster, 1998.

Schele, Linda, and Khristaan Douglas Villela. "Creation, Cosmos and the Imagery of Palenque and Copan", *Eighth Palenque round Table, 1993,* Merle Greene Robertson (General Editor), Martha J. Macri and Jan McHargue, (Volume Editors), San Francisco: Pre-Columbian Art Research Institute, 1996. (www.mesoweb.com/pari/publications/rt10/RT08_00.html)

Schevill, Margot Blum, and Christopher Lutz. *Maya Textiles of Guatemala: The Gustavus A. Eisen Collection, 1902, The Hearst Museum of Anthropology, the University of California at Berkeley.* Austin: University of Texas, 1993.

Schlesinger, Stephen C., and Stephen Kinzer. *Bitter Fruit: The Story of the American Coup in Guatemala.* Cambridge, MA: Harvard University Press, 1990.

Simon, Jean-Marie. *Guatemala: Eternal Spring, Eternal Tyranny.* New York: Norton, 1987.

Smith, A. Ledyard, and Alfred V. Kidder. *Excavations at Nebaj, Guatemala (with Notes on the Skeletal Material by T. D. Stewart, illustrator).* Washington, DC: Carnegie Institution of Washington, 1951.

Stephens, John Lloyd, and Frederick Catherwood (illus.). *Incidents of Travel in Central America, Chiapas, and Yucatan.* London: Arthur Hall, Virtue & Co, 1854 (http://tinyurl.com/84kccfr).

Stephens, John Lloyd, and Frederick Catherwood (illus.). *Incidents of Travel in Yucatan,* Vols. I & II. New York: Cosimo, 2008. Originally published in 1843.

Stoll, David. *Between Two Armies in the Ixil Towns of Guatemala.* New York: Columbia University Press, 1993.

Stoll, David. "Guatemala: The New Jerusalem of the Americas?" *Cultural Survival Quarterly*, 7.1, 1983 (www.culturalsurvival.org/publications/cultural-survival-quarterly/71-spring-1983-death-and-disorder-guatemala).

Stoll, David. " 'The Land No Longer Gives': Land Reform in Nebaj, Guatemala," *Cultural Survival Quarterly*, 14.4, 1990 (www.culturalsurvival.org/publications/cultural-survival-quarterly/144-winter-1990-land-and-resources).

Tedlock, Barbara. *Time and the Highland Maya (Revised Edition).* Albuquerque: University of New Mexico Press, 1982.

Tedlock, Dennis (trans.). *Popol Vuh: The Mayan Book of the Dawn of Life.* (Revised and expanded edition. Translated, with introduction, commentaries, and glossary). New York: Simon & Schuster, 1996.

Tedlock, Dennis. *Rabinal Achi: A Mayan Drama of War and Sacrifice* (translated and interpreted by Dennis Tedlock). Oxford: Oxford University Press, 2003.

Thompson, J. Eric S. *Maya History and Religion.* Norman: University of Oklahoma Press, 1970.

Van Akkeren, Rudd. *La Visión Indígena de la Conquista.* Guatemala: Serviprensa, 2007.

Wilkinson, Daniel. *Silence on the Mountain: Stories of Terror, Betrayal, and Forgetting in Guatemala.* Boston: Houghton Mifflin, 2002.

World Health Organization, UNICEF, UNFPA, and the World Bank. *Trends in Maternal Mortality: 1990 to 2008.* Geneva: World Health Organization, 2010.

Wright, Ronald. *Time among the Maya: Travels in Belize, Guatemala, and Mexico.* New York: Grove Press, 1989.

Basalt grinding stone.

Guatemalan cornucopia of fabulous fruits and vegetables.

ENDNOTES

1 Lovell, W. George, *Conquest and Survival in Colonial Guatemala: A Historical Geography of the Cuchumatán Highlands, 1500–1821* (Montreal: McGill-Queen's University Press, 2005), 17–22.

2 Gustavo Adolfo Montenegro, "El Lugar de Jaguar," *Prensa Libre,* July 25, 2005. Journalist Montenegro discusses the research of Dutch anthropologist, Rudd van Akkeren, into the origins and mythology of the Ixil communities and their relation to the Maya of the Petén lowlands. Van Akkeren advances the hypothesis that the name *Ixil* is derived from "Hix" (or *I'x*), one of the twenty daygods in the sacred Maya calendar that symbolized the mystical powers of the jaguar, and "Il," a common Maya suffix associated with place or source.

3 Linda Schele and Peter Mathews, *The Code of Kings: The Language of Seven Sacred Maya Temples and Tombs* (New York: Simon & Schuster, 1998), 24.

4 According to the Academy of Mayan Languages of Guatemala, Ixil is one of twenty-one distinct and living Maya languages today. Linguists believe there is evidence to suggest that a "proto-Maya" idiom developed into six major linguistic roots, from which thirty Maya languages developed. Several Maya languages are no longer spoken today, and several others are on the brink of disappearing.

5 A. Ledyard Smith and Alfred V. Kidder, *Excavations at Nebaj, Guatemala* (Washington, DC: Carnegie Institution of Washington, 1951), 5.

6 Pierre Becquelin, Alain Breton, and Véronique Gervais, *Arqueología de la Región de Nebaj, Guatemala* (Guatemala City: Centro Francés de Estudios Mexicanos y Centroaméricanos, Escuela de Historia, Universidad de San Carlos de Guatemala, Ministerio de Asuntos Exteriores de Francia, 2001), 13–23.

7 Becquelin, Breton, and Gervais, *Arqueología de la Región de Nebaj,* 217.

8 Schele and Mathews, *The Code of Kings,* 13.

9 Ibid., 210–213.

10 http://en.wikipedia.org/wiki/Popol_Vuh.

11 Schele and Mathews, *The Code of Kings,* 23–48.

12 Ibid., 34–36. The "golden mean" is achieved when the ratio of the sum of two unequal measurements divided by the larger measurement is the same as the ratio between the two measurements (Wikipedia).

13 Graphic of Maya calendar is adapted from adapted from Michael D. Coe and Mark Van Stone, *Reading the Maya Glyphs* (2005) and Alexander W. Voss, "*Astronomy and Mathematics,*" in Grube, Nikolai (ed.). *Maya: Divine Kings of the Rain Forest* (Cologne: Könemann Verlagsgesellschaft mbH, 2001), 131-136.

14 Robert M. Carmack, *Toltec Influence on the Postclassic Culture History of Highland Guatemala* (New Orleans: Middle American Research Institute, Tulane University, 1968), 62–70.

15 Lovell, *Conquest and Survival,* 40–43.

16 Dennis Tedlock (trans.), *Rabinal Achi: A Mayan Drama of War and Sacrifice* (Oxford: Oxford University Press, 2003), 35.

17 Adrián Recinos and Delia Goetz (trans.), *The Annals of the Cakchiquels* and *Title of the Lords of Totonicapán* (Norman: University of Oklahoma Press, 1953), 115–116.

18 Nikolai Grube (ed.), *Maya: Divine Kings of the Rain Forest* (Cologne: Könemann Verlagsgesellschaft mbH, 2001), 26.

19 Lovell, *Conquest and Survival,* 58.

20 Rudd Van Akkeren, *La Vision Indigena de la Conquista* (Guatemala: Serviprensa, 2007), 53–55.

21 Francis Gall, *Diccionario geográfico de Guatemala* (Guatemala: Instituto Geográfico Nacional, 4 vols., 1976, sections on Nebaj (727–728), Chajul (603–604), and San Juan Cotzal (355–356).

22 Casa de la Culture Nebajense, *Estudio de Prefactibilidad Par un Proyecto de Desarrollo Turistico en el Area Ixil* (Nebaj, El Quiché, Guatemala: Programa de Las Naciones Unidas Para el Desarrollo/ PNUD and Programa de Desarrollo par Desplazados, Refudiados, y Repartriados, 1992), 2.

23 Gall, *Diccionario geográfico,* 356, 727–728.

24 Lovell, *Conquest and Survival,* 149–153.

25 Ibid., 80.

26 Ibid., 126–129.

27 Ibid., 95–100.

28 Ibid., 121.

29 Ibid., 118–126.

30 Benjamin N. Colby and Pierre L. van den Berghe, *Ixil Country: A Plural Society in Highland Guatemala* (Berkeley: University of California Press, 1969), 54–55.

31 Lovell, *Conquest and Survival,* 91.

32 Jackson Steward Lincoln, *An Ethnological Study of the Ixil Indians of the Guatemala Highlands* (typewritten text with manuscript notes and photos, 1940; edited version published posthumously by Carnegie Institution of Washington, D.C., 1942), 49. Lincoln cites one Father Baltasar Valdivia writing in the Chajul parish records: "[T]he apostolic missionaries in these towns must face the fact that after 300 years of evangelization, they are found in a worse state than in the first century [of Spanish rule], regressing toward the old barbarism, mixed with the vices and irreligion of other races."

33 Elaine D. Elliott, "A History of Land Tenure in the Ixil Triangle," unpublished paper, Centro de Investigacíones Regionales de Mesoamérica (CIRMA), 1989, 6–10.

34 Lincoln, *An Ethnological Study,* 59–65; excerpts from Lincoln's 1939 interview with then-aging Doña Juana B.

35 Lincoln, *An Ethnological Study,* 61.

36 Colby and van den Berghe, *Ixil Country,* 69.

37 David Stoll, *Between Two Armies in the Ixil Towns of Guatemala* (New York: Columbia University Press, 1993), 33.

38 Stoll, *Between Two Armies*, 33.

39 Elaine D. Elliott, "Gaspar Ilom: Maya Resistance to the Western Ideology of Nature" (master's thesis, University of San Diego, 1998), 14–15.

40 Stoll, *Between Two Armies*, 35.

41 Colby and van den Berghe, *Ixil Country,* 192.

42 Lincoln, *An Ethnological Study,* 84.

43 Handy, Jim, "The Corporate Community, Campesino Organizations, and Agrarian Reform: 1950–1954," in *Guatemalan Indians and The State: 1540 to 1988,* edited by Carol A. Smith (Austin: University of Texas Press, 1990), 163–182.

44 Stoll, *Between Two Armies*, 43–46.

45 Elliott, "A History of Land Tenure in the Ixil Triangle," 11–13.

46 Commission for Historical Clarification (CEH), *Guatemala: Memory of Silence* (Conclusions and Recommendations) (http://shr.aaas.org/guatemala/ceh/report/english/graphics/charts/page84.gif).

47 Elliott, "Gaspar Ilom," 61–64.

48 International Center for Human Rights Research (CIIDH) and Mutual Support Group (GAM), *Draining the Sea: An Analysis of Terror in Three Rural Communities in Guatemala, 1980–1984,* English translation (Washington, DC: American Association for the Advancement of Science, 1996) (http://shr.aaas.org/guatemala/ciidh/dts/toc.html).

49 Ibid., http://shr.aaas.org/guatemala/ciidh/dts/nebaj.html

50 David Stoll, " 'The Land No Longer Gives': Land Reform in Nebaj, Guatemala," *Cultural Survival Quarterly* 14.4, 1990 (www.culturalsurvival.org/publications/cultural-survival-quarterly/144-winter-1990-land-and-resources).

51 *Agreement on Identity and Rights of Indigenous Peoples,* Guatemala Peace Accords: Key Texts and Agreements (English version). Conciliation Resources (www.c-r.org/accord/guatemala).

52 CEH, *Guatemala: Memory of Silence.*

53 Human Rights Office of the Archdiocese of Guatemala, *Guatemala: Never Again!* (Recovery of Historical Memory Project (REMHI), English translation, Maryknoll, NY: Orbis Books, 1999, xxiii–xxv.

54 Francisco Goldman, *The Art of Political Murder: Who Killed the Bishop?* (New York: Grove Press, 2007). Goldman chronicles Bishop Gerard's leadership in the truth commission, his murder, and the subsequent criminal investigations. See also the powerful documentary film, *Gerardi,* released in March 2010.

55 CEH, *Guatemala: Memory of Silence, Conclusions: Human Rights Violations, Acts of Violence and Assignment of responsiblility*, para 122. (http://shr.aaas.org/guatemala/ceh/report/english/conc2.html).

56 De La Cruz, Tabita Juana, Diego Santiago Ceto, and Lucas Mendoza Asicona, *Tilon Tatin Tenam Maya' Ixil, Monografía Maya Ixil* (Guatemala: Academia de Lenguas Mayas de Guatemala, Direccíon de Planificacion Lingüística y Cultural, 2008) (Academy of Mayan Languages, Office of Linguistic and Cultural Planning), 31–40.

57 Asociación de la Mujer Maya Ixil (ADMI) and M. Brinton Lykes, with Proyecto FotoVoz, *Voces e Imágenes: Mujeres Maya Ixil de Chajul/Voices and Images: Mayan Ixil Women of Chajul* (Guatemala: Victor Herrera de Magna Terra with the support of The Soros Foundation, 2000), 28.

58 Stephens, John Lloyd, and Frederick Catherwood (illus.), *Incidents of Travel in Central America, Chiapas, and Yucatan* (London: Arthur Hall, Virtue & Co, 1854), http://tinyurl.com/84kccfr, 334–336.

59 Lincoln, *An Ethnological Study,* 9.

60 Instituto Nacional de Estadística Guatemala (INE) (National Institute of Statistics of Guatemala). Population estimates are based on official growth projections for the Department of El Quiché published on the INE website. In the recent ten-year period since the last official census in 2002, the combined population of Nebaj, Chajul, and Cotzal has grown by an estimated 40 percent, with an average annual population growth rate of 3.4 percent. (www.ine.gob.gt/np/).

61 Instituto Nacional de Estadística Guatemala (INE), *Censos Agropecuarios* 1979, 2003; Investigacíon de Campo Grupo EPS, 2008 (www.ine.gob.gt/np/).

62 World Health Organization, UNICEF, UNFPA, and the World Bank, *Trends in Maternal Mortality: 1990 to 2008* (World Health Organization, 2010). (http://whqlibdoc.who.int/publications/2010/9789241500265_eng.pdf).

63 Michele Gragnolati and Alessandra Marini, *Health and Poverty in Guatemala*, World Bank Policy Research Working Paper (Washington, DC: The World Bank, 2003).

64 La Brigada de Medicos Cubanos (Cuban Doctors team) (Nebaj: 2006), unpublished statistics obtained from the Ministry of Health in Nebaj.

65 World Health Organization, *Trends in Maternal Mortality:* 1990 to 2008; comparative number for Costa Rica, 44; Mexico, 85; El Salvador, 110; UK, 12; and U.S., 24.

66 WINGS, U.S.-registered nonprofit organization working in Guatemala (http://wingsguate.org/).

67 David Gonzales, "Guatemalans Try to Mend Ties Snapped by War: Modern Methods and Mayan Beliefs," *New York Times*, February 27, 2003.

68 Tomás Guzaro and Terri Jacob McComb, *Escaping the Fire: How an Ixil Mayan Pastor Led his People Out of a Holocaust during the Guatemalan Civil War* (Austin: University of Texas Press, 2010).

69 Colby and van den Berghe, *Ixil Country*, 67–68.

70 Lincoln, *An Ethnological Study,* 104–105.

71 Ibid., 19.

72 Ibid., 19.

73 Ibid., 139.

74 Benjamin N. Colby and Lore M. Colby, *The Daykeeper: The Life and Discourse of an Ixil Diviner* (Cambridge, MA: Harvard University Press, 1981), 142.

75 Ibid., 43–46.

76 De la Cruz, Ceto, and Asicona, *Tilon Tatin Tenam Maya' Ixil, Monografía Maya Ixil,* 113-115.

77 Instituto Nacional de Estadística Guatemala, *Censos Agropecuarios, 1979, 2003.*

78 Instituto Nacional de Estadística Guatemala (INE) (National Institute of Statistics) ¿Como estamos viviendo? *Encuesta Nacional de Condiciones de Vida, Principales Resultados, (How Are We Living? National Survey on Living Conditions, Principal Results)*, 2006 (www.ine.gob.gt/np/).

79 Asociación de la Mujer Maya Ixil (ADMI), *Voces e Imágenes*, 24–25.

80 Colby and van den Berghe, *Ixil Country,* 68.

81 Dennis Tedlock, *Popol Vuh,* 146.

82 J. Eric S. Thompson, *Maya History and Religion* (Norman: University of Oklahoma Press, 1970), 352–354.

83 Colby and Colby, *The Daykeeper*, 43.

84 Stephens and Catherwood, *Incidents of Travel in Central America,* 162–164.

85 Lincoln, *An Ethnological Study*, 20.

86 From Guatemalan archival records and interviews, historian Elaine Daly Elliott pieced together key details of this classic land dispute in several unpublished papers and a master's thesis. Permission to cite these papers was obtained.

87 Lincoln, *An Ethnological Study,* 32–33.

88 Stoll, *Between Two Armies*, 72.

89 Ibid., 71–75.

90 Ibid., 26–59; with interesting land registry research by Elaine Elliott, Stoll describes the trends in land titling and ownership concentration that heightened tensions between Ladinos and Ixil and within the Ixil community prior to the outbreak of civil war violence in the region after 1975.

91 Instituto Nacional de Estadística Guatemala (INE), *Censos Agropecuarios*.

92 Tedlock, *Popol Vuh*, 45.

93 Elliott, "A History of Land Tenure in the Ixil Triangle," 16.

Photo by Michel de la Sabelier. Wood-saving stoves may provide this Ixil girl with more time for school work.